The Really Useful Literacy Book

Second edition

The Reall   *Literacy Book* provides inventive ideas for the classroom together with an access   informative summary of the theories that underpin them. Written for the prim   ool teacher, student or trainee teacher, this book will act as a springboard for furthe   ation. The authors of this book, all highly experienced literacy specialists, show the   how to plan units of work with flexibility and creativity, with reference to the lite   rning objectives of the Primary National Strategy. They offer a number of imagin   eracy units based on exciting ideas that are designed to motivate, engage and chall   ildren in classrooms.

This   pdated second edition contains a brand new chapter based on working with mu   and galleries in order to expand children's literary creativity. Using as their bas   'big ideas' – contexts and coherence, motivation, and content and process – the autl   d the reader through a set of principles and practices which, when applied to famili   ents of the literacy strategy, will encourage teachers to formulate their own exciting,   e and flexible literacy teaching.

Amo   literacy areas covered are:

- Narr
- Non   n
- Trad   l tales
- Poer
- Spok   written language.

This   , stimulating book is an essential companion for teachers in Foundation, Key Stag   i and 2, and those on initial teacher training courses who want to develop their literacy practice. In addition it is extremely useful for literacy leaders looking to develop whole school approaches in primary schools.

Tony Martin, Chira Lovat and **Glynis Purnell** work in the Educational Development Unit, University of Cumbria. Tony Martin (with Mick Waters) is author of *Coordinating English at Key Stage 2* (RoutledgeFalmer, 1999).

The Really Useful Series

The Really Useful Maths Book: A Guide for Primary Teachers
Tony Brown and Henry Liebling

The Really Useful Science Book: A Framework of Knowledge for Primary Teachers,
Second edition
Steve Farrow

The Really Useful Science Book: A Framework of Knowledge for Primary Teachers,
Third edition
Steve Farrow

The Really Useful Literacy Book: Being Creative with Literacy in the Primary Classroom,
Second edition
Tony Martin, Chira Lovat and Glynis Purnell

The Really Useful ICT Book: A Framework of Knowledge for Primary Teachers
Nick Packard and Steve Higgins

The Really Useful Literacy Book

Second edition

Being Creative with Literacy
in the Primary Classroom

Tony Martin, Chira Lovat and Glynis Purnell

Routledge
Taylor & Francis Group

LONDON AND NEW YORK

First published 2004 by RoutledgeFalmer
This edition published 2007 by Routledge
2 Park Square, Milton Park, Abingdon, Oxon, OX14 4RN

Simultaneously published in the USA and Canada
by Routledge
270 Madison Avenue, New York, NY 10016, USA

Reprinted 2008

Routledge is an imprint of the Taylor & Francis Group, an informa business

© 2007 Tony Martin, Chira Lovat and Glynis Purnell

Typeset in Palatino by
Keystroke, 28 High Street, Tettenhall, Wolverhampton
Printed and bound in Great Britain by
TJ International Ltd, Padstow, Cornwall

British Library Cataloguing in Publication Data
A catalogue record for this book is available from the British Library

Library of Congress Cataloging in Publication Data
Martin, Tony, 1947–
The really useful literacy book : being creative with literacy in the primary classroom
/ Tony Martin, Chira Lovat, and Glynis Purnell. – 2nd ed.
p. cm. – (The really useful series)
Includes bibliographical references.
1. Language arts (Elementary) 2. English literature–Study and teaching
(Elementary) 3. Language arts–Correlation with content subjects. I. Lovat, Chira.
II. Purnell, Glynis. III. Title.
LB1576.M3795 2008
372.6–dc22
                                        2007027723

ISBN10: 0–415–43165–4
ISBN13: 978–0–415–43165–1

Contents

Acknowledgements

We would like to thank the staff and children of all the schools that have helped us develop ideas in their classrooms. Specific work is acknowledged in particular chapters.

Special thanks to Nancy Martin for the Lucy Gray materials. These can be purchased from the Wordsworth Trust, Grasmere, Cumbria, tel. 015394 35544. Thanks also to Kate Lovat for the photos in Chapter 9, and to Jack Johnson for the photograph on page 62.

Special thanks also to the Manchester Education Partnership literacy team, especially Jana Welsby, for the bookmarks (copyright Manchester City Council). Also to Tristram Rossin who designed and illustrated them.

We are very grateful to Julie Howse, a teacher from Birchfield Primary School in Manchester, who made a significant contribution to Chapter 7 by carrying out much of the work, both in her own classroom and in the Whitworth Art Gallery. It is thanks to Julie that we are able to present all the exemplar work in this chapter.

We recognise the support always provided by colleagues at the University of Cumbria, not least the administrators in the Education Development Unit for their ICT help in preparing the manuscript and their equanimity during the virus crisis!

Source materials

A. A. Milne (1924) *When We Were Very Young*, London: Methuen © A. A. Milne. Copyright under the Berne Convention. Published by Methuen, an imprint of Egmont Books Limited, London, and used with permission.

Rosemary Davidson (1996) *One Teddy All Alone*, Cambridge Reading Series, Cambridge: Cambridge University Press © Rosemary Davidson 1996, reprinted with permission of Cambridge University Press and Rosemary Davidson.

Material from Janeen Brian (1991) *Natural Disasters*, Flinders Park, Southern Australia: Era, reprinted with permission of Era Publications.

Photograph from the Whitworth Gallery, Manchester.

Introduction

The first edition of this book had three main aims: to link the theory and practice of literacy teaching; to explore creative approaches to literacy; and to focus on speaking and listening and teaching and learning. The first of these remains very important; we believe the most effective teachers and school literacy leaders are those with a firm grasp of the rationale underpinning classroom practice. Since the first edition was published, the second and third aims have become key elements of the revised literacy framework produced by the Primary National Strategy in England.

Linking the theory and practice of literacy teaching

There are many examples of books in which theory and research are outlined and other books full of practical ideas for the classroom. We attempt to link theory and practice throughout the book in the belief that a firm grasp of theory – the rationale underpinning practice – gives us the confidence to take professional decisions when planning and teaching our work. Without theory we are all at the mercy of whatever happen to be the latest recommendations and pronouncements.

Exploring creative approaches to literacy

Sometimes there appears to be a tension between structured approaches and creativity; between teacher modelling and the voice of the child. However, we believe that structure can provide the spaces for children to be creative as they respond to reading and develop their own control of writing. High quality teaching is about providing that space.

At its worst, the impact of Standard Attainment Tests (SATs) can result in creativity being relegated to the second half of the summer term – we know schools in which concerts, plays and out of school visits in Key Stage 2 are becoming a feature of the second half of the summer term. It is as if there is a distinction between teaching literacy in preparation for the SATs (the first two and a half terms, with an interregnum for Christmas) and engaging children creatively. This book is based on raising attainment in literacy through using creative approaches to teaching it: in the Foundation Stage, Key Stage 1 and Key Stage 2.

There are references throughout to the Primary National Strategy (PNS), sometimes because the classroom work reflects the approaches recommended by it, sometimes because an alternative approach is being examined. The PNS has produced exemplar units of work for each year group, based on three blocks: narrative, non-fiction and poetry. Each of these is a number of weeks long and we fully support the recommendation to plan for depth. However, we have two concerns. First, while exemplar units are useful for teachers there is a danger that these units become the only way of approaching text types. A good example is the Year 5 classic poetry unit based on 'The Highwayman'. While the ideas in the unit are fine, they do not include the approach we take in our classic poetry unit (Chapter 13). We worry about all Year 5 classes in England doing 'The Highwayman' in exactly the same way! Second, all the units are text based. In the book we have included examples of a language based unit (Chapter 12) and a process based unit (Chapter 11). None of our units covers everything a teacher might do in the course of a two, three or four week unit. They are offered as ways of working with children in classrooms. Ways which creative teachers will take, change, develop and make their own.

Focusing on speaking and listening, teaching and learning

In 1969, the book *Language, the Learner and the School* was published (Barnes et al. 1969). The blurb on the back cover stated:

> Language is the most subtle and pervasive of the means by which we present our assumptions about role, about subject matter, and about the people we talk to, at and with. . . . And yet . . . teachers tend to talk too much (and pupils too little) . . . what can we learn about learning by looking at the language of our class-rooms?

This was written in the mid 1960s and yet here we are in 2007 still arguing the case for the importance of pupil talk in the classroom. While we are excited by the ideas now finding their way into classrooms, we are also sad that it has taken the national strategies in England so long to realise the importance of this aspect of teaching. Ways in which we manage and encourage children to use speaking and listening in different groupings for different purposes impact on the quality of literacy lessons. In addition the whole area of teaching and learning in terms of such issues as thinking skills, learning styles and the emotional aspects of learning offer us exciting ways into engaging children with their work. Combining reading, writing, speaking and listening with insights from teaching and learning, offers us a rich set of ideas for the classroom.

Structure of the book

Chapter 1 considers what we call the big ideas with regard to the teaching of literacy. There are not many! Most have been around for a long time. Some are highlighted in the Primary National Strategy while others need reasserting.

> **The Big Ideas (Chapter 1)**
>
> ➤ Contexts and coherence
> ➤ Motivation
> ➤ Content and process

These big ideas lead to a set of principles and practices explored in Chapter 2.

> **Principles and Practices (Chapter 2)**
>
> ➤ Generic teaching and learning
> ➤ Reading, writing and purpose
> ➤ Sounds and words and sentences
> ➤ Key teaching strategies

Chapters 3 to 16 outline units of work in the primary classroom and each chapter is structured in the same way.

1. An introductory discussion of the focus of the unit.
2. 'What was in the teacher's head when planning this work?' We link this 'professional thinking' to the big ideas in Chapter 1: contexts and coherence, motivation, content and process. In addition we provide links to the literacy learning objectives from the Primary National Strategy Framework for Teaching and the Early Learning Goals from the curriculum guidance for the Foundation Stage.
3. Starting points. How we start a unit always involves professional choices. In some units we suggest a number of potential ways of starting, while in others the materials have been designed for a particular starting point.
4. Spotlights. These take us into the classroom for lessons at different stages of the unit.
5. Beyond the unit. These sections contain ideas for developing the work with children in the longer term.

Reference

Barnes, D., Britton, J. and Rosen, H. (1969) *Language, the Learner and the School*, London: Penguin.

1 The big ideas

Why do we teach as we do?

Teaching literacy is not simple. The ways in which children learn to read and write, and the teaching strategies which will best help them to do so, have been debated and researched for hundreds of years. Not only because of its complexity but also because it is so vitally important, we believe it is the most fascinating aspect of teaching and learning. In the classroom the fascination constantly manifests itself. How come that 4 year old can already read, while the child sitting next to her has hardly begun? Why does that 10 year old find it so easy to produce three or four page stories in which the ideas are imaginative and the sentences flow, when the child sitting next to him sweats out, almost painfully, half a page of disjointed text? What lies behind that 7 year old's 'ability' to spell in contrast to the child sitting next to her for whom spelling seems to be a total mystery? And what sort of teaching will help each of these children?

However, while literacy teaching and learning are complex, because learners are complex, this does not mean we are just faced with a tangled web of ideas and approaches (and it can look like this on the staff room bookshelf where the ever growing pile of government publications offering advice totters against the latest literacy scheme from one of the well known publishers, which in turn slumps against the pile of journals and educational magazines advocating the latest good ideas). In fact, underpinning the ways we teach and the ways learners learn are a small number of 'big ideas' which lead to a set of powerful principles and practices. This rationale informs the ways we plan and the ways we teach. It lies at the heart of high quality classroom practice, and clarity about it gives teachers the professional freedom to think through their classroom practice.

The Big Ideas

➢ Contexts and coherence
➢ Motivation
➢ Content and process

Contexts and coherence

Contextualised literacy

Reading and writing are all around us. Young children are exposed to it from birth – on the television, in newspapers and magazines, on bottles, cans and packets. They see other children and adults engaging with print in different ways. This means that the learning of literacy does not take place in a vacuum, and the school and the classrooms within it are not laboratories. The importance of these everyday contexts in which children learn to read and write is well researched and at its most powerful with regard to very young children:

> All surveys coincide in a very simple fact: if the child has been in contact with readers before entering school, s/he will learn to read and write more easily than children who have had no contact with readers. What does this pre-school knowledge consist of? Basically in a first immersion in a 'culture of literacy': having listened to someone reading aloud, having seen someone write, having had the opportunity to produce intentional marks, having taken part in social activity where reading and writing made sense, having been able to ask questions and get some sort of answer.
>
> (Ferreiro 2000)

This quotation has two important implications in terms of 'contexts for literacy' in the classroom, whatever the age of the child. First, there are the literacy contexts themselves – the different ways in which written text is produced and used in the world around us. We can either ignore them and create an artificial 'school literacy' in which the reading and writing reflect only the school and the classroom, or we can bring the everyday literacies into our classrooms and use them as the basis of our teaching. Margaret Cook (2002) reports the impressive development in Reception children's writing as a result of such an approach. One unit of work involved a visit to the local McDonald's and the subsequent building (by the children as well as the teacher) of a McDonald's role play area. Different types of 'structured play' involving speaking and listening, reading and writing for different purposes over a number of weeks led to a range of writing from the children, all highly purposeful and all embedded firmly in a shared experience. Cook reports the impressive progress in writing attainment resulting from this work.

The second implication from the Ferreiro (2000) quotation in terms of 'contexts' is connected to the first. The literacy contexts in the home and in the example of Reception children visiting McDonald's all make sense to the child. This 'making sense' is one of Brian Cambourne's 'conditions for learning' (Cambourne 2001); learning has to be con-textualised, i.e. it must make sense to the learner. Taking this idea a stage further leads to the importance of learners having the 'big picture' clear to them in terms of why they are learning what they are learning. They see where the learning is going and how it links to previous learning and learning in other contexts. Successful learners make connections.

Research by Charmian Kenner leads her to the conclusion that the first element in what she calls an 'interactive pedagogy' for bilingual children is 'a teacher who sees bilingualism as a resource rather than a problematic condition, and wishes to expand her knowledge about her pupils' home and community learning' (Kenner 2003).

The challenge of digital contexts

All of us, teachers and children, now live in a digital age. The pace at which this has developed since the mid 1990s is incredible, shows no sign of slowing, and gives rise to both challenges and opportunities for teachers of literacy. One thing is certain: these new texts represent powerful, meaningful literacy contexts for primary school children. Locke (2003) asks two key questions:

- How can we utilise ICT to achieve our current teaching/learning objectives?
- If the rapidly changing nature of ICT is changing the nature of literacy, how are these changes reflected in our learning objectives, our pedagogy and our envisionments of the future of classroom programmes?

The first question is already being answered in primary classrooms across the UK. Many now have digital projectors and interactive whiteboards installed and being used on a daily basis in literacy lessons. Texts are displayed and annotated on screen. The writing of teachers and children is saved and returned to later in the week. Children have access to computers at school and examples of them producing presentations and web based, multimodal texts appear regularly in literacy journals. At its best such work is exciting and motivating for both teachers and children but we would like to ask a question which can be asked of any method, approach or resource we might use in the classroom. There is always a danger of classroom practice becoming 'ritualised' in the sense that what occurs, occurs every day: so, now there is the daily ritual of turning on the digital projector so that the text can, yet again, be displayed and read on a screen. Is there an issue with screens? Should we worry about the child who has already spent an hour or more staring at a screen in the morning at home before arriving at school, then spends the literacy lesson staring at a screen followed by the numeracy hour staring at a screen and who will go home at the end of the school day to spend more hours staring at a screen? We are as excited as anyone by the new technologies, but we believe schools need to carefully monitor the amount of 'screen based learning' undertaken on a daily basis by children. In terms of literacy, specifically, the question is always about the most appropriate way to present a text to children. This will depend on the text type and its purpose.

The second question posed by Locke is very challenging. We are not sure it is yet clear how ICT is 'changing the nature of literacy' but we would like to consider two particular issues. The first is the impact on written language of the new methods of communication such as email and texting. In Chapter 13 we describe a literacy unit which investigates the difference between spoken and written language on the basis that 'writing is not speech written down'. However email and, especially, texting are beginning to blur this distinction. Texting is very close to speech, used as it is to have written conversations. Exactly how will these new ways of communicating affect and alter the nature of writing? What exactly will writing be like in another fifty years? Of course, the one certainty is that it will change, language always has (or we would all be writing like Chaucer). The second question posed by Locke, then, is about how far we should incorporate emailing, texting and other digital forms (e.g. blogging) into our objectives, pedagogy and programmes? Certainly these are literacy practices which make sense in terms of context to children. Indeed we may now be faced with a striking phenomenon that for the first time ever, many of the children we teach are writing more outside school than they are inside.

Bringing that writing into the classroom, discussing it and using it as a way into other purposes and text types surely must make sense.

The second issue contained within Locke's second question concerns how nowadays a key aspect of being literate is the ability to combine different modes to create meaning. Merchant et al. (2006) describe a project involving Key Stage 2 children in two schools who were paired and communicated with each other. Over the course of the project 'they moved seamlessly across different software platforms such as PowerPoint, Photoshop, First Class, Word, and were also able to search the Web to select relevant information' (Merchant et al. 2006, p. 36). Of course we have always had multimodal texts. Maun and Myhill (2005) remind us of the illuminated manuscripts designed and produced by medieval monks (though Brother Anselm is unlikely to have used the term 'multimodal' to describe his efforts) and Victorian love letters written on appropriately coloured, illustrated and perfumed notepaper (truly multimodal: writing, illustration, colour and smell!). There is no doubt in our minds that the potential of reading and producing computer based multimodal texts must be part of a modern literacy curriculum, and the Primary National Strategy includes such work in the literacy objectives. The literacy curriculum will, then, include such texts as well as the already established multimodal texts (e.g. information books and newspapers) and also texts written in continuous prose, without illustration whether they be narratives (novels and short stories), reports or articles. Indeed continuous prose is still the literacy of power in our society and being literate means being able to read and write it.

Coherent units

This focus on trying to ensure that learning makes sense to the learner leads to the now common practice of teachers sharing the lesson's learning objectives with the children, whatever their age. The distinction is made between what we are doing and what we are learning. However, in our experience there is less sharing of the big picture, the coherence which lies at the heart of what has been planned. A literacy unit lasting a week, a fortnight or longer should be a coherent experience for the children, making sense to them in a number of ways. Teachers can share coherence explicitly with children in terms of the following.

From the beginning to the end

From the initial introduction ('During the next few weeks we are going to . . .') to the final plenary which might involve children producing a piece of sustained writing in which they demonstrate the learning from the unit as well as an oral discussion of what has been learnt.

The linking and applying of text, sentence and word work

At times these may be taught together, with the text providing the context for exploring sentence level and word level features. At other times they may be taught discretely, for example with a word level focus on the past tenses of regular and irregular verbs. (Indeed, we have to be careful not to ruin the power of a text through using it as a focus for such work. We don't read poetry to improve our spelling. However, in shared writing teachers will look to apply all elements of the unit so that examples of the spelling will be used and noted. Children will then be expected to apply this work themselves in their own writing.

Literacy across the curriculum

Texts being read and written in other subject areas can be linked to literacy units. At its simplest this means that whatever text type is being studied in literacy has the potential for being the basis of the writing in history or geography or science. For example, a focus on Victorian child chimney sweeps in history could be linked to text types in the following ways:

- **Instructions**: How to sweep a chimney.
- **Explanations**: Chimney sweep to his mother, explaining his first day: 'I got out the poles, so that . . .'.
- **Persuasive**: Ad for chimney sweeps: 'Live life at the top!' 'Nice, open aspect'.
- **Recount**: A typical day's work: 'A day in the life of . . .'.
- **Argument**: For and against child chimney sweeps.
- **Non-chronological report**: Jobs in Victorian England.

Of course, only one would be chosen depending on the current literacy focus. Children then see the coherence of working on this writing both in history and literacy. The additional bonus is that only one piece of writing, covering both literacy and history, is produced to be assessed and marked, with a literacy hat on, 'Is this a good recount?' and with a history hat on, 'Is it correct history?'

Looking back and revisiting

Flipcharts and interactive whiteboards are useful because the literacy learning can be kept and then revisited on future occasions. One of the problems associated with English and literacy teaching can be the constant forging ahead with little thought or time given to previous learning. So, we spend a week teaching adverbs and then move on to the next topic. Six months later a colleague complains, 'Hasn't anyone taught this class adverbs? They just looked blank when I mentioned them!' As adults we recognise the same problem when someone shows us how to work the latest audio, visual or computer equipment. Then two days later we try at home on our own . . .! Constant, quick revision is a key to learning.

One simple idea is to begin every literacy lesson with two minutes' quick revision, and this is where flipcharts and interactive whiteboards really come into their own. 'Who can remember what we collected when we looked at words beginning with the digraph **ch** . . . the prefix **bi** . . . sentences beginning with a subordinate clause?' Who can recall the powerful verbs we used in that story based on *John Brown, Rose and the Midnight Cat*? A flick of the pad or a tap on the whiteboard and the relevant work is back in full view.

Coherence between years can be enhanced by a teacher selecting some key work saved on flipchart sheets or the whiteboard to pass on to the colleague who will be teaching the class next year. Now the children are thinking back months and then making connections with the new work they are about to embark upon. In a similar vein, work such as a story produced during shared writing can be read and discussed by other classes in the school.

The planning of each of the units in this book began on the basis of providing children with a coherent set of lessons.

Motivation

We all (adults and children) learn when we are motivated to do so. Sometimes this learning is superficial, driven purely by purposes external to the work itself and soon forgotten (none of us can remember much of the content of the notes we pored over in preparation for A level examinations). Sometimes the learning is deeper so that it remains with us forever, either because we continue to practise it, e.g. handwriting or spelling or the way to work the DVD player, or because it makes a real impression on us, e.g the snatches of poetry we can call up or our knowledge of the ways children worked in the factories of the industrial revolution. In terms of the teaching of literacy, we need to consider the following, all of which figure strongly in the units of work described in this book.

Learning because we're interested

We believe children learn best when they find something interesting. Creating and fostering a positive ethos for learning about language means modelling our own interest in front of the children. If we demonstrate that we find this aspect of literacy exciting, there is more likelihood that they will. This modelling means a classroom in which the way the teacher refers to texts and language ('Today we are going to consider a really interesting spelling pattern' . . . 'That's an interesting rule you seem to have discovered' . . . 'Wow, what a wonderful word!') is matched by the displays around the room (Five Fascinating Facts About Fonics). This is not just work to be 'covered' or 'delivered'. The best teachers do not just model language use in shared reading and shared writing, but model an enthusiasm for texts and language. As Graham Frater wrote about his survey of schools in challenging circumstances which had high achievement in Key Stage 2, the teachers had 'a passion for language and literature' (Frater 2001).

Setting the scene

Years ago a Canadian teacher at a conference suggested that a problem in many classrooms was that children were 'surprised by teaching'. We can picture a child enjoying himself over the weekend. On the way to school on Monday morning he looks ahead mentally to the day in front of him. First up will be literacy. But what exactly will he be doing? Until he is sitting on the carpet in front of the teacher he has no idea. Oh, it's a poem. And the teacher is reading it – has read it – is asking a question. Oh, now it's the next question and the child is still trying to get himself into 'poetry mode'. While this example is something of a caricature, we believe there is enough truth in it to draw attention to the need for us to set up learning in ways which motivate children.

This need not take much time at all. An example could be that on Friday afternoon the teacher explains that Monday's literacy lesson will begin with a poem, the theme of which is bullying. Over the weekend the children are asked to think about bullying. Have they ever been bullied? Why do they think some children are bullied? Why do they think some children are bullies? In registration on Monday the class is reminded about these questions and spends time in silence thinking about them. The literacy lesson begins with paired talk about the questions followed by a brief teacher-led discussion. The aim is that everyone is now motivated to read the poem. A group of Cumbria primary teachers came up with a short list of ideas in only a few minutes.

The Friday before the Monday

- The teacher tells a personal anecdote related to the text. As a weekend task, the children are asked to think about something in their own lives related to the same theme.
- The children are given a picture related to the subject matter of the text. Over the weekend, with their parents, they write appropriate words around the picture.
- The teacher gives the children a skeleton of the short story – title, characters, situation. Over the weekend the children predict the plot.
- For a narrative or a poem, the children are given the title and theme (e.g. bullying). Over the weekend they think about these and what they mean to them in their own lives.

Purposeful reading and writing

Why do adults read and write different text types in their everyday lives in and out of the workplace? What motivates them to do so? We read and write to achieve different purposes. Some of these purposes are straightforward, e.g. I read the instructions in order to play the game. I write the letter to the bank manager in order to persuade her to lend me money. Others are more subtle and complex, e.g. I read the novel because . . . well, why do you think we read novels?

'Purpose' is one of the most important ideas underpinning the teaching of literacy. As adults we can consider the various purposes for which we read and write in our everyday lives. On in-service projects with teachers we often ask them to consider the reading and writing they do and the purposes which drive them.

Reading

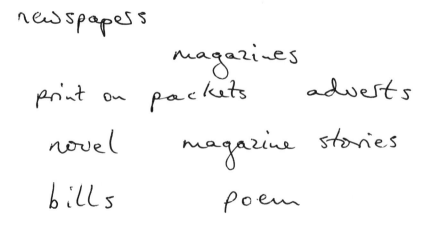

Figure 1.1

We find teachers distinguishing between the reading they 'have to do' both as teachers (e.g. the SATs regulations) and as people (e.g. household bills) and the reading they do because they want to (e.g. novels or poetry) (see Figure 1.1). There is always discussion about finding the time to read, and exchanges between those teachers who make the time because reading is so important to them and those for whom reading is not a habit.

Writing

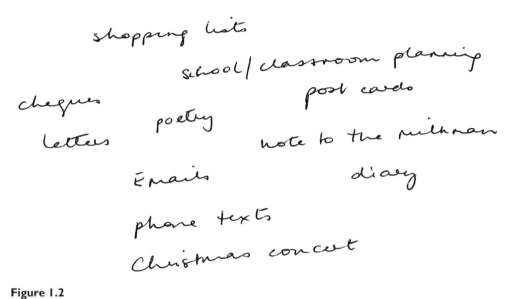

shopping lists

school/classroom planning

cheques

poetry

post cards

letters

note to the milkman

Emails

diary

phone texts

Christmas concert

Figure 1.2

For writing we distinguish between 'everyday writing' (e.g. shopping lists), writing that some people do because it is part of their job (e.g. teachers produce written plans) and writing which engages the imagination (e.g. poetry or the Christmas concert) (see Figure 1.2). Sadly, over the years, there have been very few examples of the last category. There is always discussion about why this might be, and a general admittance that lack of time is not really the issue. We find time to do other things, e.g. watch the television, but not to write. Could it be that writing is, in fact, hard work?

For each of the reading and writing examples above, a purpose can be attached, and these purposes lie at the heart of the text types making up the range of reading in the National Curriculum (NC) and Primary National Strategy: to instruct, to persuade, to narrate, to remind, to report, to recount. We therefore begin with purpose in writing and move from there to text types. Unfortunately the National Literacy Strategy in England began with text types which in our experience resulted in a great deal of 'purposeless teaching' and 'purposeless writing by children'. Writers should learn about a text type because it enables them to say what they want to say appropriately in order to achieve a writing purpose.

In addition, for writing, there is the need to consider the reader for whom the writing is intended (the audience) (see Table 1.1).

The concepts of purpose and audience have been a key idea in the teaching of literacy for many years and are examined in more detail in Chapter 2.

Table 1.1

Audience	Example of writing
Someone known to the writer	personal letter/email/phone text
A specific type of reader	
Teacher	*article in educational journal*
Four year old child	*picture story book*
Beer drinkers	*poster advertising Guinness*
A general readership	the electricity bill
The writer him/herself	personal diary

Engagement with powerful texts

If, whenever possible, we use powerful texts as the basis of our literacy teaching, we stand the best chance of motivating children to undertake the work. We almost defy a 7 year old not to be swept up in the power and excitement of a novel such as Ted Hughes' *The Iron Man*. Children cannot wait for the next reading. They jump at the opportunity to write their own first person versions of a key episode. In their research in London with Year 5 children published as *The Reader in the Writer* (2001), Myra Barrs and Valerie Cork go further and suggest that the reading of powerful texts was one of the key factors responsible for children producing high quality writing:

> Texts with . . . emotionally powerful themes communicated immediately with children in the classes we visited. They moved children and led to valuable discussions of the human situations they dealt with . . . Although it is not so easy to measure or track the effect of this kind of experience on children's writing, it is likely that emotionally powerful texts of this kind helped children to adopt other points of view, and to explore the inner states of characters, more readily.
>
> (Barrs and Cork 2001, p. 215)

Learning because it reflects my life

One of the major motivating factors for children (indeed for all of us) is reading and writing about subjects and themes which interest us and reflect our own lives. To be always reading texts chosen by someone else would soon demotivate most of us. Becoming an independent reader means being able to make independent choices about what to read. This is not to say that reading is just a free for all; there will be texts chosen by teachers for a variety of reasons, and one of the hallmarks of good teaching is being able to excite and interest children in the texts we want them to read. But within a broad and balanced reading curriculum children must begin to make their own decisions as well.

In terms of writing, while we want children to learn how to write a range of text types for different purposes, there is also the powerful idea of writing reflecting the identity of the writer. This means children being given the opportunity to write about their own lives and what is important in them. This can happen through the writing of any text type: for example a child can be encouraged to set a story somewhere they know and base the characters on people in their own lives. The child is the expert here, bringing their own life into school, knowing it has status in the teacher's eyes. If children leave this at the school gate, just producing school writing, the motivation to write can be lost. Writing journals are a powerful way of using this idea to motivate reluctant writers (see Graham and Johnson 2003) though they require sensitivity on the part of the teacher if a child is to share their own experiences, thoughts and feelings with them.

With regard to children learning English as an additional language (EAL), Eve Bearne writes:

> It is all too easy to forget that bilingual writers are bicultural writers and that making their own meanings clear is fundamental to their teachers being able to act responsibly in developing their English. Very often this means encouraging writing based on home, community and cultural experience . . . However the usual 'warnings' apply: home culture is for pupils to share with teachers when the pupils choose.
>
> (Bearne 2002, p. 24)

A belief and a route

Belief

> *If you think you can, or you think you can't, you're right.*
> (Henry Ford)

A second important area of motivation is about the self-belief of the learner (do I think I can learn?). The Henry Ford quotation is well worth discussing with children. Hay McBer (2000) in their work for the government defined classroom climate as:

> The collective perceptions by pupils of what it feels like to be a pupil in any particular teacher's classroom, where these perceptions influence every pupil's motivation to learn and perform to the best of his or her ability.
>
> (Hay McBer 2000)

None of the work described in the units making up the main body of this book will succeed unless children feel they can succeed with it. Teachers teach within the ethos they and their colleagues create and sustain. Trying to teach (and get children to learn) without establishing the aspects of motivation is really difficult. Powerful literacy teaching frequently works or does not work due to classroom ethos. It is important to remember here that learning is as much an emotional process (how I feel about myself as a learner) as it is a cognitive process (what I think).

A route

The engagement of the learner

A belief also implies the learner engaging with their own learning, thinking about it, considering strengths and weaknesses, in order to make decisions about how to progress.

Here we move into developing a child's engagement with their own learning, and the development of a route which makes sense and can be followed.

In the classroom we provide the route as we plan, teach and assess the progress of children. First, we carry out 'assessment of learning', making judgements about a child's attainment and progress, including both their skills and knowledge as well as the reading and writing behaviours we observe. Opportunities for assessment occur constantly in the classroom. We need to:

- **be mindful of it:** sometimes we plan for it, perhaps at the end of a unit of work when children write their own example of the text type we have been studying, or when we lead a guided reading group and assess the reading of the children in terms of both the strategies they use and their answering of our comprehension questions. At other times, perhaps during whole class teaching or when children are working independently, we notice a child working in new ways, for example a 4 year old writing independently, in the role play area for the first time. These opportunities to assess might be jotted down quickly at the time and then added later to our ongoing record of a child's development.
- **be flexible about it:** as is implied above, assessment does not just occur at the end of a piece of work. We can assess what children already know or can do at the beginning of a unit (far better than assuming no one knows anything about the work we have planned), during a unit and then, of course, at the end.

Second, in the classroom, assessment informs our new planning so that it lies at the heart of the route we want the learner to take. This 'assessment for learning' has the added dimension of encouraging children to think about their own work rather than just doing it. There is always a danger of children 'doing' a piece of writing and then handing it over to the teacher to 'think about it', i.e. assess it and comment on it. Assessment for learning might involve the child assessing the writing first, following a rubric discussed in class, before the teacher plays her part.

Target setting

Target setting also has an important part to play in the route agreed with a learner. Out of the assessment can be developed targets for further improvement. However, there is a danger that target setting can become unmanageable for teachers and superficial for children. A classroom dominated by a whole variety of targets runs the risk of diluting learning for its own sake discussed above, e.g. the desire to engage with powerful texts simply because they are powerful. How to use targets profitably in the primary classroom, supporting the teaching and in a way which is easily managed by the teacher of a large class is the aim.

Key questions to ask about any approach to the setting of learning targets for children are:

- How far is the child involved in decisions about targets?
- How does the child demonstrate that a target has been achieved?
- What do the child's parents know about the targets?

Whatever the system, the child's involvement is the key. In the end the motivation to move along a learning route has to come from the learner.

Boys

Yes, boys do seem to be a problem! In terms of attainment they still lag behind girls (in the 2006 Key Stage 2 English tests, 79% of boys and 87% of girls achieved level 4 and above in reading and 59% of boys and 75% of girls achieved level 4 and above in writing). A lot of research has shown that boys read less than girls (e.g. Moss 1998). Barrs (in Barrs and Pidgeon 2002, p. 10) writes that 'studies have found girls writing more, choosing to write more readily'. So motivation (or the lack of it) appears to be a crucial factor in raising the attainment of one-half of the school population. However, the actual situation is very complex (far more complex than the constant references to it in the media would imply). Reviewing the range of research – biological, psychological and social – Maynard (2002, p. 36) states: 'Having explored a number of theories which attempt to explain gender differences, we are left with a complex and confusing picture.'

We have not the space here to discuss the details. We simply point to a few ideas which have forced us to reconsider our thinking. How do you respond to each of these research findings?

- Any differences between boys and girls are small compared to variation within either sex (Campbell 1995, cited in Maynard 2002).
- 'It is a myth that boys are motivated [to write] by the use of ICT' (Essex Writing Project, in Bearne 2002).
- In Gemma Moss's (1998) research, boys in the can/do category (can read and choose to do so) nearly always had at least one parent who was a committed reader. This was not true of girls in the same category who became committed readers through their peers and the school. Boys' peer group relationships seemed to work against them becoming committed readers, but it was a key positive factor for girls.
- Moss (1998) also questioned boys' choice of non-fiction texts because they preferred them: 'Non-fiction texts allow weaker boy readers to escape others' judgements about how well they read and how competent they are. They enable them to maintain self esteem in the competitive environment of their peer group relationships' (Moss, in Barrs and Pidgeon 2002, p. 10). Non-fiction texts are illustrated (unlike novels) and the reader can pick up the gist without having to engage with all of the writing.
- 'Boys' poetry writing showed remarkable layers of understanding and sensitivity' (Essex Writing Project, in Bearne 2002).

We must be careful not to view this complex area in terms of stereotypes.

Some research projects have identified strategies which do seem to motivate boys and the same themes emerge. Barrs and Pidgeon (2002) summarise the Boys and Writing Project, referring to the need for boys to be clear about their progress and the next steps they needed to take; making implicit processes such as the writing process, explicit; focusing on audience and purpose; working with a writing partner; the use of visual stimuli, ICT and video; drama, role play and storytelling.

Trisha Maynard's (2002) research demonstrated the impact of direct teaching and the use of structure in terms of different text types. She refers to shared writing as boy friendly.

Our experience over many years has demonstrated to us the truth of these sorts of findings – for both boys and girls. The National Literacy Strategy focused strongly on some of them, e.g. a genre approach to different text types and direct teaching and modelling of writing, but not on others. Now in the revised framework some of those elements such as speaking and listening have made a comeback. Some of the units in this book are aimed at other key ideas such as making the writing process explicit to children, using visual stimuli as a way into texts and incorporating drama techniques such as hot seating and freeze frames to engage children with the work.

Content and process

It is difficult to distinguish between content and process in literacy and English teaching. We can see the content of literacy as made up of the texts we read with children and the texts they read themselves. Then there are the text, sentence and word level objectives we focus on with children. However, in terms of the latter – the 'content' of teaching and learning about texts and language – we find ourselves dealing with complex processes: the ways readers read and writers write.

The texts children read

The National Literacy Strategy distinguished literature (novels, poems and plays) from six other text types (recounts, reports, instructions, persuasive writing, explanations and arguments). This widening of the range of reading and writing undertaken by children in primary school was welcome and teaching the characteristics of these text types has become a major element of the content of literacy teaching.

The challenge for a teacher of knowing the texts is greatest with narrative for older children. A Reception teacher can take home all of the picture books in the reading corner and read them in one evening. A Year 6 teacher is faced with novels of a hundred or more pages each (and the last Harry Potter is 607 pages long!) As a start, getting to know key novels to read aloud to children plus those to read in guided reading is the aim. But it is more than just knowing the texts in order to teach them. Once children realise that we really do know the books they are reading, the whole classroom ethos changes. A range of discussions takes place from the quick one minute chat with a child who is halfway through a particular novel to whole class plenaries about their reading preferences and independent reading.

Three levels: text, sentence and word

All texts have three levels – text, sentence and word – and in England they form the basis of the learning objectives in the Primary National Strategy. This idea is not complex and certainly not new. If we take the front page of a newspaper as an example, the text level features are the design and structure of the page, the sections into which it has been divided and the content of these sections. Sentence level features are the types of sentences used and the ways they are punctuated. Word level features are the vocabulary used and the spelling of the words.

Explicit teaching of text level (comprehension and composition), sentence level (grammar and punctuation) and word level (phonics, spelling and vocabulary) lies at the heart of the Primary National Strategy Framework for Teaching and forms the basis of coherent units of work.

The reading process

The National Literacy Strategy represented the ways readers read texts as a searchlights model (see Figure 1.3). The more a reader is able to shine each of these searchlights on the text, constantly using each, cross-referring almost instantly between them, the better chance there is of successful reading. A knowledge of the reading process is vital if we are to support children as they read in guided reading and model the process in shared reading. However, it is difficult to appreciate how reading works once we have become fluent readers. We all read so quickly that the process is almost impossible to discern.

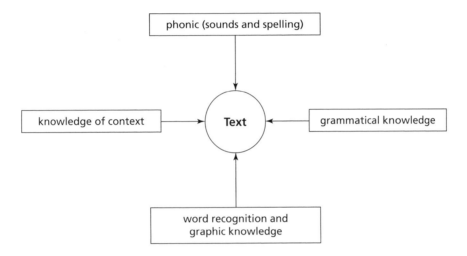

Figure 1.3

The text in Figure 1.4 is aimed at slowing you down as a reader. We will give you the context – it's a newspaper article – but it appears as if you are reading it in a mirror. Try to read it, but after a few sentences stop and reflect on the strategies you are using.

- Were you aware of scanning the words, turning the letters into sounds, and clustering the letters into whole words and bits of words ('ing', 'tion').
- Did a sentence opener provide you with a clue as to its grammatical structure and 'tune'? (For example, think of sentences beginning with the word 'If'. What 'tune' do these sentences have?) As we read sentences we use our implicit grammatical knowledge as the basis for our intonation.
- Were you just trying to work out the words and sentences or were you trying to make meaning from the text? Trying to read this text draws our attention to a major issue in reading. Every reader is trying to make meaning out of the text. This will have been the major strategy employed by anyone trying to read about Guinness. As the Primary National Strategy acknowledges: 'The ultimate goal of learning to read is comprehension' (Department of Education and Skills (DfES) 2006, p. 28). We just need to remember that 'comprehension' is *the* driving force of any reading – readers do not wait to be asked comprehension questions, they are trying to make meaning all the time! (See Figure 1.5.)

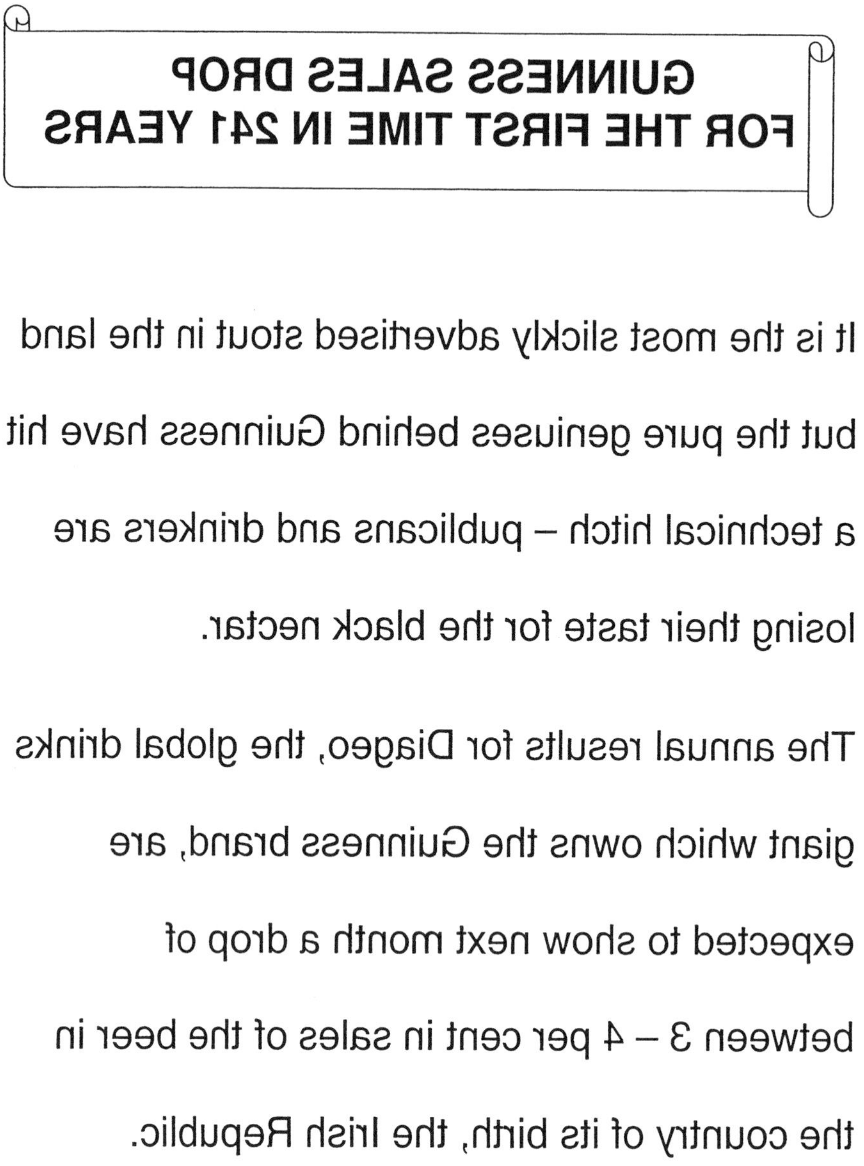

GUINNESS SALES DROP FOR THE FIRST TIME IN 241 YEARS

It is the most slickly advertised stout in the land but the pure geniuses behind Guinness have hit a technical hitch – publicans and drinkers are losing their taste for the black nectar.

The annual results for Diageo, the global drinks giant which owns the Guinness brand, are expected to show next month a drop of between 3 – 4 per cent in sales of the beer in the country of its birth, the Irish Republic.

Figure 1.4

Early readers and fluent readers: the 'simple view of reading'

The emphasis on meaning making is the same whether the reader is in the early stages of learning to read or a fluent reader. However, the extent to which the different searchlights are consciously employed differs. Fluent readers are extremely good at rapid decoding of letters, letter clusters and whole known words – so good that we are hardly aware we are doing it. This frees us up to engage with the meaning (comprehension) of the text. Early readers need to be moving towards this rapid decoding.

The 'simple view of reading' proposed in England by the Rose Report (2006) is intended to replace the searchlights model so that teachers are clear about focusing their teaching on either the development of word recognition or comprehension: 'Different

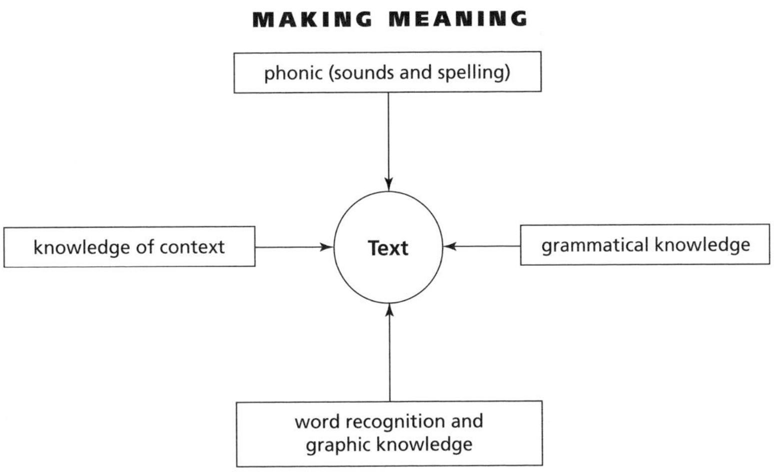

MAKING MEANING

phonic (sounds and spelling)

knowledge of context → **Text** ← grammatical knowledge

word recognition and
graphic knowledge

Figure 1.5

kinds of teaching are needed to develop word recognition skills from those that are
needed to foster the comprehension of written and spoken language' (Rose Report 2006,
p. 77).

Teaching can be differentiated for children whose reading development places them
in the different quadrants shown in Figure 1.6.

We believe that this clear focus on word recognition and comprehension will prove
useful to teachers but we have two major reservations with this latest model of reading.
The first is simply the use of the term 'simple view of reading', which implies that the
reading process, learning to read and teaching reading are 'simple'. Our experience leads
us to a different conclusion, namely that they are each complex and challenging. In fact
the Primary National Strategy paper (DfES 2006) explaining 'the simple view of reading'

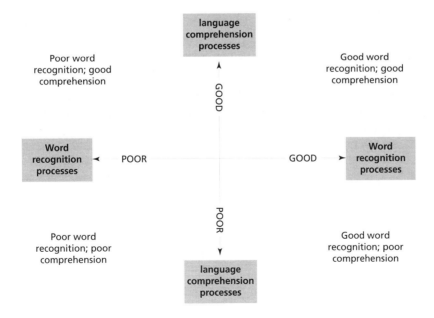

Figure 1.6

is thirty-seven pages long and focuses on such matters as how speaking and listening is the 'foundation' of phonic work, how phonemic awareness leads to phonics, semantic representation, syntax, morphology, pragmatics, metalinguistic awareness and anaphoric references (to name but a few of the issues and terms) – perhaps not so simple after all! We enjoy working with teachers who recognise the complexity of what they are doing and have developed the knowledge and understanding which make their teaching so rich.

Word recognition before comprehension?

Our second reservation is not so much to do with the model of reading but with the Primary National Strategy's assertion that word recognition comes before comprehension:

> Early on, new readers will be focused on the application of phonic skills and word recognition, but as they grow in confidence and skill, the emphasis will shift to comprehension.
>
> (DfES 2006, p. 13)

This leads to a recommendation about the teaching of early reading:

> In the early years of learning to read, teachers need to focus on helping children develop their word recognition skills . . . as children develop in their reading, attention should be paid to the transition from learning to read to reading to learn where the balance of word recognition and language comprehension changes.
>
> (DfES 2006, p. 15)

We believe these statements, and their implications for the reading curriculum in the early years, confuse two different aspects of reading. First, there is the act of reading itself – someone trying to read a written text. In this case it is obvious that the reader requires word recognition skills first, in order to comprehend – we cannot understand a passage if we cannot read the words. However, this 'act of reading' is not the same as the ways children develop as readers. We have come across many children who have developed a knowledge and understanding of written texts before they develop word recognition. More than this, their knowledge of texts means that when they come to the task of recognising words, the task is meaningful to them.

To illustrate what we mean we would like to introduce 4-year-old Simran Gill. Simran sat at home with her mother, Narinder, with a tape recorder and told a story. Narinder turned the tape player off and on at different points to allow Simran some thinking time but she did not help with the story.

Simran's story

> I am Simran and I'm going to tell a story.
>
>   Long time ago there was a little girl with a coat with golden buttons on and they sparkled in the dark and she had a nice suit like that as well that sparked in the dark so she wasn't scared of dark-ness.
>
>   A little boy came in for a golden button and [she he said, and] she said no, because you can't have one of my buttons and the little boy cried and he was a bit upset, and he told his mom.

Meanwhile a little boy came to steal her buttons but she dressed up as a monster and he ran home fast as he could and mom said 'What's the matter', but he didn't say what's the matter because he was too scared.

Ha ha ha ha ha ha . . . touch my buttons ever again because – I – dressed – up – as – a – monster.

The next day when she went to the shop nobody talked to her and nobody said 'what lovely buttons' because they heard about how she frightened the little boy.

As she went home she was very very sad and her friend asked her to tea. If you share your buttons you'll be the happier girl ever.

Listening to the tape is very different from reading the transcript. There are long pauses and false starts so that you can almost hear Simran thinking, and appreciate what a tremendous intellectual exercise it is for a young child to compose a story. To appreciate fully Simran's achievement one has to hear her voice, as many teachers on in-service projects have done: the dramatic pause at the end of dark before she adds 'ness'; the way she chants, magically, 'I – dressed – up – as – a – monster' with the tremendous emphasis on the second syllable of monster. However, even with just the words on the page, we can see how much she knows about story as a text type – and how much she has been comprehending stories long before being taught word recognition. She knows how stories begin, develop and end (even with a moral!) and that characters inhabit them and move the narrative on. She uses her 'story vocabulary – 'meanwhile', 'sparkled', 'darkness' – which shows her developing a literate vocabulary i.e. words she would not use in everyday speech. She uses written sentence constructions, for example different types of complex sentence:

- The next day, when she went to the shop, nobody talked to her.
- As she went home, she was very, very sad.

She knows that you tell a story in the past tense but is also able to shift to the present tense for direct speech. Simran and all the other children who are lucky enough to be read to throughout their pre-school years challenge the idea that early readers develop word recognition before comprehension.

Obviously teaching in the early stages of learning to read will focus more on phonics and word recognition than the teaching of older children who have developed fluent, automatic word recognition. But this does not mean that word recognition comes before a knowledge of written texts, especially story, in the development of many children as readers. In fact the early years 'language rich curriculum' recommended by the Rose Report (2006) will give all children the chance to develop the early reading knowledge displayed by Simran. Reading aloud and sharing books is singled out as a key element of this curriculum:

Indeed it is important to make sure that, over the course of acquiring phonic skills, children are also given every opportunity to enjoy and benefit from excellent literature (Rose Report 2006, p. 36).

The writing process

This can be explored in two different ways. First, there is the equivalent of the reading process above, showing what goes on in the mind of a writer during the process of writing (see Figure 1.7). Being consciously aware of the challenges writers face can only lead to better teaching of writing. Shared writing is now established in most classrooms, with its modelling of this process by teachers for children, and this has meant both teachers and children becoming more aware of the process themselves.

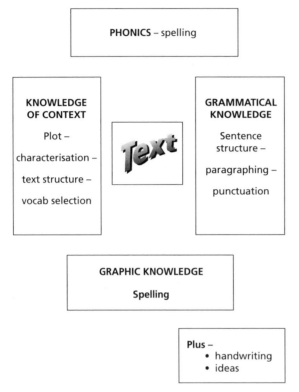

Figure 1.7

The other way of viewing the writing process is to consider the stages a piece of writing might go through (see Box 1.1). While not all writing goes through the full process, writers are always faced with the activities shown in Box 1.1.

Box 1.1

| *Pre-writing* e.g. drawing, discussing, planning | *Writing* composing | *Revising* adding, deleting, rearranging | *Editing* correcting | *Achieving purpose* e.g. informing, persuading, instructing |

The writing process can be thought of more simply in three stages

- Pre-writing – what might happen before the writing itself begins, e.g. planning.
- Writing – the process of composing, and including revising and editing.
- Post-writing – including, for example, a poem being shared or a set of instructions being used.

A 5 year old might draw a picture of what she wants to write about, have a go at some writing and then share it with her teacher. A 10 year old might plan a newspaper report, on the computer develop a writing frame for the newspaper page, import photographs or illustrations from the internet, begin to write within the frame, share the writing with a writing partner as it develops, revise it in the light of these paired sessions, finish it, take responsibility for ensuring it is correct (again with help from a writing partner), email it as an attachment to a parent, have it assessed and marked by a teacher.

Guided writing (see p. 59) means joining a group of children at a particular point in the writing process and using their efforts as the basis for teaching.

The learning process: speaking, listening and literacy

Finally in this consideration of processes, we must not forget arguably the most important: the process of learning itself, and the key role played by speaking and listening. Talk for reading and talk for writing are vitally important but why exactly do we want children 'talking in class'? Working on an inservice oracy project, some Liverpool teachers came up with the following:

Why do we want children talking in class?

➤ **Affective . . . to gain confidence and self-esteem**
Learning is an emotional as well as a rational process. Through talk we 'break down barriers'. When we contribute to a discussion and have our contributions accepted and valued we build confidence and self-esteem. This is especially powerful for children who struggle with other aspects of learning, especially literacy.

➤ **Risk taking as a learner**
Talk enables us 'to experiment without consequences'. Learning is often a risk-taking activity and it can be easier to take risks with talk than with, for example, writing.

➤ **Pedagogical . . . (inter)active learning . . . inclusion**
The challenge for all teachers is how to include all children in the lesson. Interactive learning means children interacting with the teacher and with each other. Teaching sequences using a range of speaking and listening strategies help to ensure that all children speak and listen in structured ways and feel involved in the lesson.

➤ **Psychological . . . to rehearse and reinforce ideas**
Two powerful purposes for speaking and listening are that they enable children to rehearse their learning by talking through what they are going to do and to reinforce that learning by engaging with the same 'content' in different ways, perhaps in a pair and then when the pairs move into fours. Speaking and listening are key ways of developing children's learning and thinking.

➤ **Talk for writing**
Talk as a rehearsal for writing (e.g. discussing with a partner what I am going to write about) makes the act of writing easier. Drama strategies such as hot seating, freeze frames, thought tracking and role play enable children to really engage with characters and situations which then form the basis of their writing.

➤ **Listening**
Arguably listening is harder for children than speaking! Strategies such as A/B talk (A tells B and B reports what A said) and envoying encourage children to listen actively.

> **Social/life skills**
>
> Speaking and listening are key 'skills for life'. Strategies which help children develop as confident, articulate people will remain with them for the rest of their lives. Included here are questioning skills. In the classroom do children see the teachers as the ones who ask the questions and themselves as the ones who answer questions? How might we adjust the balance and change the perceptions?
>
> A key approach for life skills is being explicit with children about how they will work with everyone in the class over time. Strategies such as 'autograph books', in which children collect the signatures of all those they have worked with, give them responsibility for their own organisation.

> **Equal opportunities**
>
> We use strategies in which all children take on different roles (reporting back what someone said; an envoy, chair of a group etc.) for different purposes.

> **Demonstrating learning**
>
> Children ought to be given a variety of ways to demonstrate their learning. If the only way of demonstrating learning is by writing about it and a child is not very good at writing, the poor writing can get in the way of the learning, both for the child and in terms of teacher assessment of that learning.

What a powerful list! Imagine if we announced we had discovered a way of working in classrooms that could achieve the results listed above. What a rush there would be to place such work in every classroom. Yet, as noted earlier in this chapter, despite all of the work in the 1970s and 1980s, plus a National Oracy Project in the early 1990s we still find ourselves in 2007 trying to establish speaking and listening strategies as a natural part of a teacher's repertoire.

The Primary National Strategy literacy framework includes four speaking and listening strands: speaking, listening, group discussion, drama. (We could ask why speaking and listening were absent from the National Literacy Strategy from 1997 to 2006? Perhaps this is one of the reasons the targets for attainment in reading and writing have not yet been met.) These strands are taken from *Speaking, Listening, Learning: Working with Children in Key Stages 1 and 2* (QCA 2003). While we welcome the status now given to speaking and listening in the teaching of literacy and the attempt to disentangle it for teachers through four strands, we would want a clearer focus on 'talk for learning' as well as the teaching of speaking and listening. Our experience leads us to argue that teaching strategies aimed at developing 'talk for learning' and 'talk for thinking' are one of the keys to raising attainment in reading and writing. What we mean can be illustrated by comparing two models of speaking and listening, both coincidentally using three interlinking circles (Figures 1.8 and 1.9).

Figure 1.8 is the model proposed by QCA. The focus is on talk itself: types of talk, the subject matter of the talk, the person talking. Figure 1.9 was proposed by the National Oracy Project (1990–1992). Here the focus is on learning: talk to develop one's own understanding; the demands of talking to others, adjusting what we say and how we say it; the skills required to interact with other people. We believe that Figure 1.9 is a more powerful model for the classroom, focusing as it does on the power of talk in learning rather than on talk itself.

So, what does talk for learning look like in the literacy lesson?

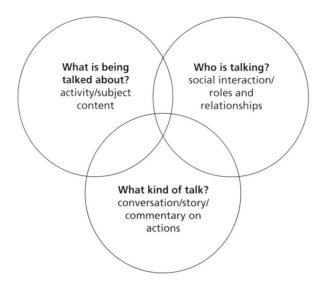

Figure 1.8

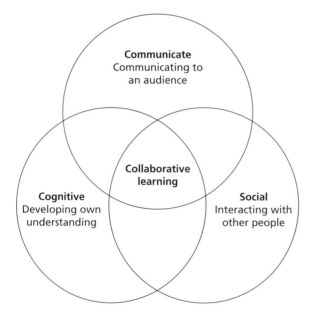

Figure 1.9

Sequences of teaching: the flow of the classroom

Let us visit some classrooms.

A Year 5 teacher is finishing her lesson with a plenary. The children sit in pairs and have a minute's silent thinking to review the lesson and come up with something important to tell their partner. In each pair, A then tells B and B tells A. When the teacher then points to a child, the child has to explain what their partner told them.

A reception teacher is planning to use the big book *The Shark with No Teeth*. On A3 paper she photocopies the first page's illustration (a huge cartoon shark with a very bright, sharp set of teeth). Copies are given out to pairs of children (one copy per pair). The children sit quietly looking at the picture. One child in each pair is holding a plastic building brick – this child is the speaker. The silent thinking finishes and he/she tells their partner what they can see in the picture. The plastic brick is swapped and so are the speaker/listener roles. Each pair is now given a pencil and they work together to annotate the picture. Almost immediately two boys agree to write 'ns' next to the shark's nose. In a whole class session the pairs then contribute their thinking about the picture and what the story might be about, and some vocabulary (extended through the teacher's own contributions).

A Year 6 teacher is struggling to improve the ability of many of his class to read inferentially. He gives out a SAT style passage and asks the children, on their own, to write an answer to question 3. Pairs are now formed and the answers compared. Each pair agrees and writes an answer. Pairs become fours and each four has to compare the paired answers and agree an answer. Envoys are sent from the fours to other fours to see what answers they have agreed. The teacher collects in the answers and displays them on an interactive whiteboard. One 'Rolls Royce' answer is agreed by the class.

A Year 2 teacher uses a digital camera to take photos of her class as they carry out a range of speaking and listening activities: silent thinking, paired talk, group (fours) hot seating. She produces a speaking and listening display and uses it to get the children to reflect on how they spoke and listened.

All of these real examples show teachers using a range of strategies to create powerful teaching sequences. The lessons flow seamlessly from one element to the next. They really do exemplify 'talk for learning'.

Talk for reading and writing

Exactly what sort of talk might help children read and write better? This is a fascinating question and one which all teachers can consider when planning or teaching. Talk for writing is now the focus of much research (e.g. United Kingdom Literacy Association and Primary National Strategy 2004) and it all seems to be pointing in the same direction: certain kinds of talk seem to contribute to higher writing attainment. So, there are talk strategies which are not just motivating and engaging for children but can also help them write better. Our own work on a range of inservice projects leads us to believe they should form a natural part of whole class teaching, group and independent work, with pairs or small groups of children using talk for a range of purposes. Drama strategies then simply become powerful teaching strategies with the focus on the learning rather than the quality of the drama as 'performance'. (The Drama strand in the literacy framework focuses too much on performance – drama as theatre – and not enough on how drama strategies might develop a child's reading and writing.) A particularly strong strategy is for children to work with a reading or writing partner – partners can be changed regularly, perhaps with the aim of every child working with every other child over time.

Talk for reading

➢ Talk to explore aspects of a text . . . drama strategies are especially powerful here.
➢ Talk to clarify and aid comprehension
➢ Talk to review texts
➢ Talk to share texts (literature circles or reading groups)
➢ Talk to recommend a good read

Talk for writing

➢ **Talk as rehearsal (1)** – with a partner, talking through ideas and plans, generating the 'content'.
➢ **Talk as rehearsal (2)** – actually composing the first few sentences orally to a partner.
➢ **Talk to review** – reading aloud writing at different points in its composition, thereby hearing one's own writing aloud in one's own voice, and then discussing and revising
➢ **Talk to edit** – reading another child's writing and trying to help by pointing out or correcting errors.
➢ **Talk for spelling** – working with a partner on a spelling investigation or challenge, or working in a group for a 'collaborative test'.

None of these strategies will work immediately. The aim, as with so much in the primary school, is to introduce them at the appropriate age and then ensure children engage with them regularly. It is this 'drip, drip' of experiences which produces results. Talk as rehearsal and to review seem to be especially important for the speaker (so even if the listening partner offers no response, the activity is still powerful). During the former, talk is used to think through ideas. In the latter, children hear their own writing aloud in their own voices (and, as a result, are often to be seen amending and adding). In terms of talk for editing, most children will miss some errors, but the constant looking at another child's writing, week after week after week, develops knowledge of aspects of spelling, punctuation and sentence structure plus the habit of considering them in writing.

We began this chapter with the idea of contexts for literacy so that the learning makes sense to the learner. Our work in many schools and classrooms, now stretching back over many years, has convinced us that structured sequences in which children speak and listen in pairs and small groups, as well as whole class sessions, means they experience a rich mixture of teacher talk and their own talk to make sense of the learning. Such sequences and talk strategies are found in all of the units making up this book.

References

Barrs, M. and Cork, V. (2001) *The Reader in the Writer*, London: Centre for Language in Primary Education.

Barrs, M. and Pidgeon, S. (eds) (2002) *Boys and Writing*, London: Centre for Literacy in Primary Education.

Bearne, E. (2002) *Making Progress in Writing*, London: RoutledgeFalmer.

Cambourne, B. (2001) 'Conditions for literacy learning', *The Reading Teacher*, 54(4): 414–429.

Cook, M. (2002) *Bringing the Outside In: Using Playful Contexts to Maximise Young Writers' Capabilities*, Royston: UKRA.

DfES (2006) *Primary Framework for Literacy and Mathematics: Core Position Papers Underpinning the Renewal of Guidance for Teaching Literacy and Mathematics*, London: DfES.

Ferreiro, E. (2000) Address at international conference 'Reading and Writing in a Changing World', Mexico, 2000. Quoted in UKRA, *Language and Literacy News*, Summer 2000.

Frater, G. (2001) 'The hardest job in the world', *Times Educational Supplement*, Autumn.

Graham, L. and Johnson, A. (2003) *Children's Writing Journals*, Royston: UKLA.

Hay McBer (2000) *A Model of Teacher Effectiveness: Report to the Department for Education and Employment*, www.dfee.gov.uk/teachingreforms/mcber.

Kenner, C. (2003) 'An interactive pedagogy for bilingual children', research paper presented at the United Kingdom Reading Association Conference, Cambridge.

Locke, T. (2003) *ICT and English, Critical English Online*, www.soe.waikato.ac.nz/english/EnglishNZ/ICT.html

Maun, I. and Myhill, D. (2005) 'Text as design, writers as designers', *English in Education*, 39(2): 5–21.

Maynard, T. (2002) *Boys and Literacy: Exploring the Issues*, London: RoutledgeFalmer.

Merchant, G., Dickinson, P., Burnett, C., and Myers, J. (2006) 'Do you like dogs or writing? Identity performance in children's digital message exchange', *English in Education*, 40(3): 21–38.

Moss, G. (1998) *The Fact and Fiction Research Project*, Southampton: University of Southampton.

QCA (2003) *Speaking, Listening, Learning: Working with Children in Key Stages 1 and 2*, London: DfES.

Rose, J. (2006) *Independent Review of the Teaching of Early Reading*, London: DfES.

United Kingdom Literacy Association and Primary National Strategy (2004) *Raising Boys' Achievement in Writing*, Royston: UKLA.

2 Principles and practices

The big ideas in Chapter 1 lead us to a set of principles and practices for the teaching of literacy.

> ➤ Generic teaching and learning
> ➤ Reading, writing and purpose
> ➤ Sounds and words and sentences
> ➤ Key teaching strategies

Generic teaching and learning

We have chosen to begin this chapter with an examination of generic teaching and learning because we believe this has as much to do with successful literacy learning as the strategies specific to literacy considered below. How teachers vary the ways they question children, provide thinking time, and organise and manage children in different ways for different purposes impacts fundamentally on the quality of any literacy lesson.

Managing whole class teaching

The challenge of whole class teaching is how to include all children in the lesson. All teachers know what can happen when they pose a question to the class and are faced with the straining arms of some children (generally the same ones whatever the question), the hovering arms of others, and the few who have no intention whatsoever of risking an answer ('I haven't put my hand up for seven years and I don't intend to start now!') and are shuffling to the edges and disappearing under the tables at the back.

For the whole class teaching sessions, basically there are two choices:

- **Each child is 'on their own'.** When the teacher asks a question each child, alone, has to decide whether to put up their hand to answer.

- **Children agree an answer between them**. This can be a 'no hands up lesson' because the teacher will ask each pair or group of children for their answer.

Neither choice is right or wrong, but varying the ways we teach maximises our chances of including all children. Sometimes a child is on his or her own, sometimes they can discuss the question within a pair or small group before contributing to the class. However, we believe that talk partner work is a key to powerful, interactive whole class teaching and one of the ways in which we can ensure the involvement of all children in the session. In one session a child can be moved from one partner to another on a number of occasions, what we call 'rolling pairs' (each child in a pair is either child A or child B, and the teacher decides that all the Bs move on to form new pairings). In addition, pairs are the baseline from which we can organise children into different groupings. A/B pairs can be split into new pairs. Pairs can join as fours, to compare ideas or written work, or to synthesise in order to contribute to a whole class session.

As well as a whole class teaching strategy, paired talk is also a key strategy during guided group sessions and when children are working independently ('independently' means independent of the teacher, not necessarily children working alone).

Other important speaking and listening strategies (now recommended by the Primary National Strategy) include:

- **Thinking time**, where children are given some silent time to think, before discussing in a pair or putting their hand up.
- **Pairs to fours**, where pairs join together for a particular purpose such as sharing ideas, comparing work or explaining what they have done or found or understood.
- **Envoying**, where one member of a group is sent to another group. The envoy's task can be either to find out from the other group and report back, or explain something from their own group.
- **Rainbow groups** (a development of envoying in which all children become envoys), where, following a group task, each member of a group is given a letter and then all the As make a new group and all the Bs, etc. In these new 'rainbow groups' are representatives of each of the original groups and their task is to report their own group's work and become part of a discussion. The original groups are then reformed to discuss what was said in the rainbow groups.
- **Listening triads**, where children are in threes, each child with a designated role as speaker, questioner or note taker. The role of the note taker is to summarise what is said by the other two.

Asking questions

The key to developing thinking lies in the asking of questions in whole class teaching and guided group work.

Questions from both children and teachers

A thinking classroom is one where children are encouraged to ask questions as well as answer them. Some children do not find it easy to formulate questions about classroom work (though they do so more readily within the security of the pair or small group than in front of the whole class) and there are examples of ways of developing this within many of the literacy units we discuss.

Quick questions and thoughtful questions

Here, in terms of literacy lessons, we would distinguish between the following:

- Questions where a quick, instant answer is expected, such as 'what long vowel phoneme is in "soap"?' (answered either by 'hands up', written on individual white-boards or 'ten second talk' between talk partners).
- Questions where some thinking time needs to be provided, perhaps followed by discussion between a pair or group of children, such as 'How do you think Hannah's feelings change through the course of Anthony Browne's *Gorilla*?' In literacy such questions are often text level questions intended to develop inferential reading.

Dialogic teaching

The work of Robin Alexander (2004) has focused attention on discussion within whole class teaching with the concept of dialogic teaching. This is teaching which is:

- **Collective:** teachers and children engaged together in the learning task
- **Supportive:** there is a classroom ethos in which children feel confident about articulating answers and ideas without fear of being 'wrong', using this to develop understanding
- **Reciprocal:** teachers and children listen to each other
- **Cumulative:** teachers and children build on each other's ideas and thus create chains of thinking
- **Purposeful:** teachers plan and facilitate dialogic teaching with clear goals and outcomes.

Posing a question such as the one above about Hannah in Anthony Browne's *Gorilla* in a class where children know they have to listen to the responses of classmates with the expectation that they can agree, disagree, build on these responses is very powerful. It breaks the problematic strategy of teacher asking a question, some children putting their hands up, a child answering, if the answer is correct the teacher repeating the answer back to the class, the teacher asking the next question. It means children seeing the point of listening to answers. It means teachers taking a step back and being more subtle in how they lead and manage the learning.

Pace

From the above it follows that the word 'pace' in terms of teaching does not mean teaching quickly. The equating of pace with quick in national strategies has been a real problem. Of course, sometimes there will be a brisk pace, for example a fifteen-minute revision session of a phonics or spelling convention is likely to contain lots of questions requiring 'instant answers'. However at other times, for example when discussing Hannah in *Gorilla* or when reading and discussing a powerful poem, the pace will be different. We will be encouraging reflective thinking and exploratory, dialogic talk, and allowing the text to work its magic. We hope nobody is teaching poetry fast under the mistaken impression that this is good teaching.

While these strategies are often listed as we have done here, their use is best considered not in terms of isolated activities which I might choose to use in a particular lesson, but in terms of sequences of teaching, such as those we described in Chapter 1.

Learning styles

The fact that learners learn in different ways has been one of the cornerstones of the current interest in teaching and learning, and there are a number of approaches to learning styles (for a summary see Ginnis 2002). While there is still uncertainty about learning styles and the extent to which they are fixed (Hall 2006) we have found the diagram in Figure 2.1 (Key Stage 3 Strategy) to be useful, not so much because of whether particular children do in fact have particular styles of learning but because it focuses teachers on the need to provide variation in their teaching. Perhaps we all learn in all of the ways at different times, but one thing is certain: we all like variation.

It is strange that they were not explicitly part of the National Literacy Strategy for either primary or secondary schools because, like the whole class teaching sequence above, they lead to creative ways of approaching texts in the classroom whatever the age of the children. Why limit consideration of them to secondary schools?

Both interpersonal and intrapersonal learning are included in the sequence of whole class teaching above, and whenever speaking and listening are happening there is

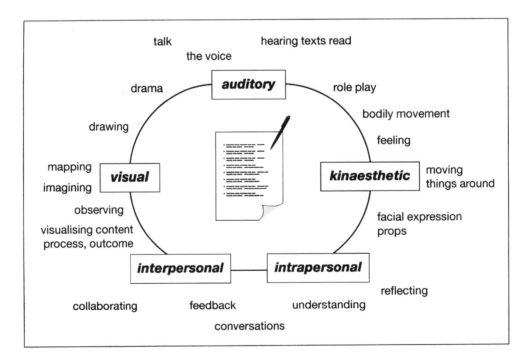

Figure 2.1

auditory learning. Ways in which literacy can be linked to visual and kinaesthetic learning are contained in many of the units. Planning with learning styles in mind is worthwhile for three reasons: first, because it means we are more likely to provide variation in our teaching; second, because it enables children to demonstrate their ability in different ways; and third, because we can develop all the ways of learning in all children – if there are such things as intrapersonal learners, it is good for them to learn how to work with other people.

Thinking skills

If the aim of teaching is not to get children to think, then we are not sure what it is about. The National Curriculum lists the thinking skills we are trying to develop in children. By using thinking skills pupils can focus on 'knowing how' as well as 'knowing what' – learning how to learn. The thinking skills listed in Box 2.1 complement the key skills and are embedded in the National Curriculum.

Box 2.1

By using thinking skills pupils can focus on 'knowing how' as well as 'knowing what', or learning how to learn. The following thinking skills complement the key skills and are embedded in the National Curriculum.

Information processing skills

These enable pupils to locate and collect relevant information, to sort, classify, sequence, compare and contrast, and to analyse part and whole relationships.

Reasoning skills

These enable pupils to give reasons for opinions and actions, to draw inferences and make deductions, to use precise language to explain what they think, and to make judgements and decisions informed by reasons or evidence.

Enquiry skills

These enable pupils to ask relevant questions, to pose and define problems, to plan what to do and how to research, to predict outcomes and anticipate consequences, and to test conclusions and improve ideas.

Creative thinking skills

These enable pupils to generate and extend ideas, to suggest hypotheses, to apply imagination, and to look for alternative innovative outcomes.

Evaluation skills

These enable pupils to evaluate information, to judge the value of what they read, hear and do, to develop criteria for judging the value of their own and others' work or ideas, and to have confidence in their judgements.

As with learning styles, awareness of these thinking skills helps to inform the ways we plan. Many teachers we know have both in front of them as they plan units of literacy and find that this influences the ways they teach and the range of activities they provide for children. Any of the units in this book could be examined with learning styles and thinking skills in mind as all were planned to incorporate variation for learners.

Reading, writing and purpose

A range of purposes and readers

One of our big ideas in Chapter 1, motivation, included the ways in which reading and writing are purposeful activities. The motivation to write is always to achieve some sort of purpose, which might be external to us (the letter to the bank manager) or internal (a personal journal).

If we add together purpose and audience (why am I writing and who will be reading it?) we find ourselves considering the best ways to construct the text we want to write (see Box 2.2).

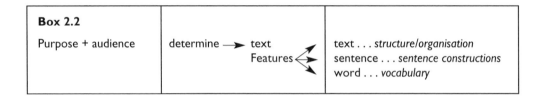

| **Box 2.2**

Purpose + audience | determine ⟶ text
Features ⟷ | text . . . *structure/organisation*
sentence . . . *sentence constructions*
word . . . *vocabulary* |

The three levels of text, sentence and word which form the basis of the termly teaching objectives are, then, based on the features of any written text. Writing is about making decisions regarding each of these levels plus the need for correctness (spelling and grammar). The features of the text types we read and write with children are based on the diagram in Box 2.2, so that instructional texts are structured and use particular sentence constructions because they are intended to achieve the purpose of instructing.

The text types in the Framework for Teaching are as shown in Table 2.1.

Table 2.1

Text type	Purpose
Discussion	to present an argument with some sort of conclusion
Explanation	to explain how something works
Recount	to give an account of something that has happened
Instructions	to provide rules or procedures
Persuasion	to persuade the reader
Non-chronological report	to communicate factual information

A sense of audience

Writers, then, write for readers, whether it be the texts driven by clear purposes such as instructions, or the story writer who is attempting to impact on the feelings and thoughts of the reader (for example a story intended to frighten). As children learn to write, one of the key ideas we are trying to develop in them is a 'sense of audience'. Put simply, this means children thinking about the reader as they write. As we struggle to write the sentences making up the chapters of this book we are faced with the most difficult writing task of all: how to compose sentences which, when read, will convey exactly what we are trying to say. This is the reason behind children writing for a range of readers rather than just solely for the teacher.

The triangle in Figure 2.2 represents three different elements of purpose and audience in the primary classroom:

➢ **Writing to achieve a purpose**
An example of what we mean will illustrate the power and importance of this. Children are told that over the course of a science unit their task is to write a booklet about the science for someone at home. The booklet is handmade, perhaps through the simple folding and cutting of a sheet of A4 paper to produce a small number of small pages. The children know that the person at home has not been in the science lessons. They are faced with the challenge of writing and illustrating the booklet so that this reader will understand the science. This is such a motivating task for children! The teacher's role is to help in the writing of these information booklets which will be taught in literacy lessons. So the science booklets move from literacy to science with children using their literacy knowledge in the science lessons – literacy across the curriculum.

➢ **Writing to engage the imagination**
We have collected many examples from teachers of literacy units which result in children becoming so imaginatively engaged with situations and characters that they

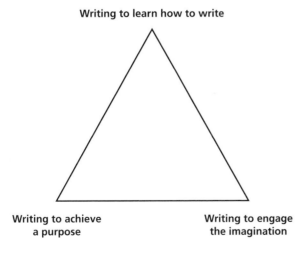

Figure 2.2

cannot wait to write. Each of the units in this book is aimed, first and foremost at engaging children, and when, for example, they have become involved in the story of Lucy Gray (Chapter 14) there is tremendous enthusiasm to write her story in the first person, as Lucy. They do not necessarily have a specific reader in mind; they just want to write! And they love sharing this writing with each other so that we develop an ethos in the classroom in which children enjoy writing for each other and reading each other's writing. This type of writing also includes the fantasy purposes and audiences which so motivate children in the early years. A letter to the children from Goldilocks, opened slowly and dramatically, holds the attention of every child. Replies, written in the role play area which is the three bears' cottage, are written by every child.

➢ **Writing to learn how to write**
Consider again the science unit above. Instead of writing a booklet for someone at home, the science is written up in an exercise book for the teacher to mark. The children know that the teacher knows the science because the teacher taught it. The only purpose for the writing can be for the children to demonstrate their understanding to the teacher.

We are not suggesting that the final approach is wrong. Regularly children will complete such tasks. However, our experience suggests that if this approach (writing for the teacher) is the only approach offered, year after year in primary school, we do not get either the quality or the enthusiasm for writing which we get from the first two approaches. Again the key word is variation in terms of our approaches.

Bringing out-of-school texts into the classroom

There are many examples of these text types all around us, and all around the children we teach. Resourcing our work with them, therefore, does not mean having to spend huge amounts of money. The first consideration ought to be whether there are real examples we can collect and bring into the classroom for free. Money can then be spent on the text types we do have to purchase. The advantage of working in this way is not just financial, but also means we bring our literacy lessons alive – children are far more likely to engage with real examples than artificial ones on the pages of literacy course books.
Some examples are:

- **Environmental print in Reception**: the children are asked to bring in something from home with print on it but not a book, e.g. shopping bags, T-shirts, packets, labels, magazines, leaflets, forms. Lots of discussion about these. What are they? Why are they produced? Why is some print bigger and some very small? Why are some words brightly coloured? What do some of the words say? Why are there pictures as well as writing? A huge display is made: 'Writing Is All Around Us'. Lots more discussion.
- **Information texts**: e.g. leaflets from tourist attractions.
- **Instructions**: e.g. recipes, games.
- **Persuasive texts**: e.g. estate agents' descriptions of houses, holiday brochures, junk mail.

We can build up boxes of examples such as these, providing free resources for imaginative lessons, both literacy and across the curriculum (see Contexts and coherence above, p. 5).

However, there is a problem with these text types, identified above so neatly. In real life, texts often contain a mixture of purposes. So, a newspaper report is usually a recount rather than a report. An information book may well contain elements of non-chronological report and explanation. A discussion will usually include some element of persuasion, especially if the writer holds strong views on the subject being discussed. We must be careful of not turning this aspect of literacy into an artificial exercise, divorced from the realities of texts in society. We need to reflect the ways texts really work in the world outside school.

Applying purpose to literature

The study of text types, based on how they are written to achieve their purposes, is a useful way of approaching a range of reading. What then of literature – narrative and poetry? Here we believe there is a danger that the study of how narratives and poems are constructed (at text, sentence and word level) will lose sight of the purposes for which readers read literature.

Since the early 1990s we have asked hundreds of teachers on in-service courses to discuss why they read stories themselves (novels, short stories, magazine stories . . .). Not once has any group included structure in their list of reasons. The constant appearance of words such as 'escapism' and 'empathy' has led to fascinating discussions about what they actually mean and then the challenge of not ignoring them in the classroom. We do not read literature for its structure and neither should children (Martin 2003).

Teaching literature is about the engagement of a child with a powerful text. The key word is response, and the exploration of how different readers respond to stories and poems is the basis of the literature units in this book. The simple diagram in Box 2.3 reminds us what happens when we read or are read to.

Box 2.3

Reader ⟶ Interaction ⟵ Text

The words of the text convey the intended meaning of the writer, but these words then interact with the reader's thoughts, feelings, personality, life history, etc. to produce a unique reading. The response of a reader to a text is, then, a combination of the text working on the reader and the reader working on the text. Most 4 year olds being read Martin Waddell's *Can't You Sleep Little Bear?* sit wide eyed and silent because their own feelings about the dark are mingling with the story. An adult who has been through a divorce will read a novel about a divorce differently from someone who has not experienced it.

Reader-response theory underpins these ideas, and it has been around a long time:

> The reader can begin to achieve a sound approach to literature only when he reflects upon his response to it, when he attempts to understand what in the work

and in himself produced that reaction, and when he thoughtfully goes on to modify, reject or accept it.

(Rosenblatt 1976)

Iser (1978) distinguishes between the meaning of the words in the text (as in 'dictionary definitions') and the significance of the text for different readers. Significance is the result of the interaction between text and reader, and will be personal, varying from reader to reader.

> Individual response to literature is fundamental . . . Readers respond to the same text in different ways at different times: readers make analogies between their own lives, current issues and those represented in texts, using the text as a fictional commentary on their own experience.
>
> (Department of Education and Science 1990)

The Primary National Strategy has a similar approach in terms of 'comprehension':

> Reading comprehension is a highly interactive process that takes place between a reader and a text. Individual readers will bring variable levels of skills and experiences to these interactions. These include language skills, cognitive resources and world knowledge. Any act of reading occurs within a particular sociocultural and emotional context.
>
> (DfES 2006, p. 28)

The study of how a literary text works begins, then, with an exploration of how readers responded to it ('it was scary') and we must provide time and space for such discussion in the classroom. Such work naturally leads into an examination of how the writer managed to produce such a response (the scary setting, the scary vocabulary, the use of short, sharp sentences for tension . . .). So, **reading like a reader** (how I responded to a powerful reading experience) leads into **reading like a writer** (how the writer did it).

In the recent past we believe there has been a danger of the analysis of texts (as in the Year 6 SATs and the National Literacy Strategy exemplar planning) leading the way, with the reader's thoughts and feelings being left behind. The Primary National Strategy twelve literacy strands show 'Understanding and Interpreting Texts' (Strand 7) before 'Engaging with and Responding to Texts' (Strand 8). While a strand devoted to engagement and response is to be welcomed, we believe the order in which the two strands appear to be a mistaken view of reading and likely to prolong the emphasis on analysis within literacy lessons. Such thinking could be the reason behind the results of the Progress in International Reading Literacy Study, carried out every five years, comparing reading attainment in thirty-five countries. The most recent survey was in 2003 (in England it involved 3,150 children in 131 schools). Two contrasting results emerged:

- English pupils were ranked third overall, and significantly better than all other English speaking countries.
- English pupils had relatively low levels of confidence and poorer attitudes to reading than the international average – 27% reported that they never or almost never read for fun compared to the international average of 18%.

While we must celebrate the good news regarding reading attainment, we seem to be producing children who can read (and that surely is their minimum entitlement) but who choose not to. We wonder at the point of a child knowing the meaning of 'metaphor' but never ever choosing to read poetry. Or the child who knows how writers might begin their narratives, but never reads or writes narratives themselves.

The reading–writing connection

Throughout the sections in this book reading and writing are either discussed together or seen to reflect each other: writers write for readers and readers read writing. The reading–writing connection lies at the heart of our work in classrooms through its consideration of the ways in which what we read influences what we write. The reading–writing connection is about **writing like a reader**. And in order to do so, writers have to have read the text type they are trying to write or have had it read to them. For example, no one could write a newspaper report if they had never read one. Of course, this begs the question how many examples of a newspaper report have to be read before someone could confidently attempt to 'write in the style of'. One? Twenty? A hundred? Inexperienced readers are very unlikely to be good writers.

  While we are all very aware of the children who are 'high ability readers' and those who are 'low ability readers', an equally important distinction is between children who are 'experienced readers' and those who are 'inexperienced readers'. Experienced readers – those who read widely and avidly – soak up the structures and sentence tunes and vocabulary of the texts they read. We then see these appearing in their writing (see Figures 2.3 and 2.4). Those of you who read *The Famous Five* will see the links clearly! The opening

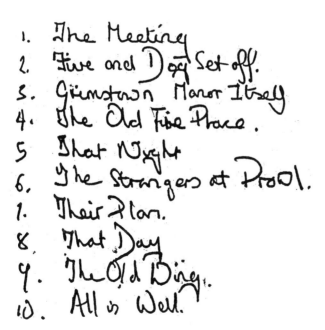

Figure 2.3

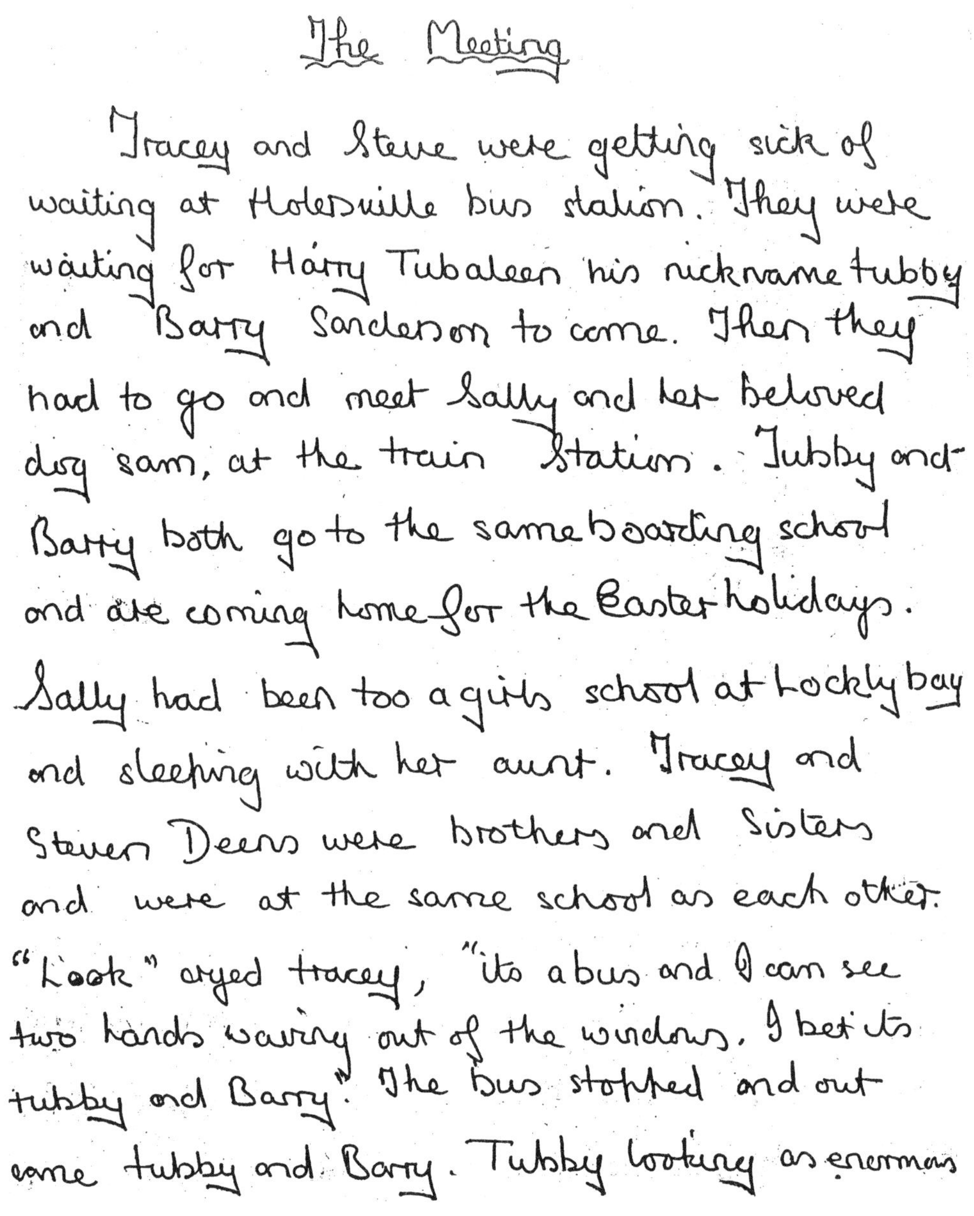

The Meeting

Tracey and Steve were getting sick of
waiting at Holesville bus station. They were
waiting for Harry Tubaleen his nickname tubby
and Barry Sanderson to come. Then they
had to go and meet Sally and her beloved
dog sam, at the train station. Tubby and
Barry both go to the same boarding school
and are coming home for the Easter holidays.
Sally had been too a girls school at Lockly bay
and sleeping with her aunt. Tracey and
Steven Deens were brothers and sisters
and were at the same school as each other.
"Look" cryed tracey, "its a bus and I can see
two hands waving out of the windows. I bet its
tubby and Barry" The bus stopped and out
came tubby and Barry. Tubby looking as enormas

Figure 2.4

of this novel, entitled *Grimstone*, was written by Carol Copsey, a teaching assistant in Cumbria, who kept a novel she had written when she was 10 years old, under the influence of Enid Blyton.

Immersion

Carol Copsey was immersed in *The Famous Five*, and writing successfully in the sense of being able to compose texts and create varied sentences links directly to how far the writer has been immersed in reading. From the experience of being read to and then wide reading, the writer builds ideas of what a successful piece of writing looks and sounds like. The more one reads the more one learns about writing. The gulf in this respect between the keen, avid readers in KS2 and the strugglers who read very little is vast. Working with a struggling writer on their writing, trying to show them how it could be 'improved', is very difficult if the child has no concept of what 'improved, good writing' is like. One issue worth mentioning here is the comparison between the amount of fiction and non-fiction read to children. Traditionally there has been far more of the former than the latter and this should be considered when choosing texts to read aloud.

Underpinning the ideas in this book, then, is the simple but powerful notion that children need to read and read and read – in order both to absorb the structures, sentence constructions and vocabulary of written texts so they become better readers and also if we want them to develop as writers. This issue arises from the start, with very young children. In his seminal paper 'Matthew effects in reading', Keith Stanovich (1986) examines the contrast between young children who read and those who do not:

> The effect of reading volume on vocabulary growth, combined with the large skill differences in reading volume, could mean that a 'rich get richer' or cumulative advantage phenomenon is almost inextricably embedded within the developmental course of reading progress. The very children who are reading well and who have good vocabularies will read more, learn more word meanings, and hence read even better. Children with inadequate vocabularies – who read slowly and without encouragement – read less, and as a result have slower development of vocabulary knowledge, which inhibits further growth in reading ability.
>
> (Stanovich 1986, p. 381)

So, from the start, the issue of how much a child reads seems to be a key in terms of the reading/writing connection. What does this mean for the school and classroom?

Three levels of reading

The three levels of reading are shown in Box 2.4.

Box 2.4

Shared	*Guided*	*Independent*
(challenging texts)	(texts at the child's reading ability)	(easy texts)

Shared reading is about working above the reading level of most children in the class. Through reading the text aloud and structuring discussion and teaching points, we enable children to access the text. We are looking to pull their reading up to the level of the text. As children get older, challenging does not mean just longer words and longer sentences! It often means the level of inference required to comprehend.

We might use a text the children can read confidently if our objective is to focus on elements of the text's structure. For children, trying to cope with a challenging text in terms of vocabulary or sentences or ideas can prevent them engaging with structural issues.

In **guided reading** the child has the support of the teacher and the group. The teacher structures the session – introduces the text, supports the child when she is reading and develops comprehension. The text is at the child's reading ability, able to be read but with challenge.

Independent reading might well be of the guided reading text or a text of similar level chosen by the teacher as being 'just right' for the child (not too easy and not too difficult). Children know all about the 'just right' book! However, we worry about children whose *only* reading is either at this level or even harder in shared reading. First, such children may not be reading enough to become a fluent reader (or a fluent writer). How many of us would read much if all our reading was at one of the above two levels? As adults just about all the reading we do is 'easy', whether it be our newspapers or the novels we choose to read for the week on the beach. Second, for such children reading is always hard, always on the edge of their reading ability. They never relax with reading. They are unlikely to develop a positive attitude to reading, or become readers for life. In terms of how much reading is done in a year, the gulf between the fluent, avid, 9-year-old reader who reads lots at home (and we guess most of it will be easy) and their peer who reads only the difficult texts in shared reading and the just right texts in guided reading, is vast. We argue for the place of **volume reading** of easy texts in primary schools as a key idea if we really do want to raise reading and writing attainment. Of course we will have to involve parents in any 'volume reading of easy books' initiative. We must address the 'why has be brought this book home when he can already read it?' syndrome (although when parents are asked whether they can easily read the texts they read . . . an interesting debate always ensues!).

One way this can be done is through the use of three bookmarks, one for each of the three levels. The appropriate bookmark is simply inserted in the book to be taken home. Manchester Education Partnership has produced superb examples for distribution to schools (see Figure 2.5).

On week one a child might take home a 'just right' book, but on week two might take home five 'easy' books – books which from a parent's perspective might not obviously be improving reading but which they can see will contribute to their child's writing development. In recent years we have received feedback from many teachers who refer to the often instant impact on the attitude and motivation of children encouraged to read 'easy' books!

Sounds and words and sentences

This section is about the ways in which we teach the sounds, words and sentences which make up the English language:

➤ **Word level:** phonics, spelling and vocabulary
➤ **Sentence level:** grammar and punctuation

In the classroom, how we approach this can be considered under the following headings:

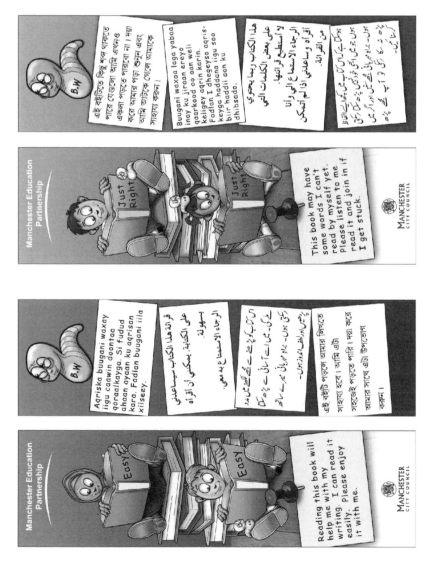

Figure 2.5 Manchester Education Partnership's bookmarks designed to suit varying levels of reading ability

- Teaching
- Children learning
- Assessing
- Marking and responding

Teaching

Much has been written (and argued) about the teaching of phonics, spelling and grammar, and there is not the space in this book to examine the details. However, we do want to draw attention to important aspects of this work, some of which have been neglected in recent years, and others which we believe are in danger in the future.

Don't forget vocabulary!

So much of the emphasis in recent years has been on phonics, spelling and grammar that there is a danger of vocabulary teaching being marginalised. Yet without words, children are not going to be able to comprehend what they read or compose when they write. Anyone who has tried to learn a foreign language as an adult knows that all the grammar and spelling rules are of little use if the words are not known.

What children require is a vocabulary for reading and writing – words they might rarely use in everyday conversation, over supper or in the playground, but which they can draw on when required. Consider the word 'meanwhile' which often occurs in stories and novels. When was the last time you used this word in everyday conversation? We would hazard a guess that 'meanwhile' is not part of your everyday vocabulary. But when you come across it in a text you know its meaning, and if you are writing you can use it. Simran (Chapter 1 page 20), who had been read to a great deal, was already using it at the age of four in the story she composed. The vocabulary that children require for reading and writing is 'literary vocabulary' in the sense that it appears in writing. A **Good Words List** can be developed every week for this purpose, the words being found in shared and guided reading texts, pulled out for closer inspection, played with and enjoyed. The list might focus on a particular type of word such as powerful verbs: glittering, creeping, emerging . . . But a good words list might also include a new, exciting word which is not part of any weekly objectives. The key, then, is that whenever we read or write with children, especially in shared writing, we must focus on the list, try and use some of the words ourselves in the writing, and encourage children to use them in their own writing.

The Good Words List

Glittering

Emerging

Creeping

etc.

From phonological awareness to phonics and on to spelling

Teaching reflects developmental learning, moving from phonological awareness to phonics and on to spelling.

> **Phonological awareness**: the awareness that words are made up of smaller units of sound: syllables, word beginnings and endings. So teaching focuses on the sounds which make up the words we speak. There is a stress on the segmenting and blending of sounds within words. Rhymes and songs often emphasise the initial sounds of words, e.g. 'Ding, dong bell' 'Little Miss Muffet' (the onset is the initial consonant sound in a syllable) and, through rhymes, the ways words end, e.g. 'Jack and Jill/ Went up the hill' 'The Queen of Hearts/She baked some tarts' (the rime is the vowel and the rest of the syllable – the part of the syllable that rhymes).
>   One important aspect of phonological awareness is **phonemic awareness** – the awareness of the phonemes which make up words. The question is do we look to achieve this awareness with children before they learn to read (Primary National Strategy) or do they actually develop it as a result of learning to read (Goswami 1995)?
> **Phonics**: the ways phonemes are represented by letters and letter combinations. So the segmenting and blending of phonemes in spoken words become linked to letters and letter combinations in written words. These phonic skills (segmenting and blending) and phonic knowledge (letter/sound correspondences) are used and applied in both reading (for decoding) and writing (for encoding). This integrated (reading/ writing) approach is vital and we would argue that once a child has grasped what phonics means and can segment the initial phoneme from a word, the drive to use phonics really does appear when the child is writing.
> **Spelling**: the morphemic structures of words (especially roots and affixes), spelling conventions and rules, irregular words, and how the phonic patterns become visual so that we see in our minds the words we write rather than attempt to sound them out.

Despite general agreement that the teaching and learning of phonics/spelling moves through these three phases, debate still rages (and no doubt will continue to rage!) about this aspect of literacy teaching. The Rose Report (2006) commissioned by the government to examine the teaching of phonics has led to the recommendations in the Primary National Strategy. If these recommendations are intended to close the debates, they have certainly failed to achieve this in the short term! We are not going to get involved in the details of current debates, which may in fact not be current in a few years' time having been replaced by a new set. However, we believe there are fundamental issues underpinning what is currently being recommended nationally and debated in newspapers, books, journals and at conferences. These issues are important whatever the debates and arguments. They are: the quality of the early years curriculum within which phonics is taught; the age at which children might begin phonics; the search for one approach to phonics teaching which will work with all children and the subsequent adoption by a school of just one programme.

A language rich curriculum

The Rose Report (2006) argues for:

> a broad, language rich curriculum: that is to say, a curriculum that generates purposeful discussion, interest, application, enjoyment and high achievement across all the areas of learning and experience in the early years.
>
> (Rose 2006, p. 16)

We fully support such a recommendation (though of course it is not a new idea and we have to wonder why in 2006 there is a need for such a recommendation to be made at all!). Throughout the Rose Report there are references to what this curriculum might look like: 'promoting speaking and listening' (p. 3), 'time to talk with children about their experiences' (p. 4), 'play, story, songs and rhymes' (p. 4), 'wide exposure to print' (p. 29), 'role play' (p. 29), 'enjoying and sharing favourite books' (p. 4). Underpinning all such activities are the big ideas in Chapter 1: children learning in contexts which make sense to them; children engaging actively with activities. There is always a danger that key teaching approaches, such as every child having time to talk to an adult about whatever they want to talk about, become marginalised in the dash to cover objectives. This 'language rich curriculum' is not just a backdrop to the teaching of phonics but rather vice versa.

Teaching about language should be a highlight of a child's time in primary school. The National Literacy Strategy was clear in its recommendation: 'The approach taken in Progression in Phonics is active, interactive, lively and fun' (National Literacy Strategy 2003). Teaching in the early years should be about 'movement, repetition, enjoyment and sensory stimulation . . . enhanced by sustained shared thinking with adults and peers' (Featherstone 2006) and phonics teaching is no exception.

The age for phonics

There has been increased pressure on teachers to begin formal phonics teaching in the Foundation Stage. However, the issue is not one of age but of who decides when a child is ready to make sense of phonics. The Rose Report states:

> The introduction of phonic work should always be a matter for principled, professional judgement based on structured observations and assessments of children's capabilities.
>
> (Rose 2006, p. 3)

We agree, and the language rich curriculum is the best way of preparing children for phonics.

Within discussion of when children should engage with phonics is the issue of gender differences. Featherstone (2006) summarises recent research on the early development of the brains of boys and girls. While warning about the dangers of thinking in terms of all boys and all girls, she states that:

> Many boys, even at the age of five, are simply not ready for sitting still, for discriminating between the sounds they hear and the letters they see or for beginning the controlled activities of formal phonics teaching. Their strengths are in large motor, visual-spatial activities . . . being active, manipulating materials and

equipment and exploring how things work. [. . .] we noted the continuing issue of boys' literacy attainment. Could it be that the seeds for this are being sown in early years classrooms?

(Featherstone 2006, p. 102)

A method for teaching phonics

A constant search for the best ways of teaching reading is obviously of vital importance. Literacy in the twenty-first century is an entitlement for all children. However, the recommendation of the Rose Report, now adopted by the Primary National Strategy, that one approach will do for all children ('the systematic approach, which is generally understood as synthetic phonics, offers the vast majority of young children the best and most direct route to becoming skilled readers and writers': Rose 2006, p. 4) is fatally flawed. Even as the Rose Report was being published, a review of all research on the teaching of phonics stated:

> No statistically significant difference in effectiveness was found between synthetic phonics instruction and analytic phonics instruction.
>
> (Torgerson et al. 2006, p. 8)

Quite what are we to make of the fact that both the Rose Report and Torgerson et al.'s research were commissioned and published by the government?

As all teachers know, learning is messy. What works for some children does not work for others. High quality teachers are those who know the complexities of the learning and teaching of reading and who are able to adjust their teaching to take account of the children in their classes. There is no 'fidelity to the programme' (DfES 2006, p. 8) with children who are not progressing on the programme. Teaching is more subtle than that.

Teaching spelling . . . not just lists for the Friday test

If the teaching of phonics is to be 'active, interactive, lively and fun', as discussed above, then what about the teaching of spelling in Key Stage 2? The subtitle of this book is 'Being Creative with Literacy in the Primary Classroom' and we believe this refers to all aspects of Key Stage 2 literacy teaching. However our experience in many schools around the country and working with hundreds of teachers in the course of a year indicates that there is a problem with the teaching of spelling. A common approach seems to be: on Monday give children a list of words to learn (these may be high frequency or patterned) and test the class on Friday. At its worst, that's it. No exploration of words, no investigations, no modelling of a fascination with the spellings of English.

As we state in Chapter 1, we believe engagement to be a key condition for learning anything in life. Therefore the teaching of spelling should be based on how to engage children with spelling. We want the announcement, 'now we're going to do some spelling' to be greeted with enthusiasm. The key is that spelling lessons are not always the same week after week, month after month, year after year. A variety of approaches, say on a three or four week rota, keeps everyone on their toes. This rota will contain different ways to approach the teaching of spelling and different ways to 'test' the children's learning. For example:

- **Week One** begins with a **spelling investigation** on Monday morning. Envelopes of small cards, each with a word on, are given out to pairs of children. The task is to sort the cards in whatever way the pairs think appropriate. Twos get into fours to compare what they did. Fours report back to the teacher. The class reaches an agreement about the sorting and the teacher teases out a generalisation or rule appropriate to the words. On Tuesday the words are revisited. Now this data will be used both to improve spelling and increase vocabulary. First, the class agrees, say, ten words which they have heard of and have some understanding of the meaning. These are the 'spelling words' to be learnt for Friday. Second, three words are agreed which most of the children have never heard of. These are the 'vocabulary words' whose meaning will be explored during the week. At the end of this week there is no test but all children have to use at least three of the spelling words and one vocabulary word in a piece of writing (see Application below).

- **Week Two** is a **spelling challenge**. This follows the same pattern as the investigation above, but now the children have to generate the data. Groups of children, each with the same spelling attainment, are given a starter: a prefix or suffix or common visual pattern (e.g. ough). Instead of taking words home to learn, this week the children go home to find words for their challenge. Which group can generate the most? Each group's data will contain words they have heard of and words they have been told or copied from a dictionary which they have never heard of. 'Spelling words' and a couple of 'vocabulary words' are agreed. The gathering and investigating of the data takes all week.

- **Week Three** the children learn the spelling words and try to use the vocabulary words. The latter appear in their writing, but can also be taken home as 'wow words' (a challenge to generate words ending in 'able' produced 'irrevocable' in one group's data; there was certainly a 'wow' from some parents when they suggested it was time for bed and received the response, 'Is that an irrevocable decision, Dad?'). This week, because each group has different words, on Friday there is **paired testing**, i.e. children testing each other in pairs. This is a very powerful strategy, first, because children enjoy it and engage with it, and second, because it reinforces the learning as each child examines the words four times in the course of the test (I look at the words to test you, I compare your answers to the list to mark your effort, I try and visualise the words when I am being tested, I watch you as you mark my effort).

  Children enjoy spelling challenges. They can be developed from the group challenge to the whole class challenge (a large sheet of paper on the classroom wall . . . all additions must be spelled correctly). There can even be whole school challenges, with the challenge somewhere in the school and anyone able to add words (children, teachers, parents, other adults working in school, visitors). This list becomes the focus of a school assembly.

- **Week Four** involves a **collaborative test** on Monday morning of a list of high frequency words. This strategy is discussed in Chapter 11 and is an excellent way of introducing words to be learnt. This strategy can be used at the end of the week with a paired spelling test, i.e. the words are called out by the teacher to the whole class and the children work in pairs to agree answers. Of course, individual learning cannot be assessed on a paired test but it can be used to generate confidence and enjoyment, so often lacking in the traditional whole class test. We are not saying whole class tests should never be used. We are suggesting their use needs to be carefully considered if we really want to raise spelling attainment.

Grammar, punctuation and vocabulary: reading like a writer

A phonics and spelling focus can be considered explicitly on its own rather than arising from within a text – words don't vary in terms of how they are spelt. However, sentence level work (like vocabulary) is all about variation – the ways writers vary their use of words and sentence structures in order to convey exactly the information or emotion that they intend. It makes sense therefore to begin such work within the context of a text, and that text's purpose. A short story will be read and enjoyed with responses shared and discussed ('reading like a reader'). We can then ask the question: 'How does the writer do it?' Immediately we are focusing on the writer's choice and use of vocabulary, particular parts of speech, e.g. powerful verbs, sentence structures and punctuation ('reading like a writer'). Any one of these can be drawn out of the text, decontextualised, studied and then applied by teachers in shared writing and children in their independent writing.

Children learning

Children learning – understanding and remembering – is best achieved through ensuring application and daily revision.

Application – by teachers as well as children

We really learn the meanings of words, how to spell them, use a variety of sentence structures and punctuate, through applying what we have learnt in our own writing. Spellings learnt for Friday but then not used are soon forgotten. In shared writing, teachers model how to apply current spellings and then encourage children to apply them in their known writing. Initially this use may be shaky, as is all new learning, but the only way to embed it is through further use. The worksheet may be completed correctly (and has its place as a tool for children to focus on something specific) but it is only when a child attempts to use their learning in their own compositions that they are forced to grapple with it properly.

Daily revision

Constant, quick revision is the other important aspect of learning (see p. 9). As we have already emphasised we all forget a great deal of what we are taught! Here we believe interactive whiteboards and flipcharts have a great deal to offer because the work on them is permanent. Following a literacy focus, whether at word or sentence level, it is so easy to begin a future lesson with just a couple of minutes of revision: 'Who can remember the work we did on . . .? What did we write on the whiteboard/flipchart? Let's have a look.' The board is tapped or the flipchart paper rolled back to reveal the earlier lesson.

If every literacy lesson began with just two minutes of quick, instant revision, we believe more children would remember previous work, and learning would move from the short-term to the long-term memory.

Assessing

Assessment of children's learning is not the same as teaching. This might seem obvious but in fact a lack of clarity has bedevilled English teaching for many years. So, a weekly spelling test will assess whether children have learnt their spellings (though without the application and revision above, this might be just superficial) but it is not teaching *about* spelling. We need a teaching curriculum and then to assess the level of understanding of children. While worksheets and tests are often used to assess word and sentence level work, real learning is assessed when children use the words or sentence structures or punctuation in their own work in the context of a real task. A worksheet rarely teaches.

Marking and responding

In the 'Teaching and learning' section in Chapter 1 we considered responding to children's work from a wider perspective, including the part played by learning targets. Here, with the focus on word and sentence level work, we consider two important principles when marking spelling in children's writing.

The first principle is that the classroom ethos should be supportive of children having a go and indicating where they are unsure. Figures 2.6 and 2.7 are the work of two Reception children in St Joseph's Primary School, North Tyneside. The first piece was written in late September when they attempted to write the nursery rhyme 'Humpty Dumpty'; the second piece was written in June. As is indicated they were both still 4 years old when they wrote their second pieces. The figures show the progress, over the course of the Reception year, in their understanding of how sounds and letters work in English. As they crack phonics they are encouraged to spell on the basis of the sounds they can hear in words, but also to indicate with a 'magic line' where they think further letters may occur. They are not only having a go but also thinking about whether that go is correct.

The magic lines idea can be developed into children having a go at the whole word and then, at the very moment they have written it, underlining it if they think it might be wrong. Again this is different from just having a go and it was a 10-year-old girl who explained:

> I don't like having a go because when my teacher reads my writing she'll think that I think that the words which are wrong are right. But I know I've spelt them wrong. I just don't know how to spell them right. And I don't want my teacher to think I think they're right when I know they're wrong!

We stress that this strategy does not seem to work as a proof-reading exercise, with the child going back to underline potential errors after the writing is finished. The underlining must happen as soon as the word has been written. This means that children are not constantly interrupting themselves to ask for words or look up words during their composing. They can focus on their ideas and their sentence structures, and then return to spelling at the end. (This strategy also turns a negative into a positive: 'Well done Tracey, you have correctly identified your 23 spelling errors!')

The second principle is that whenever possible we need to help children generalise from the specific. The correcting of the errors is now a negotiated responsibility between

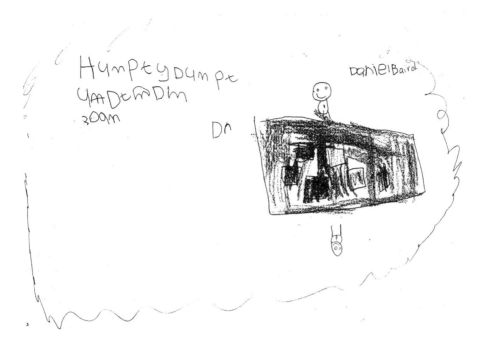

Figure 2.6

child and teacher. Certainly children should be expected to see themselves as responsible, but a high number of underlined words can be daunting. We can help by indicating which words should be corrected.

The child writes bot for boat, thinks it might be wrong and underlines it.

The child finds the correct spelling, i.e. boat.

This is indicated above the original, underlined word (if the original error is erased we cannot teach from it) – bot.

If the word is part of a pattern in English, the teacher indicates the pattern – boat, coat, load.

The child is set the challenge of finding some more examples.

I went to the beach. I jumped over the waves. I forgot to take a towel.

Kathryn Aged 4

Figure 2.7

The child writes the examples in their own spelling book, which might not be alphabetical in order to keep these patterned words together.

The words are learnt and the child's spelling partner carries out the test.

Bottom up and top down

The teaching of sounds and words and sentences needs to be explicit, with children focusing on the features of language and how English works. However, there is always a dynamic between the levels of text, sentence and word, expressed clearly by Marilyn Jager Adams (1990) in her comprehensive review of the effectiveness of different reading programmes:

> none of these programmes embodies the misguided hypothesis that reading skills are best developed from the bottom up. In the reading situation, as in any effective communication situation, the message or text provides but one of the critical sources of information, the rest must come from the reader's own prior knowledge. Further, in the reading situation, as in any other learning situation, the learnability of a pattern depends critically on the prior knowledge and higher order relationships that it evokes. In both fluent reading and its acquisition, the reader's prior knowledge must be aroused interactively and in parallel. Neither understanding, nor learning can proceed hierarchically, from the bottom up. Phonological awareness, letter recognition facility, familiarity with spelling patterns, spelling-sound relations and individual words must be developed in concert with real reading and real writing, and with deliberate reflection on the forms, functions and meanings of texts.
>
> (Adams 1990, p. 422)

Key teaching strategies

In our discussion of 'generic teaching and learning' (p. 29) we drew attention to ways of working in classrooms which underpin all our teaching, whatever the subject focus. In terms of literacy specifically there are four key teaching strategies:

- Shared reading
- Shared writing
- Guided reading
- Guided writing

In the National Literacy Strategy shared reading and writing are used with whole classes, while guided reading and writing are key strategies for working with groups of roughly equal reading or writing ability. However, viewing them simply as whole class or group activities is not the most important aspect: shared reading and writing can be powerful strategies to use with small groups or individual children. Similarly, guided reading and writing are underpinned by important ideas about how we work with children in groups but the ideas are equally applicable to working with a child one to one. It is as key approaches to literacy teaching that we need to view these strategies and then decide when to employ them in the classroom. Taking such professional decisions, based on achieving particular teaching objectives with particular children, is what makes teaching fascinating and challenging.

The aim is independent readers and writers

Shared and guided reading and writing are strategies in which teachers have a great deal of control. We normally choose the texts to be read and written, decide on teaching objectives, ask the questions. But the aim is for this control to be developed in children so that they do not require us to do this for them because they can do it for themselves. In the units throughout this book there are examples of children being involved in the process as much as possible. If the aim is independent readers and writers, how we approach shared and guided reading and writing can either help children move towards it or keep them dependent on us and the questions we ask.

The move through shared reading to shared writing to independent writing has now been established (through the National Literacy Strategy) in every classroom we visit. It is a powerful sequence through which we model how to read a text and then how to write it so that children can attempt to write it independently. However, as with all teaching approaches, it can become dry and ritualised through over use. The challenge is not to replace it (because it *is* powerful) but to enrich and enhance it (see Figure 2.8).

What might we do before shared reading? What might we do between the shared writing and independent writing? What sort of teaching strategies would you put in each of the clouds? The units making up the rest of this book are based on Figure 2.8 as we look to excite and engage children with a range of creative teaching strategies.

Shared reading and shared writing: modelling the process

The shared strategies are based on teachers sharing their own reading and writing of texts with children. Through reading and writing 'aloud' in front of children, and involving them in the processes, teachers model the way texts are read and written. In doing so, they teach children about the features of texts: the ways texts are constructed and composed. Modelling processes is a key idea for teaching, with the teacher providing a scaffold for the children, from which they can move to independent reading and writing.

Shared reading

There are five elements to the model:

- **This is why we read texts like this**. The previous section has emphasised how 'purpose' lies at the heart of reading. So, we share with children why people read the various text types, not forgetting the subtle and varied reasons for reading stories and poems.
- **This is how we read this text**. Some texts are read from beginning to end, e.g. a novel, while others are used to find information so that only the index and a particular page may be read at any one time. The reading of other texts, e.g. a set of instructions, may involve an initial read through to get the big picture followed by revisiting each

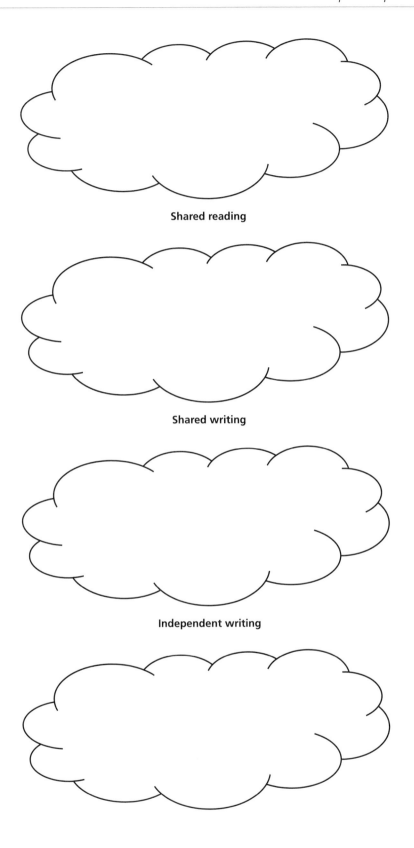

Shared reading

Shared writing

Independent writing

Figure 2.8

section. Some sections may be read a number of times. Many texts are a mix of writing and visual information, e.g. an information book, a newspaper or a website, and we show children how readers read the different elements.

- **This is the tune of this text**. One of the most important elements of shared reading is the teacher's voice. As we read aloud we demonstrate to children the reading voice appropriate to the text – the pace, intonation, pauses. Very young children are encouraged to join in the repeat readings of the same text on a number of days, imitating the way the teacher reads. With older children's shared reading, for example a short story, the whole class joining in can be difficult (and can sound like a dirge rather than a dramatic reading!). An alternative strategy is to focus on particular sections, which could be as short as individual sentences or as long as a paragraph – it depends on the text and the children. We read the section out loud, focusing the children's attention on our voice. Then, in pairs, the children read aloud to each other. Everyone is actively involved, and volunteers can then read aloud to the whole class.
- **This is how we respond to the text**. A first reading is always about 'reading like a reader' – shared reading as a rich reading experience. Through our own enthusiastic responses to the text and the questions we ask, we encourage children to join in and express how they respond. A discussion about a recipe will be different from one about an exciting story or a powerful poem. In all cases, however, the focus is on the responses evoked by the text.
- **These are text level/sentence level/word level features**. Now we move into 'reading like a writer' – how did the writer do it? Children consider explicitly the way the text is structured and organised, the sentence types used and the vocabulary. While this analysis is very useful for children in appreciating the 'craft of the writer' for their own future reading and writing, we must guard against an overemphasis on analysis. The last thing we would want is to kill the interest and joy in reading by viewing texts simply as things to be analysed.

Shared writing

For shared writing we have two choices: teacher demonstration writing or scribed writing. Teacher demonstration writing is the Delia Smith approach to teaching writing! When she announces she is going to stir fry some aubergines, there are two elements to the demonstration:

- **Visual:** we watch the aubergines being stir fried.
- **Aural:** we listen to Delia talking us through it – and what she talks about is the aubergine stir frying process.

So, in teacher demonstration writing, we demonstrate to the children how we go about composing a piece of writing. We write in front of them. As we write we speak our thoughts, letting the children hear how a writer thinks. Through many such demonstrations during primary school, the aim is for children to be able to 'think like writers' when they sit down to write.

In scribed writing we encourage children to join in with the act of writing. We share our thoughts and children volunteer ideas. Rarely do we simply accept what children offer.

In practice both methods are often used, with the former leading naturally into the latter.

The process of shared writing can be modelled as follows:

- **This is the purpose of this text**. Purpose drives the reasons for writing and the features of the text we produce (see p. 10). There is a danger of the only purpose in the minds of the children being to demonstrate to the teacher how their writing is improving. The motivation to write can quickly be lost. With most text types the purpose is clearly apparent (e.g. a letter to persuade somebody to do something), but with narrative we need to explore the type of story – exciting, scary, sad, funny, etc. Even in a test, it helps if a child decides what impact they want their story to have on the reader.

- **This is the intended reader**. This can be a real reader, known to the child (an adult, older child, younger child) or a 'type of reader' (e.g. Y2 children writing for Y3) or an imaginary reader (Little Red Riding Hood). Focusing on the reader develops a 'sense of audience' in children, so that they write with the needs of the reader in mind. Often the weakest writing suffers from children simply writing what is in their own heads, with no consideration for whoever might read it. Of course, frequently the reader will be the teacher, but children simply writing to 'please the teacher' are unlikely to develop as writers.

- **This is how we construct this text**. The text level features are about composition, organisation and structure: the ways we begin, develop and sustain a piece of writing. Frequently they relate to paragraphing so that shared writing is a key teaching strategy for demonstrating how decisions are made within and between paragraphs. Of course, this means we need to model more than the opening paragraph of a narrative if we want children to see how the whole story is sustained and the ways paragraphs work.

- **These are the appropriate sentence structures and punctuation**. Different text types are characterised by different sentence structures. This means not only explicitly referring to sentence constructions and punctuation, but also constantly rereading as the text develops. Through our intonation we emphasise the tune of the sentences. Even very young children can develop an ear for written language if they have been read to (see Simran's story, p. 20). With many such children the whole concept of 'a sentence' is an important aspect of shared writing so we constantly refer to sentences, how they sound and how they are punctuated.

- **This is the appropriate vocabulary**. Shared writing is a key way in which we look to develop the children's vocabulary – the vocabulary which they need in order to read and write. Just as in shared reading we read a text beyond the level of most children in the class, so in shared writing we are looking to create a text of a higher standard than could be managed by most children independently.

- **This is how I use the spellings**. Current high frequency words or phonic/spelling patterns can be used and noted during shared writing. Indeed it is vital that children see us applying the work from word level sessions and know we expect them to use these words in their own writing. Spellings not applied are easily forgotten.

- **These are the decisions I am making as a writer**. Throughout shared writing we talk. Sometimes we are talking to ourselves, articulating our thoughts so that children begin to appreciate how writers think. Sometimes we talk to the class, drawing attention to specific decisions or issues in the writing. The aim is for this strategy to produce independent writers but independent writers have to be able to make writerly decisions.

In the teaching of literacy we use shared reading and shared writing as powerful teaching strategies during which we read and write in front of the children, modelling the ways readers read and the purposes for which texts are written. We draw attention to the features of texts – how they are constructed and written. We model an enthusiasm for reading and writing. These two strategies lie at the heart of high quality literacy lessons.

Guided reading and guided writing

In guided sessions the children read and write. The guided teaching strategies are the times we really focus on the reading and writing processes respectively. Working with groups of children of approximately equal reading or writing ability, we take them through the processes. Working in a group also means that children learn from and support each other.

Guided reading

- **This is the context**. If it is a new text we introduce it. What sort of a text is it? What do we know about texts like these? If the group has been working on the text already there will be reminders.
- **This is the text**. With young readers and older non-fluent readers we 'walk the children through the text that they will read', perhaps using the pictures, to establish a 'map' of what will happen. We use the language of the text so that children are primed to expect particular vocabulary. We may point out some words and discuss them. Reading a novel with older, fluent readers we might focus on the title or the cover illustration or read the blurb on the back cover, or read a paragraph aloud as a model for their own reading. For other text types we manage a discussion of the text.
- **A strategy check**. We remind children about the reading process. What might they do when stuck on a word. Our aim is to establish their understanding, over time, of a range of reading strategies.
- **The children read**. With young children and non-fluent readers each child reads aloud at their own pace. With older children and fluent readers the reading might be silent, with individual children reading aloud to us. Some sessions with older, fluent readers might just involve silent reading or even no reading at all, the text having been read as an independent task.
- **We support and assess**. As individuals read aloud to us we support where necessary, reminding them about the reading process. This is also the key time to assess a child's reading, perhaps making notes for our records.
- **The text is discussed: comprehension and inferential reading**. Through our questions and the children's answers, especially establishing the habit of them finding evidence for their answers in the text, we develop comprehension. With older, fluent readers who might not have read aloud, the evidence is located and read aloud; with such readers the development of inferential reading is the key focus of guided reading.

- **We might focus on a word or sentence level aspect**. The children can search for examples which can be discussed, e.g. words beginning with a particular phoneme, speech marks or powerful verbs.

Guided writing

In guided writing a teacher might join a group at any stage in the writing process. The questions asked and the issues focused upon depend on whether the writing has yet to be started, is being written or has been completed.

- **The writing has yet to be started (pre-writing and into writing)**. We remind children what we know about the text type. We clarify the task – the piece of writing they are about to begin. We might help them plan. We might focus on the opening sentence.
- **The writing is being written (composing, revising)**. Under our direction children might explain their writing so far and/or read their writing aloud to a partner. The ensuing paired discussion might involve some revising. They might read each other's writing as an editing or correcting task. Individual children might read a sentence or two to the group so that we can teach from it.
- **The writing has been completed**. A session might involve any of revising, editing, sharing, assessing strengths and weaknesses, sometimes with the children in pairs leading to some teaching of the group.

There are examples of guided sessions with children of different ages in some of the units in this book.

References

Adams, M. J. (1990) *Beginning to Read: Thinking and Learning about Print*, Cambridge, MA: MIT Press.
Alexander, R. (2004) *Towards Dialogic Teaching*, Cambridge: Dialogos.
Browne, A. (1985) *Gorilla*, London: Magnet.
Department of Education and Science (1990) *English in the National Curriculum*, London: HMSO.
DfES (2006) *The Primary Framework for Literacy and Mathematics: Core Position Papers Underpinning the Renewal of Guidance for Teaching Literacy and Mathematics*, London: DfES.
Featherstone, S. (ed.) (2006) *L is for Sheep: Getting Ready for Phonics*, Lutterworth: Featherstone Education.
Ginnis, P. (2002) *The Teacher's Toolkit*, Carmarthen: Crown House.
Goswami, U. (1995) 'Rhyme in children's early reading', in R. Beard (ed.) *Rhyme, Reading and Writing*, London: Hodder & Stoughton.
Hall, E. (2006) 'Learning styles – is there an evidence base for this popular idea?', *Education Review*, 19(1): 49–56.
Iser, W. (1978) *The Act of Reading*, London: Routledge.
Martin, T. (2003) 'Minimum and maximum entitlements: literature at KS2', *Reading*, 37(1): 14–17.
National Literacy Strategy (2003) 'Teaching Phonics in the National Literacy Strategy', paper presented at the Symposium of Phonics, London.
Rose, J. (2006) *Independent Review of the Teaching of Early Reading*, London: DfES.
Rosenblatt, L. (1976) *Literature and Exploration*, 3rd edition, New York: Noble & Noble.
Stanovich, K. E. (1986) 'Matthew effects in reading: some consequences of individual differences in the acquisition of literacy', *Reading Research Quarterly*, 21(4): 360–407.
Torgerson, C., Brooks, G. and Hall, J. (2006) *A Systematic Review of the Research Literature on the Use of Phonics in the Teaching of Reading and Spelling*, London: DfES.

3 'Tell me a story'

Narrative in the Foundation Stage

What was your favourite story as a child? Can you remember the characters, the setting(s), the plot and the ending? Why was it your favourite? Has that got you thinking? Has it captured your imagination? It certainly started us on a trail. We asked these questions of a number of colleagues and below are some of the responses.

A story about a naughty mouse

Can't remember the author it was part of an anthology.

There was a mouse, a girl and two parents.

The main plot was based around the mouse being unable to learn how to be good – and failing miserably

I can't remember the ending!

The 'Jennings' books by Anthony Buckeridge

Jennings & Darbishire, Mr Wilson, Mr Carter, the Archbeako, the boys in Dorm 6

Jolly japes and scrapes at Linbury Court School. Prep school for middle class boys. Each book covers a term of the doings and disasters of J & D and their pals in Dormitory 6. Lots of funny moments, misunderstandings and confusion.

Extensive use of wordplay, tongue-twisters, general hyperbole and schoolboy slang. Brilliant writing style and content.

Endings usually a 'crescendo of fiascos and excitement' with Mr Wilkins explosive, Mr Carter calm and good-humoured and the boys safe at home for the end of term at the end.

Can see now I always did have a penchant for naughty boys!

Swallows and Amazons

I wanted my summer holiday to be like that. I can remember the characters and their adventures. A great book, which I reread several times.

Five Go To Kirrin Island (again!) by Enid Blyton

Julian (the macho boy), Anne (the weedy girl), Timmy the dog, the girl who wanted to be a boy . . . name??, plus a.n.o

Always the same – page one the adults are got rid of, it's the beginning of the holidays, Kirrin Island is there and waiting, there'll be picnics with lashings of ginger beer, some baddies will make an appearance, Julian and Timmy will sort them, Anne will whimper, and it all works out in the end.

Total escapism . . . and I probably wanted to be Julian!

Little Women by Louisa M. Alcott

Sisters Jo, Amy and Beth. It was so sad, I can remember thinking I was glad I didn't live in their times, I think Beth died, she was certainly very weak and Jo was a tom-boy. I think I must have liked feeling sad because I can't remember much joy in the book.

A story about a girl who had a secret house in a wood

She escaped there at every opportunity. I can't remember her name. The other characters were various woodland animals and a vagabond boy she befriended. There was also an old wise woman who watched over everything caringly. I liked the picture on the cover and I knew everything would be alright in the end but it was a real adventure, I thought I was the girl when I was reading it.

I wish I had taken notice of the title and the author!

Stories give an enormous amount of pleasure to all ages. There is no more awe-inspiring picture than that of a young child enthralled and wrapped up in a story being told.

Figure 3.1

Of all the texts we share with children, the powerful stories are those we see having the greatest impact. At the really dramatic moments children's concentration can almost be felt in the room as their eyes stare at us and their breath is held. Those who are read to regularly often seem insatiable, demanding more and more stories, while at the same time returning to old favourites again and again. Favourite stories can be told and retold to a child numerous times without the thrill or attention being diminished. How many parents and teachers have tried to shortcut a story or accidentally altered a word only to be brought up short by the child or children recognising the change made? How's that for concentration? If only the same could be true for all areas of learning! The power of story does not have to be taught. If a young child does not enjoy listening to a story well told there is something wrong. The appeal is basic. It is the desire to enter the world of story that lies behind the reading habits of so many children and adults. The question is, what can we do to harness this enthusiasm? How do we ensure all children experience the power of story (especially those who don't get the experience at home)? How do we then best utilise this power as a way into children learning to read and write?

In Chapter 1, 4-year-old Simran Gill's oral story drew attention to the implicit knowledge (of story characteristics and sentence structures) that children develop if they have been read to. We also commented on her 'literary' vocabulary – words she would not use in everyday conversation. The baseline for learning about stories is being read lots of them, and that should be a priority in the Foundation Stage. The work in this chapter uses structured story frames but we want to stress two points. First, we are not saying that this is the 'only' or correct way of approaching story; we could have worked in lots of different ways. Second, the work we describe is not a substitute for reading aloud to young children. It is a fun way of working to build on the story-reading experiences which should be one of the cornerstones of early years practice.

The chapter also raises an interesting issue about the link between recounts and stories. Arthur Koestler wrote that 'literature begins with the telling of a tale' (Koestler 1964) and we begin with the stories we tell and those we listen to throughout our lives. We think of our lives as narratives, with our beginnings, middles (often with lots of complications) and ends. We go on holiday and then cannot wait to get back and tell our friends about some key incidents. We embellish these tales just as authors do, so that over time they take on a life of their own and have little resemblance to the original happening. Young children find it difficult to distinguish fact from fiction, which is why 'news time' in the Foundation Stage can be fiction for one child and fact for another. For many young children narrative comes from their 'news' – recounts and stories are indistinguishable. They are both driven by the human need to use narrative as a way of making sense of life. In this chapter we discuss work based on traditional tales as well as on children's recount stories of their own lives.

A key focus is on children telling and listening. In order to be able to begin writing children need experience of oral language; writing means moving from oral to literate language. One key for developing talk in the classroom is to give time for children to think before responding. With the children themselves there seems to be a polarisation in this respect. There are always those children who respond almost before the question is asked and there are those who never respond, either because they have got used to not doing so in the knowledge that someone else will respond anyway or because they haven't had time to think. Others may feel intimidated in a large group. One effective strategy is to give children 'thinking time' – 20 or 30 seconds of silence, while everyone thinks about what they want to share. This ensures all children have the time to think and prepare their response and gives them the space and time to do so. Moving from thinking time to talk partners means everyone is involved as a speaker (and, with a bit of help, as a listener!).

Circle time is now used widely in Foundation Stage classrooms both for personal, social and emotional development and for communication, language and literacy development. Children learn the rules – you can speak when holding the 'teddy bear' or you may choose to pass it on without speaking; you listen to others and value what they are saying. Where circle time is managed well it is very effective in developing children's speaking skills, and it does allow time for children to think before speaking. All too often, however, the group or circle is too large and children become restless while waiting for their turn to speak. Active listening is not about waiting for a turn to speak; it is about involvement in what another is saying. Within circle time, strategies such as thinking time and talk partners are effective for the development of confidence and from there into talk.

What was in the teacher's head when planning this work?

Contexts and coherence

- I can build on the love of well-known traditional tales and favourite stories.
- I can link this to writing for different audiences.
- I can use role play to develop an understanding of the elements of narrative.
- I can use the framework for those children who prefer news and recount to fiction.

Motivation

- The children love stories and I want to use story as a powerful experience, which draws all children into the incidents and characters.
- I want to immerse them in narratives developing an understanding of story patterns and structure.
- The children love sharing their stories with other children in the school.
- The children enjoy reading books they have made.

Content and process

- Look at the construction of their favourite story.
- Use talk partners and possibly pairs, threes or fours to develop a simple group story.
- Use talk partners and possibly pairs, threes or fours to share news items (an account).
- Use a framework to look at different beginnings and endings and the 'what, where, when, who' of a narrative.
- Continue work on consonant, vowel, consonant (CVC) words, phonics and reading.
- Work on simple sentence structure, full stops and capital letters.

How does this relate to the Early Learning Goals and the Primary Framework?

The Primary Framework and the Early Years Foundation Stage (EYFS) Curriculum Guidance have been developed alongside each other, with relevant sections mirroring each other. The guidance provided in the Primary Framework (Literacy) for the Foundation Stage matches the sections in the EYFS on communication, language and literacy. Both the Early Learning Goals and the Primary Framework objectives are included below because together they demonstrate some of the fundamental aspects of learning about 'stories' and 'recounts'. You will note that a number of the Early Learning Goals are appropriately placed in more than one strand where the knowledge, skills and understanding of the various aspects of literacy overlap. The high number of learning objectives linked to story demonstrates the importance and place of story in developing literacy in young children.

Clustering the learning objectives

Speaking

Foundation Stage

- Enjoy listening to and using spoken and written language and readily turn it into play and learning.
- Use talk to organise, sequence and clarify thinking, ideas, feelings and events.
- Speak clearly and audibly with confidence and control and show an awareness of the listener.
- Extend their vocabulary, exploring the meanings and sounds of new words.

Year 1

- Tell stories and describe incidents from their own experience in an audible voice.
- Retell stories, ordering events using story language.

Listening and responding

Foundation Stage

- Listen with enjoyment and respond to stories, and make up their own stories.
- Extend their vocabulary, exploring the meaning and sounds of new words.

Year 1

- Listen with sustained concentration, building new stores of words in different contexts.

Group discussion and interaction

Foundation Stage

- Use talk to organise, sequence and clarify thinking, ideas, feelings and events.

Drama

Foundation Stage

- Use language to imagine and create roles and experiences.

Year 1

- Act out well-known stories, using voices for characters.

Word recognition

Foundation Stage

- Link sounds to letters, naming and sounding the letters of the alphabet.
- Hear and say sounds in words in the order in which they occur.
- Use phonic knowledge to write simple regular words and make phonetically plausible attempts at more complex words.

Word structure and spelling

Foundation Stage

- Use phonic knowledge to write simple regular words and make phonetically plausible attempts at more complex words.

Year 1

- Spell new words using phonics as the prime approach.

Understanding and interpreting texts

Foundation Stage

- Show an understanding of the elements of stories, such as main character, sequence of events and openings.
- Retell narratives in the correct sequence, drawing on the language patterns of stories.

Engaging with and responding to texts

Foundation Stage

- Listen with enjoyment to stories and sustain attentive listening.
- Show an understanding of the elements of stories, such as main character, sequence of events and openings.

Creating and shaping texts

Foundation Stage

- Attempt writing for a variety of purposes, using features from different forms such as stories.

Year 1

- Independently choose what to write about, plan and follow it through.
- Find and use new and interesting words and phrases, including story language.

Text structure and organisation

Foundation Stage

- Attempt writing for a variety of purposes, using features from different forms such as stories.

Year 1

- Write chronological and non-chronological texts using simple structures.
- Group written sentences together in chunks of meaning or subject.

Sentence structure and punctuation

Year 1

- Compose and write simple sentences independently to communicate meaning.

So what is the overall message of all of these objectives? Children need to experience, enjoy, be involved in, hear and relish stories and also be encouraged and stimulated to develop their own skills as story writers.

So how might the unit of work begin? In this chapter we describe two distinct and alternative ways of working with story with young children. Remember that the main text level learning objective is to be aware of story structures, to show an understanding of the elements of narrative such as openings, character and sequence of events including the use of story language.

Starting point 1: using familiar stories

The chosen edition of *Jack and the Beanstalk* is read aloud by the teacher and enjoyed by the children. The teacher's ability to read aloud is vital here, with pace, intonation and expression to the fore. A dramatic reading! There is animated discussion, especially as some of the children know it and others appear not to. The focus here is simply on personal response to an exciting story – we must never forget that for us as adults, many 'traditional tales' have almost become clichés. We know them so well that their power has faded. But 4 year olds know nothing of clichés! The power of these tales should not be underestimated.

The following day starts with a rereading, but now special 'Good Words and Phrases' are identified, queried, explained and used. A list is compiled, which is then displayed appropriately in the classroom.

Retelling the story

To start this session the children, with the teacher, identify the following significant scenes in the story.

1. Jack took the cow to market.
2. Jack bought the beans.
3. Jack's mother threw the beans out of the window.
4. The beanstalk grew and grew.
5. Jack climbed the beanstalk.
6. Jack at the giant's castle.
7. Jack and the giant came down the beanstalk.
8. Jack and his mother lived happily ever after.

In small groups the children each draw their own pictures to represent a couple of the significant scenes. The pictures are small – A5 size. Each group's collection of drawings of the eight scenes is mounted on card and laminated for use by the children.

With appropriate adult support, in pairs and then in fours, children use the laminated cards to discuss the scenes then sequence them. The cards are then used to tell the story again, with some narratives taped.

Now the action moves to the school hall, where, still in fours, one child is identified to be Jack, one to be Jack's mother, one to be the giant and one to be the storyteller. Using the cards in sequence, the storyteller retells with the other children acting the story out. Using retell and drama helps children develop an understanding of the characters involved and develops an understanding of narrative structures.

Spotlight: freeze the action – new stories from old

The children are ready to move on! When they have all had the opportunity to be involved in the retell and drama sequencing activity, one group is chosen to work in front of the class. Freeze frames will be effectively employed at various points in the dramatisation to explore options or question characters.

Children are retelling the story using the sequence prompts. Three children are acting as Jack, his mother and the giant. The teacher freezes the action right at the beginning after the narrator has said, 'Once upon a time there was a boy called Jack who lived with his mother.' The teacher asks for an alternative opening and takes 'There was a boy . . .' and also 'On a small farm a boy lived with his mum . . .'. These are noted on the flipchart and the action continues. It is stopped again when Jack has climbed the beanstalk and is about to see the giant. The teacher asks if the character has to be a giant. Could it be anything else? Responses are noted and the original story continues to the end. The teacher then 'rewinds' the story to the point where Jack is about to come down the beanstalk and the giant is chasing him; the action is frozen and the ending is discussed. The teacher encourages the children to think of different endings and displays the thought cloud. Children spend a few minutes in quiet thought (initial thinking time).

When the teacher changes the thought cloud for the 'talk time' speech bubble, the children quickly move into talk partners. They are given just a couple of minutes to discuss an alternative ending. Some of the alternative endings are recorded just like the alternative openings.

Back in the classroom, small groups of children, through illustration and writing, shared or independent as appropriate, make the alternative endings sequence cards. These can then be exchanged for the original and the 'new' stories shared with the class.

To signal 'thinking time' it is useful to have a 'thought cloud' lollipop or card. When this is held up there is no talking, it is *thinking* time. Either individual or class 'think time' clouds made on laminated card are used.

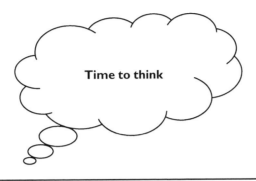

Time to think

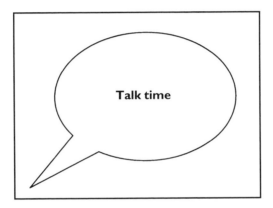

Talk time

Spotlight: using a story frame

Once children understand the options in simple story structures with beginnings, middles and ends, they can begin to move from retell and drama to recording. One way to do this is by using a story frame such as that shown in Figure 3.2.

From the drama session the children now have the information they need to learn to use story frames. Working with the children the teacher demonstrates how to fill the frame in. This is done through lots of discussion and with the use of the laminated significant scene cards as prompts. The 'Good Words and Phrases' and 'Good Story Starts' lists displayed in the classroom are referred to regularly. Separate, discrete phonics sessions mean children finding the CVC words within the texts they are using (their own and published versions).

Starting point 2: starting with children's personal stories

Here, personal recounts are used as the basis of the work. Initially over a number of whole class sessions, the teacher models the process the children are about to go through. First

Story Frame				

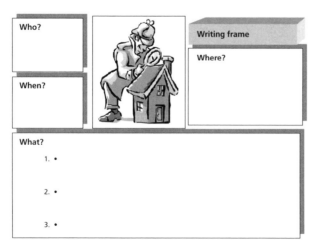

Title	Jack and the Beanstalk
Author	Traditional tale

Opening	Characters	What happened		Ending
Once upon a time	Jack Jack's mum Giant	1. Jack took the cow to market 2. Jack bought the beans 3. Jack's mother threw the beans out of the window 4. The beanstalk grew and grew 5. Jack climbed the beanstalk 6. Jack at the giant's castle 7. Jack and the giant came down the beanstalk 8. Jack and his mother lived happily ever after		They lived happily ever after

Figure 3.2

she sits and thinks in silence about some news she wants to share with the children. The children watch expectantly. Using a thought cloud, she writes some notes about her news. Now she holds up a speech bubble to signify that she is speaking and tells the class her news. In a subsequent news sharing session she introduces a set of prompts. These make the children realise that they need to include some detail to help the listener understand the context. Finally the teacher uses the strategy of shared writing to turn her spoken news into a piece of writing. The use of a writing frame such as Figure 3.3 helps the group through the process.

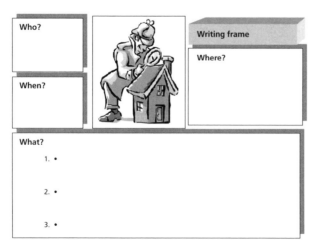

Figure 3.3

The children are now taken through the same process in a series of sessions. At the start they work in talk partners, which may be random or prearranged. The teacher asks all children to think individually about any news they may have and they use the laminated thought clouds to jot down their thoughts.

The teacher then holds up a 'Talk partner' speech bubble and in turn signals each partner to share their news, using the who, where, when, what prompts demonstrated by the teacher. The children can move from twos to fours and share their news, possibly choosing one to share with the whole class.

From telling to writing

Through a series of shared writing sessions, children's news is used as the basis for further shared, guided and independent writing. Phonic knowledge is explicitly applied by both teacher and children as they write and read the writing. The focus is on consonant, vowel, consonant (CVC) words and making a phonetically sound attempt at longer and unfamiliar words. It is important to note that children's application of their phonic knowledge is implicit in these activities and they are set within a broad and rich language curriculum.

A range of opportunities and activities

Of course no approach takes place in a vacuum. All are underpinned by a wealth of experiences and activities organised for the children. Around the classroom we might see examples of the following:

- Several writing frames displayed, some using well-known stories, some from the sharing of news items. There is a string line on which are pegged specific scenes developed by the children. They are pegged on in a sequence, which may be changed by the next child working with the writing frame. The evidence that they have been used to develop new narratives is displayed showing carefully constructed narrative.
- In the book area there are books made by the class, well used and read.
- There is a news board with the four Ws – who, what, where, when – displayed as prompts for news reporting or recounting of events with a number written into a frame.
- There are Good Word Lists around which children and staff regularly refer to and update.
- There are samples of different story starts and endings to assist children in getting variety into their narratives.

- High quality narrative texts are well displayed and accessible to the children.
- A variety of writing materials including some blank writing frames, especially the four Ws, are one resource in an enticing and exciting writing area.

Spotlight: CVC phonics session

Discrete phonics sessions enable children to focus on sounds and words, and this work is then consistently applied in reading and writing sessions. The key skills of segmenting and blending sounds in words are the basis of such sessions.

Three different coloured large foam cubes are on the carpet. Each face of each cube has a clear plastic wallet into which letters are inserted. The blue cube shows only consonants, the red cube shows only vowels and the yellow cube shows only consonants. The blue cube denotes initial consonant, the red cube the vowel and the yellow cube the final consonant in CVC words. The children take it in turns to roll the cubes and to blend the CVC to make the word. The first child rolls the blue cube and it lands on 'p', the red cube lands on 'i' and the yellow cube lands on 'n'; the child blends p-i-n and says 'pin'. The teacher writes the word 'pin' on the flipchart. The next child rolls 's-a-t', blends and says 'sat', which is written on the flipchart. So far the words make sense. The next child rolls 'f-o-l' and confidently blends and says 'fol' with a puzzled look on her face. She has recognised that this word doesn't make sense. Each child has a turn at rolling the cubes, blending the letters and saying the word. The CVC words are written up by the teacher. The words may be a real word or of course may be nonsense, but the children will be applying their knowledge and understanding of phonics.

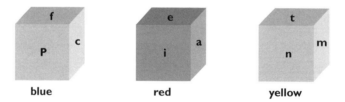

When each child in the group has had a turn, the teacher draws attention to the list of words written up from the CVCs blended from the cube rolls. The children blend the letters to form the words indicated by the teacher.

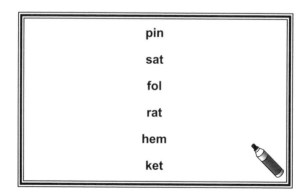

The group discuss the words and decide which are real words and which are nonsense. The more able children then segment the CVC words and find the appropriate face of each cube to represent the word.

Beyond the unit

Developing personal adventure stories

(Thanks to Dean C.E. Primary School, Cumbria, for the Reception children's work.) A big book *Where the Forest Meets the Sea* by Jeannie Baker is used as a stimulus for children to develop their personal adventure story. The children identify the characters in the story, look at how the story starts, what happens in the middle and how the story ends. Excitement is generated about adventures, with children putting themselves as the main character in the story and thinking of adventures they might have on the island. A few seed-corn ideas are shared and worked up into adventures on the island.

Adventure stories are returned to the next day but the focus is on each child developing his/her own adventure where he/she is the main character for the story, so a list of questions is developed to help children develop their stories.

- Who went with you?
- Where did you go?
- What did you do?
- What did you discover?
- How did you feel?
- What happened at the end?

The children are given a few minutes' thinking time with the thinking time bubble displayed (see p. 69). Then, in pairs, the children help each other to answer the questions, which they need to do to develop their stories. Working with talk partners and in groups of six, each child works to complete his or her own frame, which has the questions written in separate sections (see Stage 1 below). When each of the pair has completed Stage 1, they discuss what they have written, share ideas and help each other to think of ways to develop and expand on what they have written down. Throughout this process adult support is given as appropriate. The children then move to Stage 2, discussing again, before expanding the writing and moving to Stages 3 and 4. This process takes time; some children move on more quickly than others with varying amounts of adult support. We have used Stacey's work to show the development through the stages. The proforma used are A3 size (see Figures 3.4, 3.5 and 3.6).

Stacey's adventure

Stage I

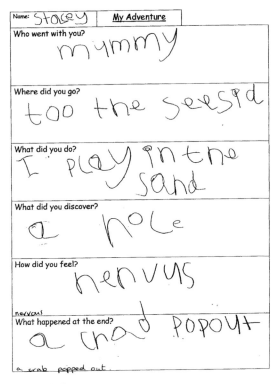

Name: Stacey   **My Adventure**

Who went with you?
mummy

Where did you go?
too the seesid

What did you do?
I play in the sand

What did you discover?
a hole

How did you feel?
henvus
nervous

What happened at the end?
a chad popout
a crab popped out.

Figure 3.4

In talk partners, the children help each other talk through and explore options about their adventures for each question, then tell and retell. In pairs, with adult support where needed, the children write in the proforma given.

It is interesting to note that Stacey dramatises her story, which gives it life. She uses words like 'nervous' and 'pop'.

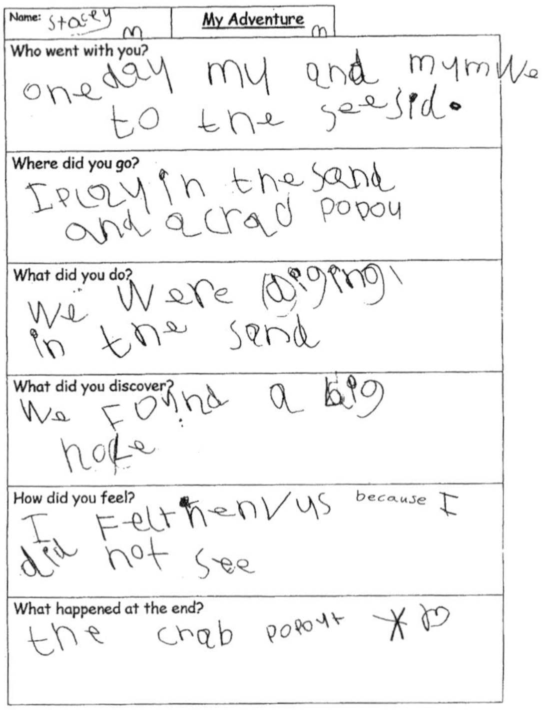

Name: stacey m   **My Adventure** m

Who went with you?
oneday my and mymWe to the seesid.

Where did you go?
I play in the sand and a crad popou

What did you do?
We were digging in the send

What did you discover?
We found a big hole

How did you feel?
I felt henvus because I did not see

What happened at the end?
the crab popout ✗ ⬡

Figure 3.5

The same talk partners are later reunited; they retell their adventures using Stage I as a prompt. They are then encouraged to expand on the initial telling/writing.

Stage 3

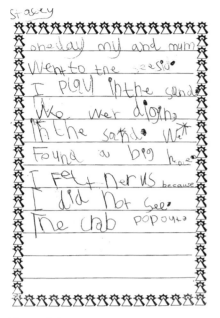

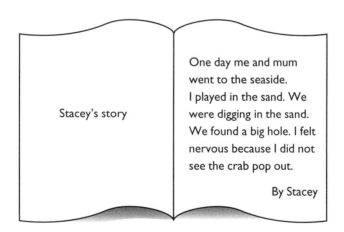

This stage is used to put the sections together to form a narrative. The adult support encourages the children to incorporate all aspects of the writing frame in the story version of the adventure and only to help with the writing if it gets in the way of developing the story. In Stacey's story, the teaching assistant added the word 'because' when the child realised it was needed. You will notice some stars * in the final adventure story. Stacey added these as she wrote; the teacher has, in previous work, drawn stars on work considered to be good. Stacey obviously was happy about what she had written and added stars where she felt she had achieved something worthwhile.

Figure 3.6

Stage 4

An illustration will complete the adventure story.

Stacey's story

One day me and mum went to the seaside. I played in the sand. We were digging in the sand. We found a big hole. I felt nervous because I did not see the crab pop out.

By Stacey

The self-esteem of children is raised in line with the impact on their learning. Stacey felt justifiably proud of her achievement.

Nursery rhymes into stories

This activity is designed to take children through a process which shows them how to transform a nursery rhyme into a series of events using the same story frame as used in the *Jack and the Beanstalk* work. Once this is done a separate step in the process is to add story language. This adds drama to the recount, transforming the events of the story into a recognisable 'literary' narrative.

> Jack and Jill went up the hill,
> To fetch a pail of water.
> Jack fell down and broke his crown
> And Jill came tumbling after.
>
> Up Jack got and home did trot,
> As fast as he could caper.
> He went to bed to mend his head
> With vinegar and brown paper.

The children chant 'Jack and Jill', two children taking it in turns to role play the rhyme. With the story frame on a flipchart, the children are asked if the story of the nursery rhyme could be put into it. They decide to have a go (see Figure 3.7).

The children decide on an opening – 'Very early on Saturday'. There seems to be no ending either. One child says her mum sings another verse:

> When Jill came in,
> How she did grin
> To see Jack's paper plaster.
> Her mother told her daughter off,
> For laughing at Jack's disaster.

So the children decided to use this verse to add to the significant events. The frame now looks as shown in Figure 3.8.

They talk the story through using story language, not the nursery rhyme language, and then decide on an ending: 'After that Jack and Jill's dad got the water from the well.'

Story Frame	
Title	Jack and Jill
Author	Traditional tale

Opening	Characters	What happened	Ending
	Jack and Jill	1. They went up the hill 2. They went to get a bucket of water from a well 3. Jack fell down and hurt his head 4. Jill fell down too 5. Jack got up and went home 6. He went to bed with a plaster on his head	

Figure 3.7

Opening	Characters	What happened	Ending
Very early on Saturday	Jack and Jill	1. They went up the hill 2. They went to get a bucket of water from a well 3. Jack fell down and hurt his head 4. Jill fell down too 5. Jack got up and went home 6. He went to bed with a plaster on his head 7. Jill got home and laughed at Jack 8. Mum told Jill off for laughing at Jack	Dad fetched the water from the well after that.

Figure 3.8

Finally, in a series of shared writing sessions the story of the nursery rhyme is written with additional story language being modelled.

Very early on Saturday morning Jack and Jill clambered up the hill. The sun was shining and they got very hot and sweaty. They were going to fetch a bucket of water from the well. All of a sudden Jack tripped over a stone, fell down and banged his head. Jill wasn't looking where she was going and tumbled over him. They both cried and cried as they ran home. Mum put a plaster on Jack's head and put him to bed. Jill laughed at Jack's plaster. Mum told her off for laughing at Jack. Jack and Jill don't fetch the water any more. Now their dad does it.

What is your favourite story? A survey of favourite texts

This survey can take place at any time. It means taking the classroom stories out into the home and bringing the home into the classroom. Parents are acknowledged as a child's first educators and working with them is important in maximising the cultural capital children bring to school. So enlisting their help with the story survey will bring a number of benefits. It will involve the parents in their children's learning; they will be in a position to help their children choose a favourite story, reread it to them or help them find it if it is in a book. Putting requests such as this up on a parents' notice board is commonplace in many schools but probably most often found in the Foundation Stage. In this instance a prompt card would be useful, indicating the information children will need to bring into school. Some schools use a parental–school comment book in which messages such as this are exchanged. A benefit linked to the cultural capital mentioned earlier is the opportunity this gives for all to learn of stories from other cultures, giving status to home culture and acknowledging and using it in a child's learning.

However, some children may have little 'book experience' at home. These children will need time and help in school to choose their story. Every child must have something to contribute. The stories will be shared and enjoyed over the next week. Some stories will be read to the class, others told by the child to a group or class. Some will be made available for others to look at and read in a carefully organised 'Favourite Book' area.

Children using the story frame with support

A teaching assistant is working with a group of six children; they have chosen one of the group's favourite stories and are working to put it into the writing frame in its original form. They have chosen Darren's story. The story is read aloud to the children, who first listen to it for pure enjoyment. Darren tells the group why it is his favourite. He says it is because it is funny and makes him laugh. They then listen again to put the opening into the writing frame. Darren writes it on the flipchart. They then identify significant scenes; these are drawn by the children (one each) and a caption added using guided or independent writing, as appropriate. The ending is then entered onto the flipchart. Children are asked for an alternative ending. They decide on one and retell the story to another group using their illustrations, captions and alternative ending.

Writing a personal story

The class soon moves on and begins to use these frames to develop their own narrative. They begin by thinking of a character (maybe one from another story) or scenario and completing the frame with just one or two scenarios in the 'What happened' section.

So we see six children working together. They have already decided the characters' names, Jack and Jake. The two boys are 6 years of age and Jack has a little sister Carrie, who is 3 years old. They are on holiday at the seaside. The teaching assistant has asked them to work in their talk partners to come up with one scene per pair. First, they are given some thinking time, which is indicated by the teaching assistant displaying the 'think time' bubble. Next, five minutes are allocated to discuss their ideas for a scene. Things get very animated and the ideas start to flow. After five minutes the discussions are called to a halt. Each pair is asked to make brief notes about their scenes. Those children who need support do this through guided writing. The scenes are then illustrated by the children and are displayed on the wall of the classroom.

Another group repeats the process. And another. Eventually twelve scenes are on display on the wall for the class to look at and read.

As a whole class group the agreed characters are revisited and one by one the scenes are discussed as options for the middle part of the story. The children can choose from the scenarios and build the framework around their choice or choices. Many different stories can be built up from the information available. All children have been involved and therefore have ownership of the content. They have worked in a supportive and supported way making this a non-threatening, creative activity, which enables visual, auditory and kinaesthetic learners to be involved. Over the next few weeks children will write the stories in groups, using their writing frames. All the stories are gradually compiled and made into a class book of 'The Adventures of Jack, Jake and Carrie' for all to share.

References

Baker, J. (1987) *Where the Forest Meets the Sea*, London: McRae.
Koestler, A. (1964) *The Act of Creation*, London: Hutchinson.

4 Playing with role in the Foundation Stage

'Little Boy Blue'

Figure 4.1 'They just don't know how tired I get looking after all these lambs'. *By Faye*

The learning potential of role play with young children is phenomenal. It brings together so many aspects of early learning that we are constantly amazed that it is not used more widely, but those teachers and schools who do use it extensively attest to its value. So, it's not about teaching literacy versus being creative – it's about being creative to teach literacy and raise attainment. A school that used the arts, including role play, to raise children's self-esteem and attitude to learning, found a significant impact on raised attainment. The infant class referred to in the quotation below spent a week working on the book *Can't You Sleep, Little Bear?* by Martin Waddell. Role play is not only about the children being in role, but also about the teacher being in role, which was the case identified in the article below, entitled 'First I was a bear, then a snail. Now I am an angel . . .'. A failing primary school has been transformed by a method of teaching that focuses on the arts.

> On the day of my visit 22 six year olds dressed as bears await the start of their literacy hour. They are spending a week studying the book *Can't You Sleep Little Bear?* (about a bear who is afraid of the dark) and are getting into the spirit by wearing paper 'bear hats' with ears attached . . . Soon the class retires to the bear cave (a sheet rigged up over the desks) for the story before splitting into groups for activities which include brain-storming adjectives and writing to invite him to tea. This arts-driven approach has been so successful that it is being studied by officials from the Department for Education and Skills who hope to spread the message to other schools . . . 'Getting into the part can help you imagine the things you are going to write about,' says one of the children.
>
> (Cassidy 2001)

What is role play and why is it so important?

Role play is a way of teaching through drama. It is a way of enabling children to explore through dialogue. It supports the development of speaking and listening, of understanding cause and effect, actions and consequences, of considering the feelings of others. But most importantly it allows children to explore within a safe and secure environment. In addition it is *fun*! Young children enjoy it and are eager to involve themselves in it. It is highly motivating – one of our 'big ideas'. It is an extremely versatile and effective form of drama. So powerful is drama as a means of learning and teaching for all ages that some primary schools do not leave it to chance and choice but include it in their learning principles. We know of at least one secondary school that has made it a compulsory subject for every pupil throughout the school. There is no doubt that through playing with and in role young children are able to grow in personal, social and emotional development. It gives them opportunities to test out social contexts, develop awareness of their own needs and views and those of others, to view the world from perspectives other than their own, to consider consequences of actions and to develop the social aspect of forming relationships with others. We could go on. It is also a powerful means of developing communication and language skills. Children do this through developing imaginative play; creating imaginary situations; extending real life experiences; practising their use of language; learning and using new vocabulary; interacting with peers and adults. This list is not exhaustive by any means. By viewing role play as a learning and teaching strategy it can be effectively used to meet many learning objectives, providing, of course, that it is well planned and children are taught appropriate skills.

The traditional role play area

Role play is a term that is commonly accepted within the early years classroom. Yet it becomes clear when talking to teachers and working with children, both in the early and later Foundation Stage, that the term is used to cover many aspects of a child's learning and of a teacher's teaching where some approach to drama is used. Traditionally role play occurs in a given area of the classroom which is set up in a themed way. Teachers of young children value the space given to role play within the classroom as a place where children can learn to develop social and communication skills within the secure environment. There are times when a child may need the security of playing with familiar objects whilst exploring how other people live; this is the thinking behind providing a 'home corner' and is particularly appropriate in the first term in school where things may be strange and unfamiliar. Other role play areas are linked to topic work, for example a vet's or doctor's surgery, a garden centre. In each case, the potential for immersing children in the language of the 'area' (oral as well as written) is huge.

Effective use of a role play area depends on the following:

- The children, teacher, teaching assistants and adult helpers being clear about its purpose.
- Children being involved in the setting up.
- All those involved being fully aware of the specific learning focus.

The focus may change over time but the involvement of the adult is central to successful learning, especially in terms of language development. Clearly effective learning through the use of role play areas depends on the appropriateness of approach to the learning intended. There is, however, a health warning to be heeded. Despite a teacher being clear about the learning expected to take place in this socially set up environment, we find that without the involvement of an adult, children tend to play out roles alone, in parallel to others, or introduce other resources to the area that alter the intended focus. Children may extend their play beyond the set-aside role play area, taking the play out into the wider classroom or outdoor area. For example the role play bus steering wheel being 'driven' out around the classroom to the outdoor area to 'crash' into the train. The work of Bennett et al. (1996) identifies the discrepancy between the purpose identified by the teacher and the use of it by the children. It is unlikely, we would argue, to be highly effective in developing social and language skills without interaction with an adult. It may, however, be highly effective in providing security through familiarity and in providing a more intimate space in which children can play.

We have entitled this chapter 'Playing with role in the Foundation Stage' rather than 'Learning through role play' because we want to consider it beyond the role play area. This may mean using the adult in role, a child in role, a group of children in role, the whole class in role or a mix of these during any one session.

Speaking, listening and literacy

In our experience there is anxiety among teachers that children are coming to nursery or reception classes with a decreasing level of listening and speaking skill. Whether or not this is true, it is important to consider both this and the different experiences that young children now have before coming to school.

> Talk is fundamental to children's development and learning has a central role to play in developing their knowledge and understanding. Speaking and listening play an important role in children's social, emotional and cognitive development. Excellent teaching of speaking and listening will therefore enhance children's learning.
>
> (DfES 2006)

Developing the skills of listening and speaking is crucial to developing the skills required of a reader and a writer. Talk for literacy is the main literacy driver when working in the Foundation Stage. That is not to say that familiarity with text as a reader and a writer is less important but that this can be achieved only through developing listening and speaking skills. It is within this context that the varied use of teaching and learning through drama is so valuable. Talk needs to be a distinct aspect of developing literacy and requires a dedicated curriculum. As developing reading and writing depend on oral language this aspect of the curriculum is the bedrock which early years learning and teaching make paramount.

In this unit there is also a focus on the need for children to discriminate sounds, which is an important skill in the development of listening. It is also a necessary skill for children to have prior to developing phonic work. There has been much discussion and research in the area of the teaching of phonics which has been highlighted in the Primary Strategy. There are a number of schemes that support a structured approach to phonics teaching. Many Foundation Stage classes use specific phonic schemes such as Playing with Sounds, Progression in Phonics or Jolly Phonics. The Primary Strategy gives importance to a structured approach to the teaching of phonics and clearly states that it is the prime approach to teaching word recognition for the majority of children. Initially this would seem to contradict one of our big ideas which states that children's learning needs to be coherent (for the child) and flowing, where children can make the links. However, the practical application of the strategy outlined above will support coherence where the text, in this case a nursery rhyme and associated narrative, are used by the children to identify and apply their phonic learning to date. Hence phonics are identified within the text rather than the text leading the phonic learning. What is important is that it is the current text that is used by children for identifying examples of the appropriate phonemes throughout the unit of work.

Inside out and outside in

This is about using communication, language and literacy development across the Areas of Learning and using other Areas of Learning within communication, language and literacy. Early years teachers and teaching assistants know that it is not effective, and certainly not practical, to see children's learning compartmentalised into boxes, or Areas of Learning. Indeed the 'big idea' of coherence in children's learning would make this a non-starter. The more the links are made and used, the more effective the learning will be. Personal, social and emotional development and communication, language and literacy development are ongoing throughout a child's time in the Foundation Stage and remain important into and throughout Key Stage 1. Playing with role is a fantastic and powerful aspect of learning and teaching which will always bring a fascinating dimension to learning objectives.

The unit of work developed in this chapter has the traditional nursery rhyme 'Little Boy Blue' as the central theme:

> Little Boy Blue, come blow your horn
> The sheep's in the meadow, the cow's in the corn.
> Where's the boy who looks after the sheep?
> He's under the haystack fast asleep.

Will you wake him? No, not I,
For if I do he's sure to cry.

Little Boy Blue is the central character with scenarios built up or suggested.

Learning and teaching strategies

Three key teaching strategies are developed in this unit:

- Talk partners
- Hot seating
- Freeze frames.

Variation and immersion are so important in the primary classroom. Using a variety of different strategies makes the work more interesting and exciting for the children and the teacher. Using **talk partners** ensures that all children are actively involved in the process and not passive receivers of information. The strategy develops listening, speaking and negotiating skills necessary for social interaction. This is not to say that children can use talk partners effectively straight away, but work with early years teachers indicates that it is quickly developed and very much enjoyed; in fact in one class the Reception children now ask if they can discuss questions with a talk partner. Those classes where this is embedded involve children in reporting the response of the partner (A–B talk). How does this work? Each partnership consists of child A and child B. Child A talks to child B who listens, then vice versa. Child A then reports what child B has said and vice versa. This is challenging for adults let alone young children. However, it really develops skills in active listening rather than waiting to talk. This skill takes time to develop but children quickly catch on with the activity and, with sensitive support from adults in the classroom, each child can respond. The essence of talk partners is the active involvement of all children in the activity. Taking this onto A–B talk may require working in small groups or even with one adult supporting the children still at the early stages of speaking and listening. A–B talk doesn't mean each child responding in front of the whole class – this would be counterproductive and extremely time consuming – however, careful managing of the activity by the teacher, using different groupings (small and whole class) over time, will allow time for the more reserved or reticent children to develop listening and responding skills.

Hot seating can be started in the Foundation Stage in a very simple way. Initially it is likely that the teacher will be in role. Toye and Prendiville (2000, p. 61) identify the different status of the teacher in role (TiR) and how this operates:

Demands of TiR	*Implications for the children*
You are in the drama with the children.	*You demonstrate the demand to take the work seriously.*
You must make clear the fact you are 'in role' by using role signifiers.	*The children feel secure because expectations and the conventions are made concrete – particularly important with young children.*

You must be willing to accept the possibility of new responses.	*The children define and decide; they see their ideas made possible, their decisions acted upon.*
You must plan carefully the viewpoint of the role and select the language and status of the role.	*The resulting authenticity draws the children into forms of teacher–pupil dialogue not possible in the usual teacher–pupil relationship.*
You must structure the role to challenge the children's ideas; this can mean taking up viewpoints that are deliberately wrong or controversial.	*You must structure the role to challenge the children's ideas; this can mean taking up viewpoints that are deliberately wrong or controversial.*
You must be prepared to take the role of 'someone who does not know'.	*The children's status is enhanced and they have the captivating experience of teaching the teacher.*
You should be able to demonstrate a change of attitude.	*Pupils experience successfully shifting opinion through their actions and arguments.*
You can create tension through the use of secrecy, reluctance to speak, revealing something new, blocking ideas, applying pressure, challenging thinking, suggesting possibilities, i.e. 'depending upon'.	*Because interaction with the TiR takes place in the 'present tense', children do not know what is going to happen next – this adds to the potency of the process.*
You can manage the behaviour of the children from within the role.	*Children respond because the control is coming from within the fictional context – something they have invested in with their ideas.*
You can give them tasks without appearing to be teacher-oriented.	*The need to speak, listen, read and write can be greater because of the demand of the fiction.*

What might a 'hot seat' activity look like?

Initially the teacher or, as children's understanding develops, a child responds to questions in character. So the teacher adopts the role, signified by a shawl or a hat or other appropriate prop, and steps into character. The children work, possibly in pairs, to think of questions to ask the character in order to gain information to further their understanding of the context, the story or the feelings of the character. If we use Boy Blue to exemplify an activity it might look like this.

The children are working in pairs or small groups with a teaching assistant to develop questions to ask Mr Rigg, the farmer. The teaching assistant, in role as Mr Rigg holding a walking stick as the significant prop and also wearing a hat, sits on the seat in front of the class and tells them that Boy Blue has been found asleep again and he's off to wake him up and get him to sort out the animals. Mr Rigg says he'll come back in a while to talk to the class about Boy Blue. The teaching assistant then comes out of role to work with the children to decide on what questions they want to ask Mr Rigg when he comes back. The questions can be worked up in pairs or in fours if the children have been introduced to moving from pairs to fours. The pair, or group, agree a question to ask 'Mr Rigg'.

What is happening during hot seating? Young children find it difficult to compose questions in order to elicit information focused on a specific scenario. It is more difficult for them to ask 'Why were you cross with Boy Blue?', than it is to ask 'Can I watch a video now?' So giving appropriate support and practice in posing and asking questions will help children develop skills of inquiry. Being able to ask questions and elicit a response also raises self-esteem, so crucial in developing as a learner. In addition it is developing an understanding of character. Children begin to work with three levels of characterisation: physical appearance, behaviour and attitude, and feelings.

Freeze frames could be used during the enacting of the narrative to pose questions. This is a particularly useful strategy to explore feelings. Children can be acting out a scene when the action is frozen (a camera is very useful at this point both to stop the action and to take a photograph to work with at a later stage). The teacher can then lead the class in exploring what is taking place at that point in time. What is happening? What are the characters thinking? What do their expressions tell us about how they are feeling? Freeze frames allow time to analyse situations.

What was in the teacher's head when planning this work?

Contexts and coherence

- Recent learning of these nursery rhymes can be built on.
- I can develop the children's understanding of characters in fiction.
- Previous drama work skills are built on.
- Speaking and listening links with reading and writing.

Motivation

- The children now love the nursery rhymes we have been learning.
- The children can have fun with linking the different rhymes.
- The children enjoy taking on a role.
- The children enjoy working with an adult in small groups.

Content and process

- Drama is a powerful way to teach children about the cause and effect of their actions and those of others.
- Nursery rhymes will be reinforced and enjoyed.
- Imagination will be enriched.
- Learning and teaching strategies used will support speaking and listening development.

- Children will have experience of narrative, explanations and recounting text types.
- Through drama and circle time children develop empathy for the character which will help them make sense of the world and how others feel.
- Listening and speaking – use of talk partners to fully involve all children in the process.
- Developing questioning skills both for open and closed questions through hot seating.
- Acting in role – the use of freeze frames allows enquiry and analysis of a moment in time.
- Phonics will be addressed through discrimination – segmenting and blending of sounds in words.

How does this relate to the Early Learning Goals and the Primary Framework?

The Primary Framework and the Early Years Foundation Stage Curriculum Guidance have been developed alongside each other, with relevant sections mirroring each other. The guidance provided in the Literacy Framework for the Foundation Stage matches the sections in the EYFS on communication, language and literacy. You will note that a number of the Early Learning Goals are appropriately placed in more than one strand where the knowledge, skills and understanding of the various aspects of literacy overlap.

Clustering the learning objectives

Speaking

Foundation Stage

- Use language to imagine and create roles and experiences.
- Speak clearly and audibly with confidence and control and show an awareness of listener.

Listening and responding

Foundation Stage

- Sustain attentive listening, responding to what they have heard by relevant comments, questions or actions.

Group discussion and interaction

Foundation Stage

- Interact with others, negotiating plans and activities and taking turns in conversation.

Year 1

- Explain their views to others in a small group, decide how to report the group's views to the class.

Drama

Foundation Stage

• Use language to imagine and create roles and experiences.

Year 1

• Explore familiar themes and characters through improvisation and role play.

Engaging with and responding to texts

Foundation Stage

• Use language to imagine and recreate roles and experiences.

Starting point

The aim is to build upon recent learning of nursery rhymes. So the starting point is using a big book of nursery rhymes and (on Friday) focusing on 'Little Boy Blue', building up excitement and anticipation about working with him next week.

Monday morning – choices

How should the work proceed? Should the intended learning for the unit of work be introduced now, the nursery rhyme read again or the children told about the letter and Boy Blue's visit?

In this example the decision is made to start with a reading aloud of the nursery rhyme, followed by the 'arrival' of the letter from Boy Blue. The letter is read aloud to the children and subsequently discussed.

Lane End Cottage
8th April

Dear children,

My name is Boy Blue and I have got into some trouble with Mr Rigg, the farmer that I work for. I would really like to come to talk to you about how I can make things right with Mr Rigg.

He thinks I fell asleep and let the sheep and cows get into the wrong fields, but I didn't. Every time I try to tell him what happened he gets cross with me and I start to cry.

Mr Rigg is a lovely man and I do love working on the farm. It's great fun. But I don't understand what I've done that's really wrong, the sheep and the cows are fine now, but I'm sure you could help me sort things out.

I'll come into school on Monday if that's all right with you and your teacher.

Love from

Boy Blue

Shared text time

The letter is read and there is discussion of its layout, words, print, high frequency words. The teacher models reading behaviour. The children are organised into talk partners to discuss possible reasons for Boy Blue's predicament. A picture is shown of Boy Blue with further discussion developing; discussion may also include the limitations of forming opinions from a picture.

Talk partners can then be used to discuss questions the children might want to ask. Once questions are formulated, they can be recorded either by the teacher or a child. Depending on the children's skill in working in this way, the teacher may ask for their thoughts in relation to the scenario set and develop this as a shared writing activity. Children are encouraged to write on laminated cards in thought or speech bubble shapes (see Chapter 3). These are used in preference to whiteboards for novelty and for the ease of photocopying for retention and reuse at a later stage in the unit of work. The choice of how to develop a list of starter questions for Boy Blue will be dependent on individual teacher choice and the level of skill of the children. The questions can then either be answered by the teacher or child in role or by group discussion amongst the children, which is what happened prior to the children explaining to Boy Blue what could have happened and what he could do about it.

Spotlight: preparing for Boy Blue's visit

(Thanks to the Reception class at Maryport Infant School, Cumbria.) The letter has been read and the children now prepare for the visit of Boy Blue. The teacher generates some questions and the children begin to discuss possible answers to the questions raised. The questions include:

- 'Why was the farmer so cross with Boy Blue?'
- 'Why do you think Boy Blue fell asleep?'
- 'What should Boy Blue do now?'
- 'Are you sure it was Boy Blue's fault?'

The children discuss each question in pairs and then confer with another pair sitting next to them on the carpet. They then agree a group response and one of the more able writers scribes for the group. The scribe writes confidently, but when unsure is helped by other children. Only in a few cases does the group have support from the teacher.

Why was the farmer so cross with Boy Blue?

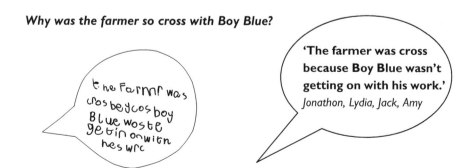

'The farmer was cross because Boy Blue wasn't getting on with his work.'
Jonathon, Lydia, Jack, Amy

Additional written comments include:

- 'He fell asleep and left the gate open.'
- 'Because Boy Blue wasn't doing his work.'
- 'He wanted to get Boy Blue into trouble so he said he did it when he didn't.'

Why do you think Boy Blue fell asleep?

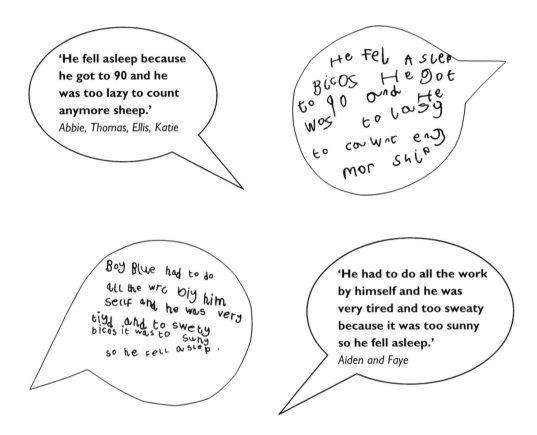

- 'He was too tired with doing all the work and closed his eyes without knowing.'
- 'He might have had to do a night shift like milking the cows so he was tired in the day.'
- 'He had to do all the work with the cows and sheep and the tractor and the farmer did nothing.'

What should Boy Blue do now?

'Boy Blue has to say sorry it wasn't my fault, I just fell asleep and the cows and sheep got over the fence by themselves.'
Olivia, Jordan, Kate, Allissa

'Boy Blue said I'm going to put it right again. He waved a stick at the animals and they all went back in the right field.'
Abbie, Ellis, Thomas, Katie

- 'Just say he didn't remember falling asleep.'
- 'Boy Blue should just say sorry and get on with his work.'

Are you sure it was Boy Blue's fault?

- 'The sheep bit the gate and the cow butted with its horns and they ran away into the wrong fields when Boy Blue was asleep!'
- 'Maybe the animals jumped over the gate and ran away!'
- 'The gate was open and the cows and sheep got out.'

Assessment opportunities

This process gives many opportunities for the teacher to make assessments of the children in their literacy development. The sequence of paired talk, group talk and group writing provides opportunities for assessing speaking and listening and also writing behaviours. The written outcomes provide assessment evidence of the ability of some children to write independently, to be able to write high frequency words and their knowledge of phonics.

Choices in managing the session

The children use these written responses when Boy Blue (teacher in role) asks for help. The character of Boy Blue could be a puppet or a teacher in role, using a prop to indicate when he or she is actually in role, for example, by holding a toy lamb or wearing a hat or carrying a shepherd's crook. If the latter option is taken then the teacher needs to explain that he or she is Boy Blue when holding the prop. Developing the learning and teaching strategy of hot seating can begin here, helping develop children's listening, speaking and questioning skills. As the unit of work develops the role of Boy Blue may be taken by a child holding the appropriate prop, with the teacher supporting the questioner or the response from 'Boy Blue'.

A bag that Boy Blue carries contains various items. The contents of this bag can be used in a number of ways, for the teaching of phonics, for extending vocabulary and for developing scenarios.

Spotlight: phonics

The puppet and his bag are used to build up the anticipation and excitement. In talk partners children discuss what the bag might contain. Boy Blue's bag contains the following items:

- map
- cap
- postcard from Bo-Peep
- train ticket
- stone
- few pence
- small plastic sheep (farm animal set)
- sheep's wool
- empty mobile phone case.

Clues are given about the articles before they are taken out of the bag. The clues relate to current phonic learning and cover a range of levels. A group of six children are working with the teacher who has put boxes on the carpet. There are four boxes, one marked for CVC words, one for 'sh', one for 'tr' and one for 'others'. The items are brought out of the bag and the children classify and sort them appropriately. The train ticket is put in the 'tr' box, the sheep in the 'sh' tray and the map and the cap in the CVC box. The pennies are put into the 'others' box. Children choose a box and write the words onto a laminated card. The items are then mixed up; the children take it in turns to pick an item, identify it, find the phonic box and the written word and then put the item back in Boy Blue's bag.

Throughout the session the focus is on the skills of segmenting and blending phonemes in the words.

Spotlight: extending vocabulary

Boy Blue's bag has additional contents in it. The teacher peeps into the bag and, using very descriptive language, is describing items. The map is being described as 'crumpled', 'smooth' and 'delicate'. An additional item is being described as shiny, cold, cylindrical and on a string. Children ask further questions like 'Is it big or small?'; 'Is there one in the classroom?'; 'What does Boy Blue use it for?' It is a whistle. The words cylindrical, whistle, smooth, delicate are added to a Good Words list being compiled for the unit of work. The children in working with Boy Blue use this vocabulary.

Spotlight: developing scenarios

The empty mobile phone case is causing much discussion. In talk partners the children are given a few minutes to discuss why Boy Blue has this in his bag. The teacher asks for feedback from some of the pairs. Opinions include 'He has lost his phone, so he couldn't let the farmer know what has happened' and 'He wants a mobile to text his friends'. In fours the children develop one of the scenarios fed back to the class. Stories soon develop. One is chosen and then acted out. The new story is recorded on the interactive whiteboard through a shared writing process.

Boy Blue's visit

Children readily engage with a scenario if the puppet or teacher is in a role where they are not 'in charge', where the children provide the answers, where the children can help. This approach is set by the tone of the introductory letter.

So the teacher reminds the children of their previous work and rereads the letter from Boy Blue. The teacher can set a background scenario; two are given below as examples.

Possible scenario 1

Boy Blue sees some of Bo-Peep's sheep in his field so tries to get them back into their own field; they are difficult to round up so he gets very tired. He manages to get them through the gate but some of his sheep follow him and run into the meadow. Some of Boy Blue's friends are leaning on a gate into the field where the cows are. They call to Boy Blue and wave but the gate breaks and the cows get into the corn. Boy Blue and his friends try as hard as they can to get the cows back but they just won't go; they are enjoying the corn too much. His friends run off and Boy Blue is so tired from chasing the animals that he has a rest in the haystack and falls asleep.

Bo-Peep has found him asleep and knows the farmer is cross so doesn't want to wake him up. When Boy Blue does wake up, Bo-Peep tells him the farmer is angry. Boy Blue knows he should have kept the animals in the correct fields and is worried that he might lose his job so he comes to ask the children what he should do.

Possible scenario 2

Boy Blue is known to be a very lazy farm worker and likes to snooze in the sun. Bo-Peep keeps telling him that he'll get into trouble and in fact recently she has been looking after his sheep and cows as well as her own flock. She finally says she cannot do that any more and he has to take some responsibility for his animals. He is always late for his breakfast and his lunch and the farmer's wife is getting a bit fed up with him. The farmer has warned him a number of times and he says if anything goes wrong again, he will be in big trouble. So, on this day he leaves gates open and doesn't watch the animals; instead he falls asleep. When he wakes up he knows he is in trouble and so asks the children to help him.

In this instance scenario 1 is decided on and explained to the class. Groups of children role play the scenario with the teacher freeze framing the action to ask another group how they think Boy Blue/his friends/Bo-Peep/the farmer might be feeling and what they should do next. Different outcomes are explored. The teacher is in and out of role.

Writing by the teacher builds prompts, on a flipchart, from information or suggestions given by the children. The suggestions made by the children can be used in developing a narrative based on the role play from the rhyme. The notes made, with references to phonic learning, will be used tomorrow to work with the children to develop the notes into a class big book.

Beyond the unit: what might we choose to develop?

All of these ideas are consistent with the learning objectives and are integral and coherent to the unit of work:

- Story sequences are developed pictorially to show why the sheep went in the meadows, how the cows got in the corn, and why Boy Blue fell asleep. This will enable children to work individually or in pairs to sequence events and then retell the scenario.
- The role play area is adapted to become Mr Rigg's farmhouse kitchen. This will give a different scenario in which children can explore the situation from the farmer's perspective, using the appropriate vocabulary on the Good Words list.
- Bo-Peep, Boy Blue's friend, comes for lunch to talk to Mr Rigg. Two children are in role using the hot seating strategy.
- The children act out the following. They are on a coach trip, stop for a picnic and help to try to get the sheep back into the fields away from the road. This would allow the exploration, through freeze frame and circle time, of helping others.
- A group of children act out the scenarios developed. With shared writing, appropriate vocabulary is used and texts written for the class to share and enjoy.
- The teacher is in role as Mr Rigg. This would support the development of speaking, listening and constructing questions.
- Shared writing of narratives developed from other nursery rhymes.
- The exploration of other text types such as letter writing, script writing and map drawing.

The potential for and impact on attainment through the use of drama with young children is immense and given the motivation factor should be something high on all teachers' strategies for developing speaking, listening, reading and writing.

References

Bennett, N., Wood, L. and Rogers, S. (1996) *Teaching Through Play: Teachers' Thinking and Classroom Practice*, Buckingham: Open University Press.

Cassidy, S. (2001) 'First I was a bear, then a snail. Now I am an angel . . .', *The Independent*, 13 December.

DfES (2006) *The Primary Framework for Literacy and Mathematics: Core Position Papers Underpinning the Renewal of Guidance for Teaching Literacy and Mathematics*, London: DfES.

Toye, N. and Prendiville, F. (2000) *Drama and Traditional Story for the Early Years*, London: RoutledgeFalmer.

Waddell, M. (2006) *Can't You Sleep, Little Bear?*, London: Walker.

5 Time for rhyme

Who's here today?
A bear for Claire
A litre for Peter
A pan for Suzanne
A pole for Joel

This is how one Reception class called the register. It began only once a week but the children have such a lot of fun with rhyming words that the teacher has split the register into groups of six names and children in the group, with their name cards selected and stuck up on the big board, have at least one turn each week to rhyme words with their name. All the children help and sometimes that help is most needed – have you ever tried to rhyme a noun with Angharad?

Children love to play with words; they love to make up rhymes even when the words don't make sense. Maybe there is a little of Spike Milligan in us all ('On the Ning Nang Nong All the cows go Bong . . .'). The existence of traditional nursery rhymes reinforces the appeal of rhyming words to young children. This sound play helps young children develop an understanding of language and its structure within familiar and recognised speech or text. Next time you recite 'Humpty Dumpty' to a young child you are highly likely to emphasise 'wall', 'fall', 'men', 'again' (even if you do have to pronounce 'again' as 'agen'). Those children who have experience of nursery rhymes during their first few years seem to understand the rhyming games more quickly than those with limited experience. These children often take great delight in changing the rhyming word to a different one – 'One, two, buckle my shoe, three, four, knock at the *floor*, five, six, pick up *bricks*'.

The continuing popularity of rhyme is clear to see. Go to your local bookshop or library and seek out the children's poetry shelves. There are numerous books included which are collections of rhymes but also rhyme is used in many picture books. Both sets of shelves are very popular with young readers and we need to capture this fascination. Playing with rhyme is a national tradition, which dates back hundreds of years.

Traditional stories and rhymes were, and still are passed down from generation to generation verbally. While the family should be the main conduit of the tradition, schools have always seen their part in this as being very important. It is rather sad that many children now enter nursery or primary schools without knowing any of the traditional nursery rhymes; hence the inclusion of traditional stories and rhymes within the early years and into Key Stage 1. The richness of the language used in traditional nursery rhymes is timeless and priceless; all children deserve to have these in their repertoire. Children from different cultural backgrounds bring different traditional rhymes and these are welcomed into the classroom and enjoyed by all. Traditional rhymes give children the tools with which to practise using language, to play with words, to invent alternative rhyming words and enjoy hearing themselves speak them – out of their own mouths. The appeal is also about rhythm, patterns of the sounds of language. Rhyme and rhythm draw attention to the language itself and this differs from other forms of language where we are often more aware of the context rather than the language. Usha Goswami (2002) draws attention to this 'phonological awareness', especially to initial phoneme (onset), such as the alliteration in 'Baa, Baa, Black sheep' and 'Peter Piper picked a peck' and rhymes at the end of single syllable words such as 'Little Bo-Peep has lost her sheep'. Through songs and rhymes children can develop phonological awareness and take this awareness to their writing and reading.

If we accept that rhyme plays an important role in developing the reading–writing connection, then it must be planned for carefully. Acknowledgement of different learning styles is important and we would always try to plan a range of activities within the learning objective that allows all children to be fully involved, and actively so. For example, activities would include working through illustration for the visual learners; through telling the text for the auditory learners; and through role play for kinaesthetic learners. A very high percentage of young children are kinaesthetic learners and need the 'action'. Acting out of number rhymes is always popular with children and is a powerful aid to learning. All of the approaches would have the same learning objective but would approach the learning in different ways. Sharing the reading of a familiar rhyme enables teachers to model the art of reciting rhymes and poems, using intonation, pace and rhythm, which children join in with thus learning how rhyme is read. Rhyme is used throughout early education and is most often offered as a long thin strand; thus it goes on continuously throughout the Foundation Stage and Key Stage 1 and beyond. This is desirable but whether it is done through linking specifically to an Area of Learning, such as mathematical development, or to a topic, such as 'animal homes', or to the Primary Framework for Literacy objectives, it needs to be explicitly planned and taught. If we are to maximise children's learning of rhyme, the links must be made, planned and implemented in terms of not only aural discrimination but also visual. The link to phonics is imperative if rhyme is to support the reading–writing and most importantly the speaking–listening–reading–writing connections. Immersion in rhyme could be, for example, a unit of work in the Reception class with a focus on rhyme and CVC words, during which activities support children's development from speaking and listening to shared reading to shared writing.

In the early years explicit teaching of phonics is emphasised in the Primary Framework and recommends systematic and discrete phonic work as part of the wider literacy curriculum.

> Phonic work should be set within a broad and rich language curriculum that takes full account of developing the four independent strands of language – speaking, listening, reading and writing – and enlarging children's stock of words.
>
> (DfES 2006)

Working with rhymes by recognising the phonics within them gives coherence to children's learning. It is not a case of choosing the rhymes to fit with the current phonics being taught, but rather that current phonics can be identified in the rhymes being used in the unit of work and children using their knowledge of phonics in their writing.

Rhyme deserves to be enjoyed, played with, spoken and shared for its own sake. If love of language is to be promoted then starting in early childhood with rhyme chanting is a sound start. However, if activities are motivating (a big idea) then the move from speaking–listening to reading–writing will ensure that rhyme keeps its appeal. The richness of language in rhyme is tangible and can be evidenced in the sheer enjoyment that children exhibit in joining in with and learning rhymes.

What a unit of work on rhyme looks like for Reception and Year 1 children is shown in this chapter. As with many concepts within the early years, this work is an ongoing process. Experience in the home and pre-nursery environments are brought to Reception and on into Year 1 and onwards.

The reading aloud of rhymes and playing with words form the foundation on which children's understanding of language develops. The richness of language used is identified in the Early Learning Goals and develops through into the Primary Framework objectives for Year 1. Where children have experienced a rich literate home environment and a stimulating early Foundation Stage, some will be ready for Year 1 objectives before the end of their Reception year.

What was in the teacher's head when planning this work?

Contexts and coherence

- I can build up their experience with rhymes.
- It can develop from word play sessions.
- I can link it in with topic work in term 2.

Motivation

- The children enjoy the nursery rhymes because they are familiar and give a feeling of security.
- The children *love* playing with words (words said fast and words said slow; tongue twisters; making up words).
- The unit will empower children to speak rhyme expressively.

Content and process

- The reading aloud of familiar rhymes, modelling rhythm, pace, intonation and volume.
- Use of rhyming books.
- Build on word play.
- Develop phonological awareness.

- Develop an understanding of patterns in words.
- Develop good speaking and listening habits and skills.

How does this relate to the Early Learning Goals and the Primary Framework?

The Primary Framework and the Early Years Foundation Stage Curriculum Guidance have been developed alongside each other, with relevant sections mirroring each other. The guidance provided in the Literacy Framework for the Foundation Stage matches the sections in the EYFS on communication, language and literacy. You will note that a number of the Early Learning Goals are appropriately placed in more than one strand where the knowledge, skills and understanding of the various aspects of literacy overlap.

Clustering the learning objectives

Speaking

Foundation Stage

- Enjoy listening to and using spoken and written language and readily turn it into play and learning.
- Use language to imagine and create roles and experiences.
- Speak clearly and audibly with confidence and control and show awareness of the listener.

Listening and responding

Foundation Stage

- Listen with enjoyment and respond to rhymes and poems and make up their own rhymes and poems.
- Extend their vocabulary, exploring the meanings and sounds of new words.

Understanding and interpreting texts

Foundation Stage

- Extend their vocabulary, exploring the meanings and sounds of new words for Year 1.
- Explore the effect of patterns of language and repeated words and phrases.

Engaging with and responding to texts

Foundation Stage

- Listen with enjoyment and respond to rhymes and poems and make up their own rhymes and poems
- Use language to imagine and create roles and experiences

Rhyme across the curriculum

It would not make sense to focus on the unit of work for this chapter without putting rhyme in the context of an early years classroom. It is one of the most powerful ways of developing the language of young children and happens on a daily basis in one form or another. One of our big ideas is coherence and another context; ongoing use of rhyme is crucial to both these elements. It is an effective strategy in engaging children with language.

No matter what the particular topic or unit of work, rhyme will be found running alongside. Young children learn using rhyme in many ways. One of the most powerful is through singing the rhymes; this can be found in all curriculum areas. The singing, enacting, sharing and enjoyment of rhymes is embedded in early years education and is often linked to a particular Area of Learning, for example number rhymes for mathematical development such as 'Five little ducks'.

Five little ducks went swimming one day,
over the hills and far away,
Mother duck went quack, quack, quack
But only four little ducks came back.

One, two, buckle my shoe,
Three, four, knock at the door,
Five, six, pick up sticks,
Seven, eight, lay them straight,
Nine, ten, a big fat hen.

When number rhymes are used in a practical way where children act out the rhyme, the one to one correspondence of number and symbol is demonstrated in a way that young children relate to. For example 'Ten green bottles', an age-old favourite, can help children to understand counting down from 10. Ten children, one at a time, fall as the rhyme dictates; counting the children still standing helps children 'see' the sum; the use of rhymes aids the reinforcement of the concept. Hughes et al. (2000) encourage the use of stories and rhymes which have a mathematical bias in order to help children make sense of real world mathematics.

Starting point

(Thanks to the staff and children at Broughton Moor School, Cumbria.) Playing with words and rhyme is a lively and much loved part of life enjoyed by children from the time they first come into school. The majority of children transfer from the village pre-school and come knowing some nursery rhymes and the staff in Reception quickly build on this experience. They regularly recite nursery rhymes and sing rhyming songs. They play with words, making up nonsense ones, and listen to adults reading nonsense poems aloud. The children choose to look at, share and read from a wealth of poetry and nursery rhyme books in the classroom. With this rich climate as a foundation, the class begin to work with a specific text. In this instance it is *One Teddy All Alone* by Rosemary Davidson (1998). The book is read aloud and the children listen quietly. They enjoy the rhythm of the rhyme and the repetition within it. They look at the illustrations and discuss them, noticing much of the detail to be found. The book is left in the book area for children to look at, read and share. The next day the book is reread with the children starting to join in. The rhyme is enacted with seven children each taking the role of one of the teddies. The class recite the rhyme with the seven children jumping up and miming action to the lines of the verse.

> One teddy all alone
> Two teddies on the phone
> Three teddies with a kite
> Four teddies in a fight
> Five teddies up a tree
> Six teddies in the sea
> Seven teddies *all for me*.

By the end of the week the children know the rhyme well and have read and reread the book. The text becomes the focus for the unit of work developing children's knowledge and understanding of rhyme.

Spotlight: rhyming strings and things

The rhyme is being written on a flipchart and the children are sitting as a group reciting the rhyme as it is being written up. They are helping the teacher to write it correctly. The teacher is saying some of the words incorrectly and in the wrong order and the children are quick to tell her where she is going wrong and what the correct word is. The rhyme is now correctly written up. The children are asked to listen for the words that rhyme when it is read aloud. They are asked to listen quietly the first time. On the second reading they listen carefully and put a hand up or jump up when they hear any words they think rhyme. Before the teacher gets to 'phone' some children are saying 'alone–phone'! The words that rhyme are underlined on the flipchart using different colours for different rhymes. They think of other words that rhyme with 'phone' and come up with 'bone' and 'groan'. 'Kite' and 'fight' soon have 'bright' and 'night' written up, with 'me' and 'bee' in the same group as 'tree' and 'sea'.

The different spelling patterns are pointed out to the children who also identify spelling patterns that are the same – bright and night; bee and tree.

Spotlight: the next day – extending the rhyme

The children really know this rhyme well now and recite it without the text. The teacher and a teddy are pointing to the words to emphasise the rhythm of the verse. How could the rhyme have gone on? The children are encouraged to think of a different line for the seven teddies.

> Seven teddies watching telly

is agreed on. The children count up from one to seven and get the next number, so there are eight teddies now. What will go with seven teddies watching telly? What word can the new line end with to rhyme with telly? 'Jelly' is the first choice. Starting from the beginning 'One teddy all alone' the children reread and extend the rhyme to include their new rhyming couplet:

> Seven teddies watching telly
> Eight teddies eating jelly.

The last two lines follow:

> Nine teddies sleeping in the night
> Ten teddies get a fright!

The children are delighted with their rhymes and read the rhyme through from start to finish including their work.

Later in the unit of work the pattern of the rhyme 'One teddy all alone' is used as a basis for the children writing their own rhyme about a different subject. This is quite an undertaking for Reception children, but given the support, permitting circumstances and appropriate learning and teaching strategies, this is a very satisfying and purposeful activity. The end result is a book written and illustrated by the children (for an example see Figure 5.1).

> One teddy on a plane
> Two teddies down the lane
> Three teddies on the sand
> Four teddies coming to land
> Five teddies making tea
> Six teddies all for me.

The strategies used to develop this new work are illustrated on the facing page.

Spotlight: rhyming words

Children are playing with words at every opportunity. One child is reading a favourite book, *Walking in the Jungle* by Richard Brown and Kate Ruttle (1998). The book is well known by the class and several other children soon join the one who has picked the book out. The teacher models language by reading the story aloud. The children identify the rhymes and repetition in the text. The rhyming words are put up on the whiteboard for

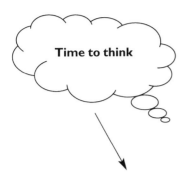

Time to think

Giving children thinking time allows each child the time to gather his/her thoughts before talking about them. This strategy also enables those children who don't respond instantly to still be involved. We all recognise the child whose hand goes up immediately a question is asked, leaving others thinking the moment has passed! It also helps by slowing some children down; it is not always the first thing that comes to mind that is the best!

The children are given time to think about what a new rhyme might be about. Will it be about teddies or another animal or a person?

How might the first line go:

'One . . . ,'

Working in pairs means each child is able to share his/her ideas with at least one other person. This encourages children to share their initial thoughts and whilst listening to a partner they may take on different ideas, refine or modify original thoughts.

Each child tells his/her partner the ideas he/she has about whether he/she wants teddies in the new rhyme or another animal or person. Each listens carefully to the other and starts talking about which idea (or combination of ideas) they will agree on. When the teacher asks for a response from *some* of the pairs, each will be ready to respond.

Each pair may try to think of a first line.

Talk partners

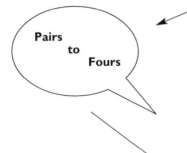

Pairs to Fours

Where talk partners is firmly embedded children may be ready to work with another pair. If this is the case each pair takes their agreed idea to the new group of four. This strategy requires more social skills than working in pairs and also needs an understanding of negotiating. With young children this will need to be developed gradually with a lot of adult support. It is complex but not impossible with Reception children.

In fours the children tell the group the two ideas they have for (i) the character and (ii) a first line (if one has been thought up). Again, as with talk partners, the teacher asks for a response from *some* groups.

The teacher models the writing process, scribing the suggestions made by the children. This is read and reread with the children, refined and polished. Once agreement has been achieved the process of making this into a class book begins.

Whole class

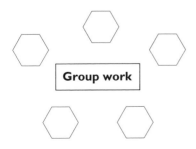

Group work

The children then work in small groups using expertise within the group. One child (or group) may illustrate, one word process, one compile. Where necessary the teacher and teaching assistant help. Illustrations are drawn to match the text. The result is a class rhyme with a book used and enjoyed by the children who wrote it.

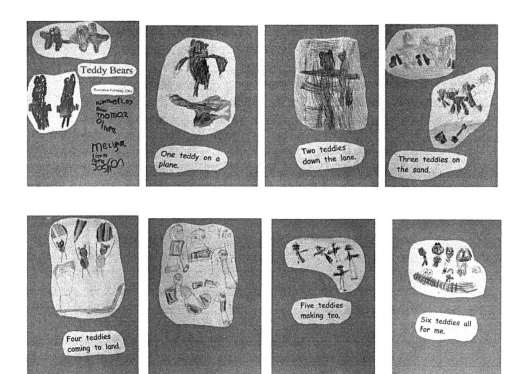

Figure 5.1

all to see. Children are given thinking time to decide what they might 'see' in the jungle. They draw a picture of what they might see and write the text underlining the words that rhyme. Some children require help from one of their peers or an adult.

Walking through the jungle
What did I see?
A big hairy bear
Looking at me.

Later that day children are given a different verse start

Walking down my street
What did I find?

In pairs they discuss what they might find 'down their street'. After a short time several pairs are asked what they have found. (This strategy keeps the activity lively and also helps provide ideas for those who are struggling at this stage.)

Some children orally develop their own rhymes from this point.

Walking down my street
What did I find?
A big scarey dog
But I didn't mind.

Running through the jungle
What did we see?
All the tiny animals
Having their tea.

Spotlight: Year 1

The book is also used with Year 1 children. They look at and identify the parts of the rhyme that use repetition. In learning to extend sentences the children are adding adjectives. They are using this knowledge to make interesting verses in the same pattern as the *Walking in the Jungle* text.

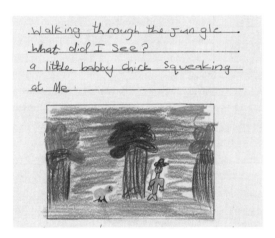

Walking through the jungle.
What did I see?
a little babby chick Squeaking
at Me.

> This Year 1 child enjoyed the repetitive nature of the rhyme and developed adjectives to fit in the verse.

Spotlight: 'Buckingham Palace' by A.A. Milne

But what if we don't start with a rhyme? What if we start with some pictures – what would this look like? How would this develop? The visual images given to the children would need to capture their interest and motivate them to explore the pictures further.

Each child has a set of the pictures shown in Figure 5.2. Following a sequence of strategies, the children talk to share and develop understanding and as a rehearsal for writing. The sequence ensures all children are actively involved in the activity and have a chance to think individually, to share thoughts with a number of others in a non-threatening situation and then to put forward a group response.

In talk partners they take it in turns to talk about each of the pictures. The listener can add his or her ideas once the first speaker has finished. To keep children focused it is useful to ask for a few responses at each stage of the procedure. Then in A–B partners, 'A' moves on to a new partner and explains the understanding from the previous partnership.

Figure 5.2

Having used talk to really 'get into' the pictures, the teacher notes information on a flipchart or on an interactive whiteboard. The benefit of using the interactive whiteboard is that the notes can be added to the pictures on screen for use by the whole class.

The class have a discussion about what the building might be and agree it is a palace. They discuss who might live in a palace. The teacher has a book about the British royal family with pictures of Buckingham Palace and of the Queen. One child tells the class that he has been to Buckingham Palace and that he went on the train to London. They look at a picture which shows the changing of the guard and look at the pictures they have been given and find the picture of the guard. In pairs again they discuss who the boy and the woman might be and what they are doing; they discuss the wedding picture and the picture of the socks, musing on how it fits in with the rest.

At this point, and only after the sharing has happened, the two verses of the poem are read aloud. The children are really involved with the rhyme now and look at the pictures in relation to the poem being read to them.

They're changing guard at Buckingham Palace –
Christopher Robin went down with Alice.

Alice is marrying one of the guard.
'A soldier's life is terribly hard',
                              Says Alice.

They're changing guard at Buckingham Palace –
Christopher Robin went down with Alice.
We saw a guard in a sentry box,
'One of the sergeants looks after their socks',
                              Says Alice.

It is then read aloud in full (six verses) so that the children know the story of the poem. The teacher explains that the pictures are about only two of the verses and these are then read again. The poem is read aloud slowly. As it is being read, in pairs, the children put the pictures in order as they occur in the verses. The children are beginning to match the text to the pictures. They are asked if the 'story' told through the poem matches the story they have developed from the pictures. The beauty of working with this poem by A.A. Milne is that it has a rhythm and repetition, which appeals to young children (as well as adults).

The two verses of the poem can then be given out to the children, who match the pictures to each verse. Then, using shared reading, the teacher reads the poem aloud modelling intonation, pace, volume and pitch with the children joining in.

This process can be used with older children to explore poetry using other strategies such as hot seating and freeze frames (see Chapter 14, 'Whatever happened to Lucy Gray?').

Spotlight: phonics

In a discrete fifteen-minute session, groups of eight children play a game with laminated fans. The children are sitting in pairs; they have one fan between them. On the board are three columns. The first is a list of six graphemes representing initial consonant sounds (onset), the second is a list of graphemes representing six medial phonemes and the third consists of one final phoneme. The partners choose one from the initial sounds list and write it on the fan, then one from the medial sounds and finally one from the final column. They write the word, blend the sounds, and check with each other that they have blended them correctly. They turn to another pair and swap fans. Each pair takes it in turns to blend the sounds and say the word aloud. The children are encouraged to confer with their partner throughout the process. When each group of four has blended the rhyming word, each one is written on the right of the board, as shown in the box.

The teaching assistant then works with the group to identify words that rhyme and asks if anyone knows any other words that would rhyme. The children tell her that 'hatch' and 'latch' rhyme and that 'flash' would rhyme with 'mash', so the teaching assistant writes 'flash' on the right-hand side of the board and, giving help when needed, asks the pairs to work together to try to segment the word so the letters can be added to the columns.

h	a	tch	1. latch
m	oo	sh	2. mash
c	i		3. stitch
l	u		4. hatch
st	e		5. flash
cl	o		
fl			

Beyond the unit

Playing with a much loved rhyme

Children are enjoying playing with words and reciting one of their favourite nursery rhymes, 'Hickory, Dickory Dock'. The children are encouraged to try different words to see if they rhyme. They try:

Hickory, Dickory Dock
The mouse ran up *the road? the street? the block?*
The clock struck *two*, the mouse ran *up? down? through?*
Hickory, Dickory Dock
Tick, tock, tick, tock.

The hilarity and laughter generated when it clearly doesn't rhyme helps those children beginning to learn about rhyme to join in, with this familiar yet different rhyme. The children agree on the following and correctly identify the rhyming words:

Hickory, Dickory Dock
The mouse ran up the *block*
The clock struck *two*, the mouse ran *through*
Hickory, Dickory Dock
Tick, tock, tick, tock.

Rhythm in rhyme

This helps children understand syllables. Children sitting in a circle copy a clapping rhythm started by the teacher.

1. 'One slow clap followed by three faster claps.'
2. Once it has gone around the circle once, the teacher changes it to five equal claps and the children follow in turn.
3. A child then models a rhythm and again it goes around the circle.

4. The teacher then claps the rhythm of 'One, two, buckle my shoe' and the children follow on.
5. Words are added to the clapped rhythm of this line.
6. The teacher models and children follow for each line of the rhyme.
7. The teacher draws attention to the change in rhythm for line 3 of the rhyme.
8. The rhyme is then chanted in its entirety with very soft rhythmic clapping.
9. A child chooses another favourite rhyme – 'Hey Diddle, Diddle, the cat and the fiddle' – and claps the first line.
10. This rhythm is taken around the circle.
11. The rhythm of the second line is attempted.
12. All children join in that and subsequent lines.
13. Children clap the rhythm of the rhyme and sing the words.

This process can be visited regularly. Children develop the skill of listening for the 'tune' of the rhyme.

Rhyming word matching

A bit like matching pairs – the cards have pairs of rhyming words written on them. The cards are placed face down, the children take it in turns to reveal two cards until the rhyming word is found, collecting pairs as they go.

Inventing rhyming words to fit the story

Children enjoy making up words. As mentioned earlier in this chapter Spike Milligan is a good example of using invented words (see Milligan 1968). Children will happily follow this pattern. Some of the nonsense rhyme books can be shared with the children in advance of developing their own nonsense words.

Personalising the rhyme

Using books such as *Mr. Morse's Horse* (Graham 1996), which is a big book with sets of rhyming words, captures children's imagination. They very quickly start to substitute rhymes from, for example, Morse–horse; Clare–bear; Bruce–moose; Jake–snake found in *Mr. Morse's Horse* for their own. It is an easy step from substitution in a rhyme book to developing different uses of rhyme; hence we can arrive at rhyming registers such as:

> A bear for Claire
> A litre for Peter
> A pan for Suzanne
> A pole for Joel

One way to call the register!

References

Brown, R. and Ruttle, K. (1998) *Walking in the Jungle*, Cambridge: Cambridge University Press.

Davidson, R. (1998) *One Teddy All Alone*, Cambridge: Cambridge University Press.

DfES (2006) *The Primary Framework for Literacy and Mathematics: Core Position Papers Underpinning the Renewal of Guidance for Teaching Literacy and Mathematics*, London: DfES.

Goswami, U. (2002) 'Rhymes, phonemes and learning to read', in M. Cook (ed.) *Perspectives on the Teaching and Learning of Phonics*, Royston: UKRA.

Graham, A. (1996) *Mr. Morse's Horse*, Hong Kong: Era Publications.

Hughes, M., Desforges, C. and Mitchell, C. (2000) *Numeracy and Beyond*, Buckingham: Open University Press.

Milligan, S. (1968) *Silly Verse for Kids*, Harmondsworth: Puffin.

6 Outside in, inside out, or reading and writing out and about

Environmental print

Year 1 term 1

Last year, in term 1, the Reception's topic was 'Ourselves', not uncommon and very appropriate. So here we are in Year 1 term 1 and we are going to build on the learning from last year's work. How will we do that? – through a focus on 'Where we live'. One aspect of the work this term is *print in the environment*. In Chapter 1 we highlighted the importance of contextual learning for children: 'Reading and writing are all around us. Young children are exposed to it from birth – on the television, in newspapers and magazines, on bottles, cans and packets.'

If you have not already done so, turn to Chapter 1 and read the paragraphs under the first of our big ideas – 'Contexts and coherence'. Print in the environment is literacy in the real world; it makes sense to children; it addresses a range of audiences through different genres; it is familiar to all children. The National Literacy Strategy has highlighted the need to extend the range of reading and writing, recognising that environmental print is powerful and accessible to children. Traditionally it is an underused resource and may not always fit Standard English, e.g. 'Kwik Save'. However, its familiarity and accessibility to children make it an excellent starting point for all children but particularly for those children who experience barriers in accessing other forms of literacy. All children come to school with 'cultural capital' (Marsh and Millard 2000) in terms of their home and community experience of literacy. Using environmental print is valuing these experiences and building on what children know and understand from outside school. But how can this be used to best effect in the classroom?

The range of fabulous, high quality resources targeted on developing children's reading and writing that can be found in a Key Stage 1 classroom is extensive. However, if many do not link directly with some children's home experiences, what message does this give to children about reading and writing? Environmental print, on the other hand, links to the experience of *all* children. It's out there so we should be using it!

A paper presented by Dr Jackie Marsh at the UKRA Research Day in Cambridge in July 2003 focused on the texts that children between the ages of 2.5 and 5 years are most likely to become familiar within the home. These include text messaging, with very young children playing with mobile phone toys, on-screen text in the form of computer games, the internet and emails as well as junk mail, newspapers and magazines, video and CD covers, labels, posters and stickers. To what extent are we making use of this environmental experience of text and how divorced is it from 'school learning' of text?

The class has been working on the topic of 'Our school' and is now going to broaden its understanding of their environment beyond the confines of the school gate. The opportunity for using environmental print is built into the block of work. Children will have vastly differing home backgrounds and vastly different levels of confidence about their ability to interpret the written word. At the beginning of Year 1 the reading abilities will range from a virtually fluent reader to one who appears to retain little information about word or text level work, despite the best efforts of the parents, Foundation Stage teachers and teaching assistants. Immersion in speaking and listening, then in reading and writing, will begin to make links for all children, and the many and varied opportunities offered in school (and at home) will have an impact on each child's development towards becoming literate.

As adults we all know there is a wealth of print around us. We see it every day. Children also see it every day and many 'recognise' the message that the text is sending out. Recognising the 'M' of McDonald's for example is an early start for children in understanding print in the environment. The context is the cue that children work with in understanding and interpreting text. So if the word McDonald's was in a different colour and was not displayed above a fast food outlet but was, for example, displayed in blue on a chocolate bar, it is unlikely that a child would register the word as the McDonald's with which they are most familiar.

In addition to environmental print being highly contextualised for children, it is also cheap to use, is real and is highly motivating. Making a display of print brought into school from the environment (our 'outside in') involves all children and can be made lively and interactive. Children can discuss the display in pairs, choose recognisable texts and share that with a bigger group. Discussions around where the text can be found, what it means and how children recognise it are all very worthwhile activities.

Using environmental print in a role play area

Traditionally role play areas or corners were set up in classrooms as a home corner to facilitate social play and to give an element of recognition and security to children in the early stage of schooling. This really has now developed into an important feature in many classrooms as a means of developing aspects of learning and teaching. The areas are usually linked to topic work, so we see travel agents, vet's and doctor's surgeries and garden centres springing up each term. We should never underestimate the value of role play in children's learning. Young children learn best by doing. The old Chinese proverb

I hear and I forget
I see and I remember
I do and I understand

really does relate directly to learning in young children (and many adults), hence the value of using role play. We are firm believers, however, that the purpose of role play must be explicit and clear to adults and children. In the case of our supermarket café, the initial objective is to extend children's vocabulary and, through appropriate play, to use this vocabulary accurately. It is also to enable children to develop knowledge and understanding of the function of the café within a community. The café will be full of environmental print relevant to the specific focus of the role play area at that time. Children will need support and direction in using a role play area effectively. Sharing a Good Words list and possibly setting scenarios to be played out will support children's learning. Clearly there is also a place for what tends to be known as 'free play' within the area. Our experience, however, shows that where children have been involved in the development of the area then, out of choice, the children choose a focused approach and will frequently build up their own scenarios. Opportunities are planned to incorporate writing for particular purposes within the area. So the café may have notice-making resources, labelling materials for goods, writing pads for orders, a telephone pad for messages and a visitors' book (yes, some cafés do have them) to write customer comments in. Again the reading–writing connection is developed.

What was in the teacher's head when planning this work?

- This builds on previous learning, thus contextualising the work and giving coherence to previous units of work.
- We can use the topic of 'Where we live' to focus on geography and literacy. Literacy is cross-curricular; whether we use literacy to access curriculum areas (another inside out) or other curriculum areas use literacy (outside in), it is all-embracing.
- There are opportunities to differentiate for different abilities and learning styles.
- This will be linked to the supermarket café – and incorporate role play.
- Parents will be engaged in this unit of work, using their expertise.

Contexts and coherence

- Offering this block of work under the topic of 'Where we live' gives coherence to the work and enables cross-curricular links to be genuinely made. The planned opportunities to link geography and literacy are clearly stated.
- There will be spin-offs with links into mathematical development.
- The children will have a level of knowledge and understanding about their community.
- The work will include approaches to appeal to visual, auditory and kinaesthetic learners and to all levels of literacy within the class.

Motivation

- All children live near to school but will have their own experiences, thus bringing a rich variety of knowledge and understanding.
- The children love talking about the community; they are the experts!
- Most children go to the local supermarket but will not have seen it in this way before, as a reading lesson.
- It offers the opportunity to take children out of school.
- This will motivate those four very reluctant readers.

It is important that the children and parents really get enthused about this project. The fact that they will almost certainly have shopped at the supermarket gives them a level of security and expertise to which we then add something out of the ordinary (we don't go shopping with school, do we?).

Content and process

The whole project is about the community immediately around the school. The specific environmental print foci come early in the topic:

- An environmental print walk from the school to the supermarket – designed primarily to raise the self-esteem of four reluctant readers by putting them in the role of experts who will then work with the other children.
- Print within the supermarket – to inform the planning and development of our role play area 'The café in the supermarket' and leading to a range of writing opportunities.

To make the process successful for different groups of children, the amount of scaffolding and input will be varied appropriately. Initially there will need to be discussion about the project and what we want to learn from it, including what is already known. One option is to start with the mind-map. This will require a recap of the process and a practice.

- Mind-mapping can be used as a benchmark at the beginning of the project. Comparing mind-maps at the beginning and then at the end of a project gives an indication of development and learning. The children have made a mind-map before although only once so it needs to be planned carefully to ensure all children can be involved.
- The generation of ideas, expectations and predictions followed by the analysis of what actually was seen requires specific thinking skills, particularly analytical and evaluative skills.

How does this relate to the Early Learning Goals and the Primary Framework?

The Primary Framework and the Early Years Foundation Stage Curriculum Guidance have been developed alongside each other, with relevant sections mirroring each other. The guidance provided in the Literacy Framework for the Foundation Stage matches the sections in the EYFS on communication, language and literacy. You will note that a number of the Early Learning Goals are appropriately placed in more than one strand where the knowledge, skills and understanding of the various aspects of literacy overlap.

Clustering the learning objectives

Speaking

Foundation Stage

- Use talk to organise, sequence and clarify thinking, ideas, feelings and events.
- Extend their vocabulary, exploring the meanings and sounds of new words.

Year 1

- Experiment with and build new stores of words to communicate in different contexts.

Listening and responding

Foundation Stage

- Sustain attentive listening, responding to what they have heard by relevant comments, questions or actions.
- Extend their vocabulary, exploring the meanings and sounds of new words.

Year 1

- Listen to and follow instructions accurately, asking for help and clarification if necessary

Group discussion and interaction

Foundation Stage

- Interact with others, negotiating plans and activities and taking turns in conversation.
- Use talk to organise, sequence and clarify thinking, ideas, feelings and events.

Year 1

- Take turns to speak, listen to others' suggestions and talk about what they are going to do.
- Ask and answer questions, make relevant contributions, offer suggestions and take turns.

Word structure and spelling

Foundation Stage

- Use phonic knowledge to write simple regular words and make phonically plausible attempts at more complex words.

Year 1

• Spell new words using phonics as the prime approach.

Understanding and interpreting texts

Foundation Stage

• Know that print carries meaning and, in English, is read from left to right and top to bottom.
• Extend their vocabulary, exploring the meaning and sounds of new words.

Creating and shaping texts

Foundation Stage

• Attempt writing for a variety of purposes, using features of different forms such as lists and instructions.

Year 1

• Convey information and ideas in simple non-narrative forms.

Text structure and organisation

Foundation Stage

• Attempt writing for a variety of purposes, using features of different forms such as lists and instructions.

Sentence structure and punctuation

Foundation Stage

• Write their own names and other things such as labels and captions.

Year 1

• Use the space bar and keyboard to type their name and simple texts.

Setting the context and assessing through mind-mapping

The children have five minutes to jot down things they know about the school. To give them a start they are given a sheet with the school at the centre and thought bubbles around. They can put what they like in the bubbles. One child writes a list, another draws small pictures, another writes notes or captions around the centre of the page, another ignores the bubbles and writes a few sentences, another matches jobs to people, drawing a picture of the person and writing the name beneath. One child explained her mind-map

Figure 6.1

(Figure 6.1) from top left: 'Different size people from little ones to big teachers; signs; food; paint and books; trees, a flower and a seat and a football; I can't think of anything else.'

Then moving beyond the school, into the wider community, the children are asked to contextualise the supermarket in relation to the rest of the community by constructing a mind-map. The community has been talked about so the children understand the word. As we have worked with mind-maps, they know they may represent their understanding as they wish.

They first construct their mind-map on their own and will then get into pairs and talk to their partner about their mind-maps, taking it in turns to explain the links. Each child's mind-map will be carefully kept for assessment purposes, comparing it with one completed at the end of the project. Figure 6.2 shows an example of a child's mind-mapping.

The children will build up a class community mind-map by using recognisable environmental print. For example the school could be represented with appropriate text, by the crossing patrol lollipop or the school badge or logo; the garage by the BP sign; the pub by a wagon and horse with its name underneath. This approach encourages children to start looking for print in the environment and bringing this into school. Parents will need to be involved in the whole project but particularly in this aspect as children will need (and want) to draw or make notes to bring from the community to this display. The display gives a powerful message of valuing, understanding and using print from the local environment.

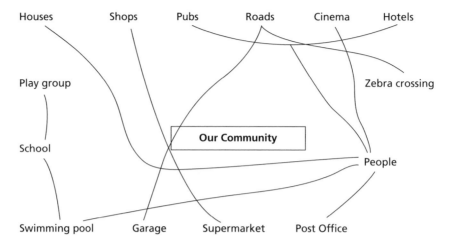

Figure 6.2

Starting point

Developing the supermarket café

How did a café become the focus for our role play area? Over the period of a couple of days the children in the class discuss what they want as a role play area. It is crucial to involve children at this early stage to stimulate an interest in the planning and the development and ultimately in learning through playing in it. So a win–win situation!

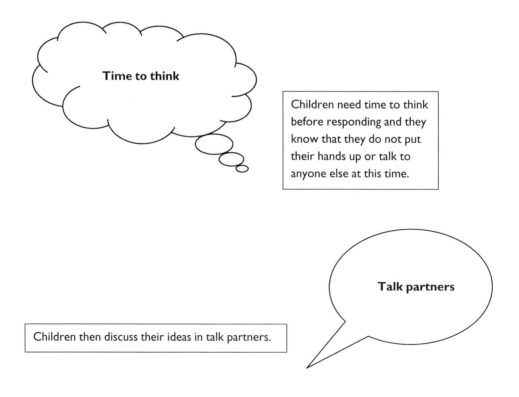

A vote is taken. It is between a café and the petrol station. The children decide on the supermarket café. But before it can be planned the children need to know what one looks like, what it does, what it offers, who works in it.

Planning the café: a visitor to school

Everyone agrees this is a good idea. Through shared writing a letter is written to the manager of the supermarket asking if someone could come to school to talk to the class about the café. The letter explains the intentions of the children to develop a role play area as a supermarket café and their need to know as much as possible about the one in their community. The supermarket manager writes back with offers of help with the print for the role play area and volunteers the services of the café manager to come and talk to the children.

Some of the children have been in the café and this gives them some idea of function. Their experience will be shared with a group or the class before the visit happens. The children will need to plan what to ask the visitor. Finding out what they need to know and how to go about it needs thinking through carefully. Will the teacher lead questioning? How planned should the session be? How are the questions thought out? Will they be written down?

One of the challenging tasks for young children in this planning phase is eliciting what it is they need to know. Not easy! Imagine you, as an adult, needing to plan questions to ask a visitor who has come to talk to you about travelling in a space shuttle. It is, we guess, outside your personal experience. You may have seen it on television or film but what do you need to know? So it is with children who have a more limited experience of life and language than we do.

Working with a full class with the teacher as scribe is likely to end up with very few children really being involved and the teacher leading the questioning focus. How much better it is to work in talk partners so that every single child has a say.

Spotlight: what might we see?

The class is split in two. One half is planning to ask questions that can be answered only with a 'yes' or a 'no'. The other half is planning to ask open questions, which cannot be answered with a 'yes' or a 'no'.

Each half of the class is working in talk partners. The partners come up with one or two questions, which they note down on their laminated speech bubbles (see Chapter 3). They join with another pair in the same half, share questions and through negotiation decide on one or two questions. The questions need to be *good* questions. In order to ensure this, the teacher and teaching assistant do a 'test' run of the questions by being in the 'hot seat', role playing the café manager. Working with one half of the class at a time the questions are tried out, refined and modified as required. The whole class listens to the questions and the laminated bubbles are stuck up on a board. These give a purpose for focused discussion during the visit.

So the questions are ready, and the supermarket café manager arrives. The questions, well planned, are asked and the children begin to build a picture of what is involved. The preparation that has gone into the visit supports literacy development at a number of levels. Useful vocabulary is noted and is displayed in the classroom as Good Words linked to the topic; these will be added to following the walk and the visit. So we have menu, drinks, coke, chips, burgers, apple, crisps – literacy that is highly relevant to the children. Children are writing words for the Good Words list and are recognising them.

The print walk

Four children, carefully chosen, are preparing for a print walk. These four children are acting as scouts and on their return they will be 'experts' in leading the class on the same walk and pointing out the environmental print en route. One of the four is an able reader but a child who says she doesn't like reading, so does as little as possible. A second has no specific learning difficulties but came to school with very limited language skills and although he is developing, he is still struggling with speaking and listening, let alone word and text level, but he wants to be able to read like the others. Another child wants to know only about Pokémon (current craze), so developing his interest and motivating him is the main drive. The fourth is a very shy child who is wary of all things different; she joined the school only at the beginning of this year.

Spotlight: visualisation of the walk

A decision has been made. Following a lot of discussion, the four children are 'walking in their minds' from the school to the supermarket, trying to think of any print they see. They are asked to close their eyes and imagine they are standing at the front gate of the school, looking around for any print, words or signs they recognise. As they visualise something, they draw or note it down. They are gradually taken through the journey, mentioning things 'seen' en route (but not print), for example 'We are just passing the florists, the flowers outside in the buckets smell lovely, I think they are stocks, they are white, lilac and yellow.' This acts as a sort of positional prompt for children to make sure everyone is travelling at the same pace. It also acts as a print spotting prompt, for example the children recognise the shop name 'Blooms'. The drawings or notes made will be used later in the unit of work.

The walk

So (ensuring risk assessments are carried out and full permission gained) the four children set off with the teacher on their print walk from the school to the supermarket. They look for recognisable print, stop when they recognise some and read the text. The children are enthusiastic and stop each other every other step as one of them recognises some text. They take it in turns to take a photograph of the recognised print as well as jotting things down on their clipboards. Once at the supermarket they go into the café, buy a drink (all pre-planned) and then return to school noting, once more, the print recognised on the way there and any they missed on the outward journey. Once back in school the children help print the photographs and set about word processing text to place alongside them. The photographs provide a powerful context for writing. Later in this unit of work, they are used by the teacher to help children recall the order in which the print was gathered.

They will be displayed at the correct places on a route map. They will also be used in word recognition games. Copies of the photographs will be made into a class book with associated word processed text appropriately inserted.

Spotlight: book making

Each of the four children makes his or her own reading book with support from the teaching assistant. This involves constructing sentences to include the environmental text at a level appropriate to each child. The environmental print will also form the first part of the display for the development of the café, 'The route to the café'. The four children talk others through the walk and share the text found in their local environment. This process helps build their self-esteem and confidence.

The books are produced in a variety of ways. One is conventionally bound; one is made as a zig-zag book, which can be opened conventionally or displayed opened in zig-zag form on a work surface; one has the photographs transferred to the computer with text word processed beneath them; and the fourth has flaps over the photographs with text handwritten beneath, encouraging the reader to read the text before checking through the photographs. Now the class sits in four groups and the four children show and read their book to a small group of children, explaining what they have done and answering questions. They move on to the next group to share their book again. They do this to each of the four groups so every child has seen each book and heard from each of the 'experts'.

The links between reading and writing are being made at every opportunity during planning and the activities of the 'virtual walk', the real walk and the book making and sharing.

Spotlight: the class walk to the supermarket

This is where the four print walk experts come into their own. They are children with the 'Mantle of the Expert'. Although Dorothy Heathcote and Gavin Bolton (1995) use drama for this role, these children do become the experts for environmental print en route to the supermarket. Prior to the class walk they:

- read their books to groups of children
- help take a group through a virtual journey
- talk about the print they remember and then what was actually seen
- display the photographs and large versions of the words they recognised on the journey and sequence them around the room.

Parents are invited to join the walk. They have been involved in the project from the start and are kept informed by information posted on the parental notice board. The class is split into two halves to make the walk more manageable.

The first half of the class do the print walk. They point out text referred to by one of the 'experts' and note any other significant text. They reach the supermarket and are met by the manager, who takes them through to the café where the café manager is waiting for them. They enjoy the welcome drink and fruit waiting for them. Working in pairs they have discussion time, focusing on print around them for replicating in their classroom café.

Working in pairs allows the children to:

- be fully involved – active participants
- 'test out' thinking
- refine thoughts
- take on new ideas
- clarify thoughts
- ask questions.

The walk back is used to reinforce and recognise print identified on the way to the café, adding any new information as it is seen.

Back in the classroom there are two aspects to this project:

- Environmental print from the walk.
- Environmental print needed for the supermarket café.

Spotlight: environmental print from the walk

The print is displayed around the classroom (in addition it is displayed on the route map in the hall). Some of the text is put onto cards for a matching pairs activity. Links are made to the print brought into the classroom by the children; this display is already being used by the children in pairs and in small groups for word recognition.

Using the books made by the four 'experts' and the additional print from the full class walk, the class write a book about the walk. Using a sequence of teaching strategies from individual (thinking time), through paired talk (talk partners), to A–B (each talk partner is either A or B – each B moves on to form a different partnership), and then from pairs to fours. The purpose is to make a brilliant book full of Good Words and extended sentences, which will effectively lead others from the school to the supermarket. The book uses the photographs taken on the walk together with the developed text. The first seven words and phrases from the walk are as follows:

1. No cars please | Photo 1 |
2. Riventhorpe Way | Photo 2 |
3. Blooms | Photo 3 |
4. e.flowers | Photo 4 |
5. The Soames Town News | Photo 5 |
6. Magnums | Photo 6 |
7. Lotto tickets | Photo 7 |

The children turn the environmental print from words and phrases into sentences. Although the initial draft does include the environmental text, it is rather boring and the children agree it would be unlikely to capture a reader's interest. It reads:

Go out of the 'no cars please' gate and go to 'Riventhorpe Way' and cross the road to 'Blooms' with 'e.flowers' on the door. The paper shop has 'The Soames Town News' and 'Lotto tickets'.

Through shared writing on the interactive whiteboard, encouraging children to extend the sentences and make them more interesting for someone reading, they arrive at the following:

When you go out of school through the low white gate with 'No cars please' written on it you will need to turn into 'Riventhorpe Way'. Once you have crossed the road, straight in front of you is Blooms the flower shop which will have 'e.flowers' written on the door. It is Mrs. Wilson's shop and she has some flowers outside as well as inside. If you look to your left you will see the paper shop which sells 'The Soames Town News' and 'Magnums'. I bet you go there to buy 'Lotto' tickets too.

Spotlight: making the role play area

The role play area is developing. Children are fully involved in its development. They make and display appropriate labels and captions, which they have word processed; the text is derived from information captured from the café manager's visit and from the children's visit to the supermarket. Various Good Words and Phrases lists are compiled and displayed; these give specific support to the different aspects of the unit of work. The lists are expanded over the weeks and smaller new ones compiled and displayed alongside each other. In week one items to be sold in the café are the focus; week two is about advertisements; week three is 'signs and instructions'. The change of focus keeps the role play area a lively, dynamic real learning environment. Children have opportunities to use a range of writing in the supermarket café. Notices are made using large eye-catching print (see Figure 6.3).

In addition there are customer satisfaction letters and a display of children's work from the local school for a competition. The range is wide, giving sufficient choice to interest all types of learner and to extend current skills.

Spotlight: Croaker

In a discrete fifteen-minute session the class play Croaker, a phonic game. Objects from the café are in an opaque shopping bag. The puppet, Sam, is having great difficulty in saying what the objects are and wants the children to help. A child pulls out an object and tells the group what it is. It is a tin of beans. The puppet says 'a bin of beans'. The children tell Sam he has said it incorrectly and repeat a 'tin of beans'. Sam says 'a fin of beans'. The children tell Sam he is still saying it incorrectly and repeat again 'a tin of beans'. Sam then says 'a tin of beans' and the children cheer and tell him he has said it correctly. He asks the children which part of the word 'tin' he kept getting wrong and they tell him the initial phoneme.

Another child pulls out of the bag a cup. The process is repeated with Sam saying it is a cut. Eventually he gets it right and the children tell him he kept getting the final phoneme wrong.

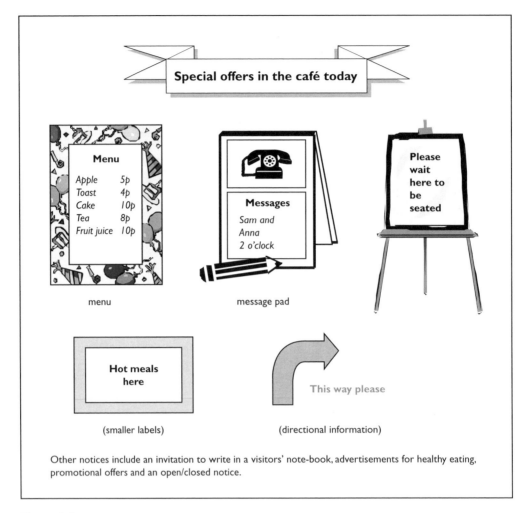

Figure 6.3

The objects ensure the process works with the three phonemes in CVC words. While these are discrete sessions, with a focus on language, the fact that it links to the unit makes it doubly meaningful for the children.

The use of environmental print is very powerful: don't underestimate its value. Have fun!

References

Heathcote, D. and Bolton, G. (1995) *Drama for Learning: Dorothy Heathcote's Mantle of the Expert Approach to Education*, Portsmouth, NH: Heinemann.

Marsh, J. (2003) 'Firm foundations for the 21st century', paper presented at UKRA Research Day, Cambridge, July.

Marsh, J. and Millard, E. (2000) *Literacy and Popular Culture: Using Children's Culture in the Classroom*, London: Paul Chapman.

7 Dance your way to a story

This unit offers some unusual ideas about making and writing stories. It provides ideas for engaging and active approaches to writing traditional stories. In the unit, children literally dance a traditional story they have created. This is part of a larger series of scaffolding and rehearsal activities for writing.

Another exciting part of the process we are going to show you is how children gathered some original and imaginative ideas for the content of the story during a visit to an art gallery in Manchester. The gallery has a fantastic collection of traditional textiles (see Figure 7.1). Children used the patterns in the textiles to get ideas to make their own traditional stories.

Figure 7.1 A sample of a woven tapestry from the textile gallery in the Whitworth Art Gallery

The unit presents an array of innovative and dynamic ways to both stimulate and inspire children's writing, alongside coherent sequences of learning activities which provide plenty of opportunities to embed and develop their ideas.

The work in this unit is based on an ongoing project in Manchester, in which there is collaboration between teachers and museum and gallery educators. The project focuses on improving children's writing by developing collaborative and tightly structured sequences of teaching. The work shown here is based around a visit to the textile collection in the Whitworth Art Gallery in Manchester.

The Manchester Project

It will probably be helpful to say a bit more about the project, because there are many ideas that were developed that will support teachers in planning work in museums and galleries individually. The Manchester Project was originally called MAGPI, which stood for Museums and Galleries Pilot Initiative. A main aim of this unusual initiative was to raise standards in writing through visits to museums and galleries.

Mutual understanding was needed so that teachers and museum and gallery educators could develop ways of working together in more coordinated ways that were focused on identified writing outcomes. Joint professional development days were provided by the authors for the two groups. The aim of these was to develop important ideas about:

- the importance of 'talk for writing' in classrooms, museums and galleries
- the power of specifying an audience and purpose for writing.

This facilitated the development of skills to jointly plan teaching sequences.

What is vital in this unit is that a highly structured approach to developing the sequence of teaching activities evolved as part of the project. The teaching and learning activities that were planned centred on some out-of-school learning in the art gallery. The activities were planned in detail by the teacher and the art gallery professionals. The particular approach to planning the work centred on the three separate phases of activity – what happened before, during and after the visit. Three questions framed our thinking:

- What would happen in the gallery which would help prepare children for writing?
- What needed to be done in school before the visit?
- How would that be used and followed up in school to move children towards independent writing?

The three parts needed to work together coherently to provide children with powerful and motivating learning experiences which would facilitate high achievement in writing.

This unit will show some unusual ways to inspire and sustain children's creative impulses, as they move through a series of stimulating activities towards writing. This unit looks into a teaching sequence which builds towards telling and writing traditional oral stories. It has been written for Year 2, but would work in any year group where the class is being prepared to write traditional stories.

This way of working is a far cry from the early days of the National Literacy Strategy, when the model for developing shared and independent writing out of shared reading activities was often narrowed to an inflexible formula. It is very different too, from the 'creative writing' approaches that teachers used before the introduction of the National Literacy Strategy. Instead, this unit offers a powerful model for developing creative approaches to writing which links to a number of subjects from across the curriculum.

What was in the teacher's head when planning this work?

The overriding priority for this teacher was to provide powerful and motivating experiences for this group of mainly Year 2 children with English as an additional language (EAL). The teacher wanted them to be able to organise their stories better, 'shaping' their texts effectively around characters, plots and settings. At this point, she was more concerned about structure and less about the use of really ambitious language and sentence structure (that was needed too and would come later).

With the gallery educator, she selected traditional stories as the writing outcome they would work towards. There were two reasons for this:

- the simple language and simple strong plots and characters in traditional stories
- the powerful links with the traditional nature of the artefacts in the textile collection at the Whitworth Gallery.

The teacher wanted to plan the classroom and gallery activities effectively, ensuring that the experiences were coherent. The teacher was determined to make this a progressive set of experiences, so her thinking about how to bring it all together is illuminating. There was a set of steps which the teacher needed to go through herself, before talking to the gallery educator. We will look at these here:

- To identify possible writing genres and topic areas to link together.
- To check out possibilities in the local galleries (or museums) – was there an existing educational session offered by the educators that could fit in with the topic and planned writing outcome? (Or could one be adapted to help children gather ideas for the writing?)

It was decided that the writing genre would be traditional story. This would be linked to dance and drama, also, through art, to maths work on different types of pattern. The visit would be to the textile collection so that children could use the images in the textiles for their stories.

Once this was agreed, the thinking and planning centred on the three questions we looked at earlier. These divide the planning into three parts – **during** the visit to the Whitworth Art Gallery, **before** the visit, and activities back in school **after** the visit. The teacher started by thinking about the visit itself.

What shall we do at the gallery?

The visit itself is the pivot around which the activities in school are arranged. It will be an important and memorable event for children, yet time is very limited. So it needs some careful thought about what we actually want children to experience during the visit.

For this teacher it is about ensuring two things happen during the visit: the first is that children are motivated and inspired, the second is to organise concrete and enjoyable experiences which will provide the raw materials for making a traditional story.

She wants children to experience the unusual and vibrant space of the textile gallery in an appreciative and exploratory way and to collect clear ideas in their sketch books and on storyboards, which they will use for the story.

So, activities in the gallery will be planned to be both open ended and exploratory, and organised to connect explicitly with the story writing outcomes around which the unit has evolved.

There are other significant opportunities here that we need to consider briefly. Entry to museums and galleries is free. It would be a real bonus if children's enjoyment of the experience can sufficiently whet appetites, so that they can persuade parents to revisit the gallery with them. The experience offers opportunities to broaden horizons and create contexts for family learning too.

What shall we need to do before we go?

The teaching sessions in school before the visit are focused on getting children familiar again with traditional stories, since these are what they will be writing at the end. The focus is mainly on reading, but reading with a difference. The character of the Snow Queen will also need to be explored, as the children will be bringing her forward into their new stories. The learning will be 'active' and include a lot of talk, drawing and drama. The teacher wants children to be inspired and excited by the work of the unit before they go out of school.

What shall we need to do afterwards to move towards the writing?

The main literacy focus of the next couple of weeks in school is on using the experiences children have had so far, to craft and write a whole story. Children at this point know about traditional story plots, settings and characters and they have their own ideas for a 'new' traditional story. The teacher will now plan some scaffolding activities to move children towards completing some pieces of writing. Also, some spelling activities, will be worked into the teaching sequence which will link with the traditional stories children have been reading.

After they come back from the visit the range of activities will broaden and extend into other subjects. More cross-curricular activities will be developed – in this case, dance, art and maths. These are important both in their own right, as separate subjects with their own learning outcomes and to enrich the experiences leading into story writing.

Contexts and coherence

- Out-of-school learning provides exciting and engaging experiences for learning. Children love a change of setting, and different kinds of places to explore the curriculum. The space and the atmosphere in the gallery itself is awe-inspiring to children. The sense of specialness they get feeds into the outcomes they achieve.

- The unit links subjects in a way that helps children make sense of their experiences and connect the learning. Making sense of the world and their learning in this integrated way is intrinsically motivating for all children. For these EAL learners, visiting and revisiting concepts and contexts scaffolds their skills in learning and using new language.

Motivation

- Children appreciate working with 'real' objects and resources. The artefacts are totally new to them too, so there is a real sense of surprise and wonder around them.
- There is a lot of novelty and variety in the unit to keep children engaged and excited.

Content and process

- Collaborative planning between the teacher and gallery educator was an essential first step for this unit. They needed to identify exactly how the learning activities during the visit could be designed to generate ideas for the structure and content of the traditional story.
- In the work before the visit children will be asked to become familiar with traditional stories by using structured drama sessions to explore settings, plots and characters. They will encounter the story of the Snow Queen, so they can bring this character with them into the new stories they are creating.
- During the visit ideas and content for new traditional stories will be collected and enriched through discussion and drawing.
- After the visit , back in school, experiences will be organised to further explore, enrich and build on that content, scaffolding the creation and shaping of written pieces.

Primary National Strategy Objectives

Clustering the learning objectives

While most of the objectives have come from Year 2, some have been brought in from other year groups. Sometimes this is to bring in an objective from another year group which will enrich and extend the topic. At other times, objectives from earlier years are brought in to meet specific learning needs in areas where the teacher knows there are gaps.

Speaking

Year 2

- Tell real and imagined stories using the conventions of familiar story language.

Group discussion and interaction

Year 2

- Work effectively in groups by ensuring that each group member takes a turn challenging, supporting and moving on.

Drama

Year 2

- Present part of traditional stories, their own stories, for members of their own class.

Year 3

- Use some drama strategies to explore stories or issues.

The drama activities will be less about 'performance' than as an ongoing tool so children can generate, explore, define and redefine their emerging ideas. In fact all the speaking and listening activities are more about enhancing thinking and learning, than about presentation skills.

Understanding and interpreting texts

Year 2

- Draw together ideas and information and from across a whole text, using simple signposts in the text.

Engaging with and responding to texts

Year 2

- Engage with books through exploring and enacting interpretations.

Creating and shaping texts

Year 2

- Draw on knowledge and experience of texts in deciding what and how to write.

Text structure and organisation

Year 2

- Use planning to establish clear sections for writing.

Dance outcomes

- Use motifs to create phrases for dance sequences including the use of gesture.

Starting points – tuning children in to the activities around traditional stories

Before the unit of work starts (this could be the Friday before the Monday or another time that week) in pairs children are given an illustration from the Snow Queen and asked to look and think about it individually. (They haven't been told that the image is from a story.) They are asked in A/B pairs to take turns to say or write what they think about the picture.

This is done in a very structured way, which helps children organise themselves and move towards the group interaction and discussion objective of 'working effectively in groups by ensuring that each group member takes a turn challenging, supporting and moving on'. Because this needs to be done in an exact way it is modelled in front of the class by the teacher and a child, one being A and the other B. Once this is done, the class has a very clear idea of what they need to do.

- A starts with the pencil and writes down what B says (B can help with the spelling too).
- The pair swap roles – B writes what A says.
- They go on doing this so that together they collect ideas using a jotting sheet like the one in Figure 7.2.

Figure 7.2 Jotting sheet

Each pair now joins another pair. Children in the fours take turns to tell each other their reflections and speculations about the picture. This can be done in a more or a less structured way. The decision about how and whether to structure the group task will depend on the experience children have had of group discussion and interaction. If in doubt, structure usually supports the discussion! Here is just one way of doing it:

1.   Pair 1 – A tells one idea to pair 2, then B does the same.
2.   Pair 2 – A tells one idea to pair 1, then B does the same.

Next we could add a bit of 'challenge' (from the objective above). So far the children have been working together supporting each other and moving things forward. The challenge will be created by asking children to use a couple of 'challenging' question prompts. They are challenging in the sense that they ask others to explain their thinking: instead of merely saying what they noticed and inferred about the picture, children now have to make clear what led them to think like that.

One way to do this is to get each pair to select certain comments that the other pair made which interest them. This makes the activity both more manageable (there aren't too many things to ask about) and more authentic, since children are asking questions only about those aspects they are most interested in. (We don't normally ask questions about things that don't interest us: perhaps asking children to generate questions when they aren't interested in the answers robs them of taking a genuinely enquiring attitude.)

So, for example, the first pair might have said, 'She looks like a witch'. The task of the second pair is to ask a 'Why?' or 'What makes you think that?' question. It is helpful here if they have physical prompts, written on cards. They say, 'What makes you think she looks like a witch?'

Again, decisions need to be made about how to do this. Will it be left open ended, with children organising themselves within the fours? Or should the teacher decide to model and even write up a sequence on the whiteboard? One way of doing it could be:

1.   Pair 2 chooses one of pair 1's ideas and asks a question about it – pair 1 answers.
2.   Pair 1 chooses one of pair 2's ideas and ask a question about it – pair 2 answers.

This will need careful modelling. Unless the process has been explicitly demonstrated, it is difficult for children to understand exactly what the teacher wants them to do. They may well need a bit of practice. It is often helpful if the teacher moves round checking how groups are managing this. Is one child in each pair dominating in either the asking or answering of questions? If so, it might be that children need further modelling, this time by fours who have taken turns well.

Throughout this session, the teacher makes specific evaluative comments about children's skills as they speak and listen to each other. The teacher does this to:

•   give high status and value to specific speaking and listening skills. We need to comment on this because children get a lot of contradictory messages about 'listening' (to the teacher), and not 'talking'. Children will be helped here by greater clarity about teachers' expectations about when talk or listening are expected from children.
•   provide assessment for learning feedback information about children's developing skills in both supporting and challenging each others' ideas.

Before the gallery visit

This part of the teaching sequence is about becoming familiar with traditional stories. Children will be given lots of opportunities to browse, read and hear traditional stories in a variety of forms – books, comic layouts, internet material and alternative versions.

Whole-class shared text sessions

The first session is a reading of the Snow Queen story. This starts with a standard shared reading session, in which the teacher reads the story with good pacing and expression, and children listen, following the text on paper or the whiteboard.

During the next series of sessions during the week, the teacher stops the reading at significant moments to encourage a broader response to the story. This will involve two main elements: drama and drawing. These were chosen because:

- both involve talk and collaborative decision making
- careful pairings here could help children develop their ideas by utilising home languages
- both require children to use inference and deduction to make sense of the detail of the text.

The sequence could look something like the following.

Drama

Creating some whole class movement or drama around some important moments in the story, for example:

- the making of the magic mirror by the magician
- the pieces of the mirror shattering and spinning around the world until they pierce the eyes and hearts of children
- those children becoming cruel and hard hearted towards other people, and the sorts of things they might do if they felt like this
- children playing, then struggling in the icy storm on the day that Kay disappears with the Snow Queen.

All of these movement activities offer rich opportunities to develop vocabulary. This could extend children's knowledge and use of the 'feeling' language around unkindness, and develop into an understanding of the intensity of feelings. One way to do this would be to reorder the following list:

cruel
harsh
nasty
loving
vicious
malicious

unkind
gentle
mean

The movement and drama activities could be developed into whole class or small group re-enacting of the whole story

Drawing

Asking children to visualise or create pictures in their heads about significant moments from the story: moments such as the splintering of the mirror, Kay's departure in the sledge of the Snow Queen, or Gerda's encounter with the old woman.

The process of drawing their ideas, rather than only talking or writing about them, helps children negotiate a better understanding. Different children will imagine the picture differently. This provides a powerful resource for discussions around the details of a scene. Further discussion about what is included and how to draw it, adds to children's familiarity with the language needed to retell the story and the story itself.

So children can then be asked to talk about and draw those moments in pairs. If they do these drawings on small squares of paper, they can then be used in the next activity.

Spotlight: drawing a sequence of the main events of the Snow Queen story

This part works best in pairs. Using the pictures they have already drawn and additional ones which they decide capture the main events of the story, children create a 'storyboard'. Children then practise the oral telling of the Snow Queen story.

This is modelled first by the teacher and a child, who take turns to 'tell the story' of each picture. The teacher demonstrates the use of some of the challenging language used in the original story and built upon in the drama sessions. Children share their stories in the plenary session by retelling the story to another pair. (This could be similar to the oral storytelling sequence in Lucy Gray in Chapter 14.) The role of the teacher during this work in fours is to listen in to the storytelling. Interestingly, this activity often surprises teachers. It is not always the highest achieving children who do well at this. Children who struggle to include all their ideas in their writing are freed up to include as much as they like when they don't have to write the story.

This will provide interesting and important assessment information about the gap between children's ability to 'tell a story' orally and in writing. It will inform the teacher about the children's storytelling and writing skills.

It could be developed into a peer evaluation activity, with children in the other pair commenting on the parts or phrases they like best in the story and making one (or two) suggestion(s) to make it more exciting. There are opportunities later to adjust and improve the oral storytelling. Some children do this in pairs, different ones this time, and some to individual children in another class. This will provide further feedback and discussion if it is needed. They write their comments about the feedback on self-adhesive notes to remind themselves of the new ideas.

The children have now had some experiences of reading and exploring traditional stories. They are ready for the work out of school which will provide a memorable and exciting context for getting some ideas for their own stories.

What about the visit itself? How was this two hour session shaped to contribute to children's writing?

This session is being led by the educators at the Whitworth Art Gallery. As we know, it has been carefully planned with the class teacher beforehand. The planning took place before the unit of work started, because the visit itself had to be at just the right time in the sequence of learning activities. This was important because the visit is a pivotal element of the scaffolding of the activities preparing the children for writing.

Textile 'patterns' have been chosen as the focus for the visit because they use a vast range of images which will become a rich resource for discussion of possible story elements. The textiles themselves are intricately and elaborately patterned with traditional images from other cultures and times. Children will enjoy getting lost in the intricacies of the patterns as they seek out the separate images.

It is significant that the textiles include symbols and motifs from varied cultural and historical backgrounds. This values and includes at least some of the family backgrounds of learners in this group. Some of them will have knowledge of the symbols and images in the patterns from familiar objects elsewhere.

Because the story 'elements' for the new story will come from the 'images' patterned into these fabrics, the activities in the gallery literally become the 'material' for building ideas for the new stories.

Spotlight: what happened during the visit to the Whitworth Art Gallery?

Children are brought into the main textile gallery. The surrounding exhibits of traditional fabrics in glass-fronted cases draw fascinated gazes from the children. The large space in which they are now asked to sit down is unlike any other learning context they have experienced. Their sense of anticipation is almost tangible and high engagement levels are guaranteed. The first activity in pairs is to go round and 'just look' at the textiles, noticing what they are like and talking about them. Shortly they will be asked to look back at the textiles and carry out specific tasks, but for now, it is important to just take in and appreciate the experience. This is really an opportunity for awe and inspiration: an amazing new experience in an art gallery, away from the normality of everyday environments of school and home. It seems important not to make the experience in the gallery totally task-oriented at the outset. This open-ended activity at the beginning allows children to engage with these artefacts in their own ways in a reasonably leisurely way.

To process this 'appreciation' each pair joins another and talks about what they have seen. It is a good idea to get them talking at this point, simply to articulate and open up their thinking. So the questions are important: they start off asking children about what they liked and why, then focus in on some of the details and contexts. So the sequence of questions to the fours could look something like this:

- 'Which textiles did you like?' (And why?)
- 'Were there any textiles you didn't like?' (Why not?)
- 'What did you notice about the textiles?'

Then some follow-up questions to pairs in response to what they noticed:

- 'What sorts of patterns?'
- 'What were the images in the patterns?'
- 'Where have the textiles come from?'
- 'Who made them?'
- 'Why did they make them?'

After this the children are more familiar with the display. They will have some ideas about the backgrounds of the textiles and the textile makers. They understand that the symbols on the textiles come from the places and times these people lived in.

Children now embark on the first task: in fours, they look again at the textiles, noticing and collecting the images or symbols which make up the patterns, so they can make sketches on plain paper individually. Because these are traditional designs, there are many symbols which represent aspects of traditional settings, together with the artefacts and characters which might live there.

Within their groups of four, children now work in pairs. They choose from the symbols and patterns they've sketched, a place, an object, a character and a creature. At this point, children are told that they are getting ideas for a traditional story that will include the character of the Snow Queen, whom they now know so well. These choices will become the basis for the generation of a first series of ideas for a story. Children use a planning sheet provided by the teacher to record their ideas (Figure 7.3).

They talk about possible stories, in pairs, and share the ideas in the group of four. Using the space in the gallery, they have an opportunity to improvise their stories in fours, with the option to go back to the textiles for inspiration or amendment of ideas.

The gallery visit has provided the inspiration, ideas and content for the stories. Children will now take these ideas and content back to school, to develop further.

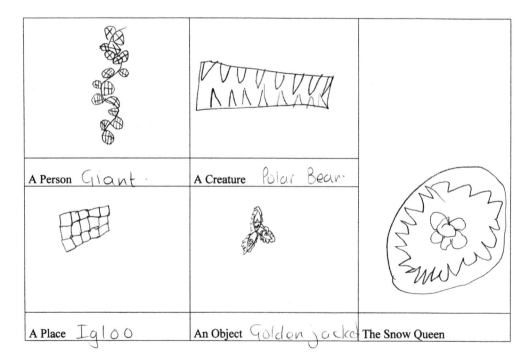

Figure 7.3 One group's storyboard

Back in school

This whole back-in-school part of the teaching sequence is about crafting the story itself (and linking in to the learning objectives about spelling). Children were given opportunities to gather their ideas for the story during the gallery visit. So they have the ideas, now they need to work with them, planning, trying things out, fixing parts together in different ways.

Spotlight: making decisions about the story – audience and purpose

In pairs children are talking about who they want to write the story for. After some suggestions, there is a vote and the class agrees that it will be for a Year 3 class. In a similar way children agree that the purpose of the story will be to scare the audience a little, but to have a happy ending. These 'purposes' can be used later as an assessment for learning activity. The Year 3 class to whom the story is presented can give feedback. They can be asked the questions 'Were you scared?' and 'How did you feel at the end of the story?' Being clear about an exact audience and purpose supports the development of skills in writing, because the clarity creates specific criteria against which children can be evaluative.

Spotlight: making decisions about the story – a shared version for the whole class

The class now needs a single version of the story which they will all work on. The shared version is important here because the teacher wants the children to dance the story as a whole class.

This single, whole-class version of the story is selected randomly by the class. A chosen child selects (unseen) one of the plans completed by the pairs (Figure 7.4). The

Figure 7.4 Chosen class storyboard for the story

teacher chooses, on this occasion, to do it in this way, because it is equitable and inclusive – any storyboard can be developed as well as the next.

Spotlight: dancing the story

These sessions enable children to really get to know the chosen class story. By the end of the dance activities, which take place over a number of days, children are very sure of the sequence of the story, the drama and tension in the plot and how it all is for the characters. Enacting the story through dance allows children to 'live' the story (Figure 7.5). Working in this way is a strongly kinaesthetic experience.

Figure 7.5 Children dance the story

The teacher may:

- select musical sequences herself which represent the sequence of the agreed story
- ask children to compose music which sets the mood for the scenes to be danced
- work on small scenarios, for example when the little girl wakes in the morning and finds her parents gone, or when the group walk on and on down the long road until they are too tired to continue
- ask children to dance the whole story.

Children are asked to create motifs for the movements of the dance (Figure 7.6). They do this in A/B pairs, taking turns to use their ideas to capture the pace and movement of the dance sequence.

Figure 7.6 Motifs used by children to record the phrasing of dance sequences

Dance and music will appeal to many learners whom we may not reach in the more conventional ways in which we expect them to learn to plan and write stories. For some children, the connections which are being made between sound, language and movement will impact powerfully on their ability to orally recall and retell the story.

Spotlight: pattern making

In an art session, various maths objectives about pattern link to the creation of different sorts of pattern using the symbols from the traditional textiles. Throughout this 'after the visit' part of the unit, children work in different groups at different times to:

- choose one of the symbols to enlarge and colour (Figure 7.7)
- make a pattern using the symbols from the gallery (Figure 7.8)
- use the symbols with colour to create repeating patterns like those they had seen in the textiles (Figure 7.9).

The decision to link the literacy work with art and maths in this way means that children will re-experience and reuse the language connected with the images from the art gallery. This will support language acquisition and particularly the use of new language in a range of contexts.

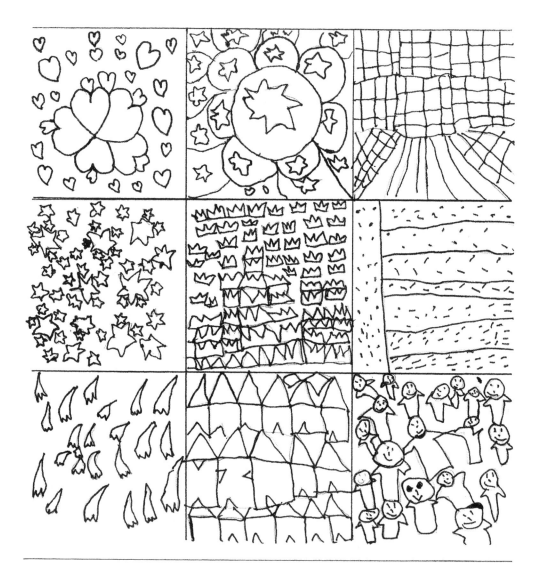

Figure 7.7

Figure 7.8

Figure 7.9

Spotlight: orally telling the new story and demonstrating how to use the individual pictures in the storyboard to create separate paragraphs

Children in A/B pairs are working together, telling each other the class story image by image. They take turns, with A telling the story of the first picture, B the second and so on. This is modelled first at the front of the class by the teacher and teaching assistant. The modelling is intended to do three things:

- To demonstrate the process of A/B pairs turn-taking.
- To demonstrate the expected level of detail and language use: children are being shown what a paragraph might be like. It is more than the short sentence which children might have come up with if they had been left to their own devices.
- To reinforce the use of story language, with phrases like 'Once long ago . . .', '. . . the long, long road' and so on.

Pairs come out to the front to tell their versions of the story, again taking turns between A and B. At the end of each telling children are asked to feed back. This could use an approach like 'three stars and a wish'. This involves noticing three parts they like and making one suggestion. The focus at this point, is on the story making sense and including plenty of the detail obtained through the dance.

Spotlight: one group writes sections of the story collaboratively

Every child in this class now knows the story really well. One group of children, who struggle to capture their thoughts in writing, is working in pairs to write one paragraph of the story from the class storyboard. This simplifies the task for them, enabling them to really focus on doing that part really well.

Some children write with flipchart pens on sugar paper, others are using laptops. Both these ways of recording are designed to allow the teacher to display the work in an enlarged format on the wall. This could become part of a 'process' display onto which the same group of children can stick self-adhesive notes to add ideas or make suggestions in the days and weeks that follow.

Spotlight: some children write up all of the class story individually, others use their own storyboards from the art gallery

Children are so fired up by all the creative inputs in and out of school, that all they want to do now is write the whole story. Some children will write using the class storyboard, around which so many activities have taken place over the past weeks. It is at this point that all of these scaffolding activities – the visit, discussion, drawing, dance and oral retelling – are integrated by children as they write the stories individually.

A group of high achieving children decide they want to go back to their own stories, planned out at at the gallery. More able children in the class may need this challenge. They write in a confident and accomplished way combining their own ideas with ideas from those which have been developed from the class story. Giving them free choice allows them to demonstrate their skills and abilities in a way that using the class story would not.

Beyond the unit

The teacher decides to use these writing outcomes to inform decisions about what to teach in the next block of work about story writing. She needs to take stock of where the children are up to: what they can now do and what they still need to learn.

She needs to see the work of this unit as part of an ongoing process in terms of attainment in writing. It is vital she sees the work of the unit in the larger context of continuity and progression across not only the year, but also the key stage and whole primary experience.

We said at the start of the unit that the work here is aimed at helping children to be able to sequence and structure stories effectively and that traditional stories are an ideal medium for this, because of their simple, clear structures and language.

So really that is what we are looking for. We will be asking the following questions:

- Can this child write a well sequenced traditional story, which has an appropriate plot and characters?
- Can the child use simple but effective story language to write the story?

Figure 7.10 provides an example of individual writing from a middle ability boy in the class. The child has English as an additional language. This piece of work, undertaken with confidence and enthusiasm, is of a very high standard for this child.

What conclusions could the teacher draw from this? She could spend a lot of time analysing and diagnosing this piece of writing. We will do it very briefly here by looking at aspects of 'creating and shaping texts' in relation to:

- what the child can do
- what the child needs to learn next.

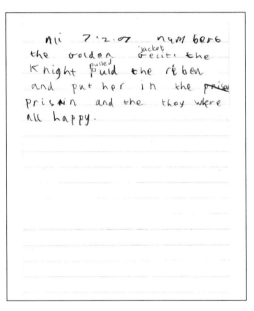

Figure 7.10 Writing sample produced at the end of the block of work

In relation to what the child can do, it seems clear that this child has through the unit learned to:

- write a well sequenced, detailed traditional story, which has an appropriate plot and characters
- use simple but effective story language to write the story

The child is using simple and effective story language, very suitable to writing traditional stories. He does though need to have some experiences of writing different types of stories in which more expressive and descriptive language becomes a major focus of the activities.

So the next unit of work around story writing could include the following 'creating and shaping texts' learning objective (Year 2): to make adventurous word and language choices appropriate to the style and purpose of the text.

8 Reporting back

Reading non-fiction and writing non-chronological reports

Year 2 term 3

This unit provides exciting opportunities for developing some integrated approaches to learning and teaching in topic areas. Children really enjoy topic work. This topic is particularly interesting for children, beginning as it does with places they have visited, and linking to a shared class experience of a seaside visit. The unit of work starts with children's real life experiences and builds upon them using a variety of learning activities which develop thinking and talking for reading and writing.

The teaching in this unit is based on the ideas of the EXIT model. EXIT stands for 'Extending Interactions with Texts' and was devised by David Wray and Maureen Lewis (1997) to provide just that – extended interactions with (non-fiction) texts. It was designed to give children real purposes for reading factual books, to find things out and write about them. In the past, project or topic work has sometimes lacked a purposeful structure, with children unsure of how to use the books they found that linked to the topic. Lacking clear purposes for reading and writing, some children simply copied from texts which they did not understand. The EXIT model provides a process approach to working with non-fiction texts for real research purposes. It provides a structured approach to reading non-fiction, extending knowledge and understanding in a subject or topic area, and scaffolds the gathering of the information so that it can be presented or written up. The model takes us through a linked series of ten collaborative activities and discussions, with specific teaching *strategies*. The EXIT model is remarkable in its practical common sense approach to research work with children. It provides a really coherent way to use factual sources to get information.

Other sources of information can be very productively used with the EXIT model. These include films, photographs, artefacts and people. Key Stage 1 children often need to develop and refine questioning and answering skills. Because this chapter is based on information about children's actual recent experiences, the children themselves have extensive knowledge and expertise. This can be used initially by modelling and making questions, in whole class and smaller groups. Later this can be extended by research using books and ICT.

The EXIT model is shown below. It is set out as a series of steps, each step stating first the strategy the teacher is using with the class at that point, and next asking a question which suggests the intended focus of children's thinking.

1. Activating prior knowledge: 'What do I already know about this topic?'
2. Establishing purposes: 'What do I want to know about this topic?'
3. Locating information: 'Where and how will I find this information?'
4. Adopting an appropriate strategy: 'How should I use this source of information to get what I need?'
5. Interacting with the text: 'What can I do to help me understand it better?'
6. Monitoring understanding: 'What can I do if there are parts I don't understand?'
7. Making a record: 'What should I take a note of from this information?'
8. Evaluating information: 'Should I believe this information?'
9. Assisting memory: 'How can I help myself remember the important bits?'
10. Communicating information: 'How should I let others know about this?'

It is not essential to proceed sequentially through each step in the EXIT model every time a unit of work based on information books is planned. Some steps in the process can be used very productively in other ways. Steps 3, 4, 5, 6 and 7 for example are extremely useful as teaching strategies for shared and guided reading in all the primary year groups; step 10 is a fundamental aspect of all non-fiction writing, communicating information for a particular purpose to a particular audience.

The EXIT model was an integral part of non-fiction reading in the first NLS framework and remains a powerful tool to give purposes for reading information books and using the internet for research.

The work in this unit also uses 'DARTs' activities, first devised by Eric Lunzer and Keith Gardner (1979). The acronym DART stands for 'directed activities related to texts'. These activities link particularly with step 5 of the EXIT model: they create a variety of interesting ways to interact or work with the text, providing vital opportunities for children to process information making sense of it in their own ways. Figure 8.1 gives some examples of DARTs activities which are about processing information.

Making new information meaningful and relevant to children is always a challenge. It is particularly demanding when we are inexperienced with a subject or year group, and have no experiential insight into children's current interest or understanding of the material we are about to introduce to them. Using the EXIT model, with its starting points of what children already know and would like to know, gives a form of scaffolding, a framework around which to build skills.

Teachers do sometimes express anxieties about the need to cover all the subject matter in the National Curriculum. What will happen if children ask a lot of questions which don't cover what is in the QCA scheme unit that they are meant to be covering? The question is really about whether we should attempt to cover all the factual stuff, the content, or whether we believe that the learning experiences and processes we set up for children are of equal (or even more) importance. If we opt for delivering the *content* over valuing the learning *process*, we are making children into passive recipients of information – not active constructors of knowledge and understanding. We are not required to cover everything with our classes. We *are* required to make informed professional decisions about what and how we teach. This is compelling stuff. We are expected to have worked out views and values about how we believe children learn best.

Just as convincing have been some teachers' experiences, that when time is spent on developing children's questions, children often ask the very questions we want them to ask – the questions that will lead to most of the content being covered anyway.

Wide angle questions	Two or three questions are given to pupils for which there is no obvious single correct answer and which will involve ranging over the whole text. When answers have been found, pupils report back.
Statement game	Pupils are given a short list of statements about a text – some contradictory and/or controversial – which can stand as comments on the piece. Pairs or groups are asked to consider their importance and/or appropriateness, identifying those with which they agree, those with which they disagree and those about which they are not sure.
Question setting	Pairs of pupils are asked to make up a small number of questions about a text to which they would really like to know the answers. It must be possible to answer such questions by reading the text or by reading between the lines. A selection of these questions can be used as an agenda for class or group discussion, or one pair's questions can be swapped with another pair's and answers shared.
Marking the text	Pupils are asked to underline or annotate parts of the text that deal with certain issues, or which identify patterns or connections. For example, one group of ideas might be underlined in one colour, another group of ideas in a second colour and so on. Alternatively pupils might note responses to the text in the margin.
Diagrams and pictures	Pupils are asked to present information or ideas from the text in a visual form, such as a drawing, a diagram or a table.
Genre transformation	Pupils are asked to rework a text or part of it into another text type. For example, an extract from a short story might be reworked into a film script; a recount of an experiment might be presented as a set of instructions.

Figure 8.1

Progression and continuity through the school

The use of the approaches in this unit needs to be part of a whole school approach to reading and writing for information. Continuity across the school would benefit children enormously in developing these reading skills in a clearly progressive and coherent way.

What was in the teacher's head when planning this work?

Contexts and coherence

- This unit is deliberately planned as a coherent topic-based approach for the summer term.
- The topic approach makes coherent connections between subject areas, while retaining explicit subject objectives.
- Sources of information used in the topic start with the children themselves (their concrete experiences), and extend outwards into more abstract print-based information.
- The reading elements in the unit work to support or service the information gathering required for the geography topic. The processes of the EXIT model themselves develop geographical enquiry and skills (asking questions, using geographical vocabulary and secondary sources). These in turn increase geographical knowledge and understanding.

Motivation

- This unit involves a lot of collaborative work, providing highly enjoyable opportunities for children to talk, read and write together in purposeful ways.
- This unit gives children status as key sources of information and expertise about places they have visited.
- This unit develops work linked to the summer visit to the seaside – a much longed-for event in the school year.
- Children will produce a class big book using ICT – this will give a very satisfying result.
- ICT is to be used as a research tool, something which children always enjoy and engage with.
- The unit of work is based on children's own questions. Children love this: it gives them a central value and place in what goes on in the classroom, putting their interests and concerns back at the heart of the learning process. (The effects this has on their motivation to 'read for meaning' is amazing to witness, as is their sense of ownership of the writing process.)

Content and process

Skills will be built through the following sequence of activities which are also stages in the EXIT model (the numbers in brackets refer to the stages in the EXIT model).

- Brainstorming onto a flipchart what we already know about the topic (step 1).
- Grouping these ideas together into a concept map: the 'areas' here will become our subheadings within the non-chronological report, big book page or chapter headings (step 1).
- Asking different types of questions about each area of the (concept) map (step 2).
- Finding answers to these questions, modelled through shared reading and applied in guided and independent reading (steps 3, 4, 5, 6).
- Keeping records or notes of information that answers the questions (step 7).
- Exploring and/or presenting this orally; then writing it up (steps 8, 9, 10).

Primary National Strategy Objectives

Clustering the learning objectives

Speaking

Year 2

- Explain ideas and processes using imaginative and adventurous vocabulary and non-verbal gestures to support communication.

Listening and responding

Year 2

- Listen to others in class, ask relevant questions.

Understanding and interpreting texts

Year 2

- Explain organisational features of texts, including alphabetical order, layout diagrams, captions, hyperlinks and bullet points.

Engaging with and responding to texts

Year 2

- Explain their reactions to texts, commenting on important aspects.

Creating and shaping texts

Year 2

- Maintain consistency in non-narrative, including purpose and tense.
- Select from different presentational features to suit particular writing purposes on paper and on screen.

Text structure and organisation

Year 2

- Use planning to establish clear sections for writing.

Year 3

- Group related material into paragraphs.

Sentence structure and punctuation

Year 2

- Use question marks.

Presentation

Year 2

- Form and use the four basic handwriting joins.

Geography

Geographical enquiry and skills

Pupils should be taught to:

- ask geographical questions (e.g. 'What is it like to live in this place?')
- express their own views about people, places and environments
- communicate in different ways (e.g. pictures, speech writing).

They should develop the following skills:

- Use of geographical vocabulary (e.g. hill, mountain, river, motorway).
- Use of secondary sources of information (e.g. CD ROM, pictures, photographs, stories, information texts, videos, artefacts).

Knowledge and understanding of places

Pupils should be taught to:

- identify and describe what places are like (e.g. in terms of landscape, jobs, weather)
- recognise how places compare with other places.

Starting points: the Friday before the Monday

1. Tell children on Friday that we are going to be starting some exciting work about their memories of visits to other places. Ask them to draw a picture about one or more of these to bring into school on Monday.
2. Ask children to collect memories from mums and dads, brothers and sisters, and add them to their pictures in think bubbles.

The first shared session: EXIT model step 1

On the first day of this work, we will be creating a flipchart record that may look something like Figure 8.2. This will be done by brainstorming ideas, using the drawings and ideas children collected from home. Children will be organised first in pairs to gather ideas, so that they are tuned in to their own prior knowledge, memories and experience of different places. The teacher writes down (preferably on a flipchart, so a record remains and can be referred to) all the 'disconnected' pieces of information that children have about the topic. Part of the challenge we have now is to help children *organise* these ideas, grouping them under sensible headings. This facilitates an important part of the learning process, in which children think and make connections between ideas.

If we write the ideas on pieces of paper and stick them with reusable putty adhesive onto the flipchart, we can move them around – this could be helpful later.

So now the teacher has gathered together a whole series of children's ideas about different places. What can be done with them? Instead of a random scattering of

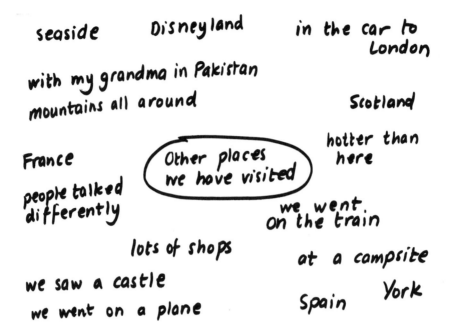

seaside   Disneyland   in the car to
                                          London

with my grandma in Pakistan
mountains all around   Scotland

                                  hotter than
France   Other places   here
              we have visited

people talked
differently   we went
                                  on the train

        lots of shops
                          at a campsite

we saw a castle
                          Spain   York
we went on a plane

Figure 8.2

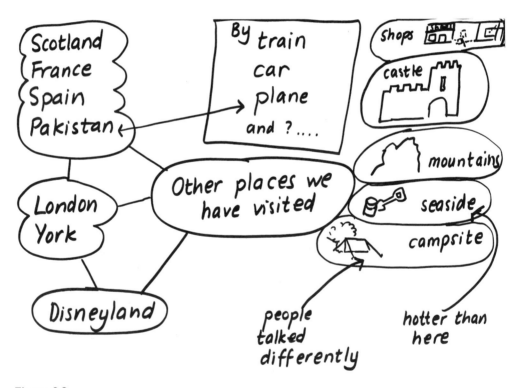

Figure 8.3

words and phrases, we could 'arrange' or 'classify' the ideas in particular ways, using 'thinkalouds' as we do so, to let children in on our thinking. If we don't use the 'thinkalouds' (metacognitive modelling), we miss an important opportunity to show children *why* we group or classify some ideas together: *why* we think they belong together. (See an example of how this could be done in Figure 8.3.)

Another way to do this is to put questions to children in pairs, scaffolding a thinking process with children to help them group the ideas in explicit and reasonable ways. Alternatively, pairs of children could be asked to group the ideas independently of the teacher. (This requires some preparation: the ideas would have to be written up onto A4 paper and cut up, so it would be easier next day or next session.) This way, children's groupings could become the subject of a snowballing activity, in which they follow up the initial categorisation by comparing it to that of others. Choosing to do it like this increases children's engagement with the task – they are all discovering how ideas can be linked and connected in different ways. This activity is rich in thinking skills; it requires children to compare and evaluate ways to group the ideas so that the big book can be made. You may need to act as a mediator here, perhaps by using the large version of the words at the flipchart.

Spotlight: asking questions

We are now at the stage of getting children to ask questions about different places. This will give a 'purpose' to our 'research'. It will give us clear questions to answer when reading. How will we get children to ask questions? It is an odd paradox that many young children ask endless questions at home, yet seem to lose this curiosity in school. Perhaps it's a matter of the climate we create as teachers. As long as we explicitly encourage and promote questioning from children there doesn't seem to be a problem. Here are some ideas.

Children could be asked in pairs to think of things they'd like to find out about any of the places that other children have visited. The children come up with a range of questions at this point. These questions could be recorded again on a flipchart, or put in the class book. Figure 8.4 gives a selection of questions gathered from one class. The quality of the initial questions is a useful assessment of children's questioning skills. The children will enjoy asking and answering these initial questions. This activity could also be used to assess children's oral skills in answering the questions.

The questions in Figure 8.4 create an interesting starting point. They are very general though and fairly closed. Children need support if they are to extend the range and types of questions they ask. Ideas for this are given in the next spotlight.

Spotlight: asking and answering questions together as a class and in small groups

One very successful way to develop the questions is to focus children's thinking on one place at a time. A confident, willing child is invited to be the expert on the place they have visited. In pairs the class write and ask questions, using some teacher-provided prompt question words: What? Where? When? How? How long? Who? Why? Some examples of these questions are collected in Figure 8.5.

Samples of children's initial questions

Where was the seaside?

Where does your grandma live?

How hot was it?

What did you do at the beach?

What rides did you go on at Disneyland?

What was the caravan like?

What did you do in London?

How far is it to Spain?

What do the people look like?

Who went with you to Disneyland?

Was there snow on the mountains?

Figure 8.4

The 'expert' child will answer some of the questions better than others (even with some support and prompting from the teacher and class). Some, she or he may not be able to answer at all. This creates a purpose and context for finding the missing information about questions from books.

Spotlight: teaching the skills involved in locating additional information from books

Children are now learning how to use books to locate information to answer questions more fully. This involves modelling and scaffolding a linked series of skill-developing activities. These are the same skills that we as adults use, without any real awareness of the process, when we are 'searching for information'. These skills are now modelled in shared reading and revisited, with differing amounts of support, in guided reading. The aim is to get children using information books efficiently.

Follow up questions using hot seating and group work

<u>Pakistan</u>

Where did you go in Pakistan?
How did you get there?
What did you do when you got there?
Who else did you visit there?
What were the houses/shops/schools like?
Why are the houses like that?
Do they have McDonalds?
Do all children go to school?
What was the television like?
Do they have computers?
How long did you stay?
What else did you do?
Did you like it?
How is it different from here? (Tell us 5 things)
Why are houses different?

Figure 8.5

- First, we need to identify from a range of possible books which is the most likely to answer our question. How do we know which one to choose? We do this based on a series of informed guesses, using the available information on the cover – title, illustrations and blurb about the book. We may well get additional information by flicking the pages open and browsing the pages, or maybe by checking out the chapter headings, contents pages or index (if the enquiry has a very specific focus). Whichever checking and refining process we use, we do it to find a way of using time sensibly – we wouldn't start reading the first book from the selection at page 1, and reading it through from cover to cover. We need to make the steps in the processes of information retrieval and processing explicit, so that children don't waste time or lose heart being unable to access the information they need.
- Once a likely book is identified, children need to learn how to use the contents page and/or index well. The contents page may present particular problems if the child's

question is not framed in the exact terms of the headings – and it rarely is. So this becomes an exercise in inference – finding the chapter which is the most likely to contain what is needed. If the question is 'Do children go to school in Pakistan?' and the two most likely chapters are 'Children and families' and 'Going to a village school', which should we go to first? Children need to be shown how to try it out. They can be shown how to go to the most likely section, skim the page, look at headings, captions, photographs, sections. They need to be shown how the teacher reflects on whether it still seems the best option. If at this point it does seem to be promising they need to be shown how and where to start looking for the information they need. They also need to know that it is sometimes easier to use the index.

- It is important next to think about the reading strategies children need so they can locate this information quickly. To do this the teacher models how to scan for key words and skim for the main ideas.
- The teacher asks children in pairs to notice what their partner's eyes do as they scan the page for the key word.
- Do their eyes do the same thing when it comes to skimming a page with lots of illustrations and subheadings?
- Once we think the information has been located, children are shown how to read and reread, checking they do understand it and it does really answer the question.

Spotlight: some examples of guided reading

Children in a guided reading session are applying the skills of skimming and scanning which have been demonstrated in the whole class session. The sequence of activities looks like this:

1. Children all work on the same double-page spread of an information book, with the same few questions, some of which are and some of which are not answered in the text.
2. Children are asked to remind themselves of what the two strategies of skimming and scanning are, and when they might need to use them.
3. Children start by underlining the key words in the first question. They know to start by skimming across the sections on the page to find the section which is most likely to contain the ideas raised in the question.
4. Children use the section they have identified to scan for the key words or others meaning the same thing.
5. Children highlight sections of information which answer the first question. (To do this they have to read around the key words to see which part of the text is relevant. This involves a third strategy, close reading, or reading for meaning.)
6. Children are asked to self-assess: did they use the strategies well? How do they know?
7. They repeat the process with the next question. This time their partner watches how they do it, asking them what they are doing, encouraging them to explain where they are making their eyes go. Together they evaluate the child's use of strategies and swap roles.
8. The teacher assesses children's use and explicit awareness of the two reading strategies.

In a second guided reading session, another DARTs activity is being used. Children need some practice at reading the text closely to consider what the place being described looks like. The teacher has therefore selected the DART activity which asks children to draw a picture. Here she wants children to illustrate fully the place described in the text, putting captions on the drawing to add any information from the text, which tells them more about the place. These 'answers' become sections of the class non-chronological report about the places they identified and asked questions about.

Spotlight: children browsing through and sharing the fascination of information books during independent time

Children are browsing and enjoying various information books about places. While it is important that children are able to read *efficiently* using a research process approach like the EXIT model, this doesn't mean that the reading of non-fiction should be only about purposeful research. In their encounters with factual books, children need time to simply browse, enjoy and make their own personally significant connections with the real world represented there. This is part of the 'awe and wonder' we associate with understanding of the natural world.

To give the browsing a significance in the unit of work, children are asked to collect some of the things they find interesting in the books they look at, thus assembling some 'fascinating facts' to put in the class information book. To support this, they are recording the book names and page numbers.

Spotlight: supported reading activity – noting some fascinating facts

Using the book names and page numbers they wrote down while browsing through the factual books, children are now making a record of the facts they find fascinating. This has just been modelled in shared reading, so children know not to just copy the bit out of the book. A teaching assistant works with the group to help them put the ideas into their own words. This is a difficult process for several children, who want to copy the text directly from the book. The teaching assistant helps children change each sentence by choosing different ways of saying the same thing.

Spotlight: making the class book about places

The class is writing up various parts of what they are putting in the class big book, which will become the non-chronological report. (The contents page, clearly derived from the original brainstorm (Figure 8.2) is included in Figure 8.6.)

Picture a number of scenes taking place at different times in the unit, in which children are busy on a range of writing tasks, which will be incorporated into the sections of the report. One group is drawing and writing up some of the 'fascinating facts' they have found for the class big book. They take out their previously compiled 'notes' and make a picture to illustrate the interesting and amazing fact they have discovered.

Later, these are used for a guided writing session. Children are supported as the teacher works with the group to make the tone of the writing more dramatic and sensational. She shows them how to select stronger words to exaggerate the amazingness of the facts.

In another area a shared writing session is taking place to show children how to write up a section of the non-chronological report. The section being worked on is entitled 'Towns and cities'. Children's questions are used as starting points; information was gathered in oral interviews and then in shared, guided and independent reading sessions. Now the teacher models how to write it up, using quite a formal tone. This is done in the structure of a series of questions and answers in each section of the book.

In a guided group, children work in pairs to write their own answers from the questions they researched and the information they gathered and highlighted. They share these in fours, checking the writing of others for:

- correct use of question marks
- correct use of handwriting joins
- whether the questions have actually been answered.

Places we have visited

CONTENTS

Page

Figure 8.6

The teacher assesses their skill in noticing the punctuation and handwriting. She listens in to the discussions about whether the questions were answered, prompting children to explain more fully where necessary, justifying their opinions. She uses questions like:

- 'How do you know that was a good answer?'
- 'What else did you need to know there?'
- 'Did Sam need to put that bit in?'

Beyond the unit

It's very simple to transfer parts of this approach into any curriculum area. The process is to start with children's questions, find relevant books to answer these, work through the EXIT model and use DARTs 'processing' activities to help children actively engage with and make sense of the text.

Some examples of what this might look like are as follows:

- Children making paired mind-maps about their understanding of a topic area at the beginning and end of a unit of work – then explaining this to another pair.
- Children using the suggested DARTs activities to make new sense of the information they have found about a topic area.
- Children presenting the information they have found out, e.g. as a poster, play, piece of captioned art or design work.
- Children becoming experts in an aspect of a history topic like Florence Nightingale, browsing some books, completing some DARTs activities, making a poster or doing a drama. As experts they show their posters or dramas, then answer others' questions in role. Again, some questions may need to be researched further. Equally important though, is that this provides a context which provokes new questions – extending the enquiry!

Adapting the EXIT model for use with ICT resources

Table 8.1 shows how the EXIT model could look if we use this type of approach to finding information on the internet.

Children in the ICT suite can go through different stages of the EXIT model. Some parts of the process are particularly applicable to ICT, while others are less so. Those aspects which seem really relevant in ICT teaching are:

- using search facilities effectively to obtain information and answers
- using reading strategies which promote the ability to locate information
- using reading strategies which promote the ability to efficiently interact with and understand the text
- using editing facilities to locate important pieces of information, copy, paste and transform the information into a variety of formats.

Table 8.1

Stage in **EXIT** model process	Specific skills which need to be taught
What do I already know about this topic?	
Activating prior knowledge	Brainstorming and concept mapping
	Organising ideas into subheadings and groups
What would I like to know?	
Establishing purpose	How to ask different types of questions
How will I find it out?	
Locating information	Generating and refining 'smaller' questions
	Changing the key words for search engine
	Refining search (use sheer number of sites as a guide)
	Selecting sites
How will I read what I've found?	
Adopting an appropriate strategy	How to read each part (Where do eyes go? Why?)
	• list of sites
	• scanning/skimming/close reading
	What happens during scrolling?
How will I know which are the important bits?	
Making notes or a record	Bookmark sites
	Underline, **bold** or *italicise* text
	Copy headings, explanations, important ideas
	Paste them into categories
How will I work on the important parts?	**Teacher intervention through guided reading**
Interacting with the text	Copy and paste parts of the text
	Use of DARTs activities to increase understanding
How will I know whether I've understood it?	Explain it to another group
Monitoring understanding	Put your copied text into your own words
	Make a mind-map
	Create questions for another group
How fair or balanced is this information?	**Important with information from the web**
Evaluating the text	Underline parts which seem questionable
	Children need to be taught to be critical
How will I share my information?	Interactive whiteboards, PowerPoint, drama, art or
Communicating to others	writing presentation

Writing stories set in some of the different places the class has visited (using some appropriate narrative objectives)

An interesting way of providing meaningful contexts for writing stories is to link these during or after the unit of work to some of the places children have visited. This can be done in various ways: through modelling of class stories, or through guided and independent writing. It will be done as part of ongoing work about writing whole stories with children, using learning objectives about writing narrative.

This provides helpful scaffolding for lots of children: geographical vocabulary will be reinforced by being used and applied, and children's familiarity and experience of places is utilised and developed. (The writing of the story as a class can involve drama work in which children explore and make discoveries about the setting.) This in turn can lead to new questions arising about what the place is like, what sorts of jobs exist there, how people travel and so on. It also creates an imaginative challenge to abler writers who could explore such settings independently through drama and story writing.

References

Lunzer, E. and Gardner, K. (eds) (1979) *The Effective Use of Reading*, London: Heinemann Educational for the Schools Council.

Wray, D. and Lewis, M. (1997) *Extending Literacy: Children Reading and Writing Non-Fiction*, London: Routledge.

9 Shapely poems and calligrams

Starting not from text, but from language and visual images

Year 3

The first version of the National Literacy Strategy created a practical and powerful model in the explicit connections it makes between the teaching of reading and writing. Showing children how to 'read like writers', identifying how texts are built up at word, sentence and text level, has offered teachers an indispensable tool to guide learners through a scaffolded process of reconstructing similar texts.

While the clear structure of the literacy hour has created patterned predictability, offering a secure learning environment to children, this very predictability *can* become limiting and boring. While children may thrive on security, too much of it may feel like a straitjacket – children also need variety, risk taking and novelty. It is with these concerns in mind that this unit of work has been planned. It moves away from the typical pattern of writing always being preceded by a shared response to and analysis of text.

A further reason why this may be particularly productive in this context, is that we want to tap into children's *creativity*. Without entering into the complex debate about what exactly constitutes 'creativity', it seems obvious that there are different aspects of creativity, and that the way into writing poetry texts in this unit provides for this. The way in which the first NLS framework used imitation and innovation of fiction and non-fiction texts to write is an ingenious and supportive way to both deconstruct and recreate stylistic and structural aspects of the original texts (particularly as the texts upon which the writing is based are often layered and complex). Shape poetry is different. Here the creativity emerges in the witty interplay between design and language use. Reading text as a starting point here could therefore simply inhibit children. How can you imitate a shape poem without just copying it? To develop writing creatively here, we need to provide scaffolding so that children play with language and visual elements. Shape poetry will be read later in the unit, to build on children's ideas.

This chapter also takes seriously recent ideas about different learning styles. It develops approaches that will encourage children to think and learn in a range of different ways. Starting from visuals, because it is different, will enable children to make and develop different types of connections in literacy learning.

Talk strategies and thinking skills are going to be really important in this unit of work. Children love to talk! They enjoy using a variety of speaking and listening strategies – in itself, talk makes them active as learners.

What was in the teacher's head when planning this work?

Contexts and coherence

This unit can be embedded in practically any curriculum area.

- I can use subject-related visual aids (photos, artwork or drawings) and develop subject-related vocabulary from this (linked to the QCA schemes of work), photographs of a landscape, a historical scene or artefact, a piece of technology.
- I can start with some subject-specific vocabulary such as the mathematical language of shapes, together with an aerial photo of a cityscape or piece of artwork that will provide a context for the use of this language.

Motivation

- Children enjoy drawing. Here they can combine this with the fun and cleverness of noticing and creating cartoons, calligrams and shape poetry.
- Children enjoy thought provoking and novel ways of presenting their ideas in writing.
- Children love it when they are asked to produce only small amounts of carefully thought out writing.
- Children enjoy language play and word games – this is the way in to vocabulary development with them.

Content and process

- Start by using subject-related visual aids (see the Contexts and coherence section), modelling how to develop some language with a visual resource, to begin to write some shape poetry.
- Support children as they develop some collaborative strategies to find and collect the vocabulary they need to compose their own shape poems.
- Link this to thesaurus and dictionary work.
- Find opportunities for children to use and apply newly encountered language.
- Lead an investigation into the various types or categories of published shape poems.
- This investigation can feed into evaluative discussions about how the poetry 'works' – perhaps in shared, guided and independent reading time. Ideas from this may be used to transform or 'redesign/redraft' previously written poems.
- Focus on finding ways to generate and refine language to describe and represent the visual images.
- Demonstrate how to think divergently rather than narrowly, and integrate this with developing alternative drafts.

Primary National Strategy Objectives

Clustering the learning objectives

While most of the objectives have come from Year 3, some have been brought in from Years 4 and 5. This is to bring in an objective from another year group which will enrich and extend the topic.

Speaking

Year 3

• Develop and use specific vocabulary in different contexts.

Year 4

• Respond appropriately to the contributions of others in the light of differing viewpoints.

Listening and responding

Year 3

• Follow up others' points and show whether they agree or disagree in whole class discussion.

Group discussion and interaction

Year 3

• Actively include and respond to all members of a group.

Word structure and spelling

Year 3

• Recognise a range of prefixes and suffixes, understanding how they modify meaning and spelling and how they assist in decoding long complex words.

Understanding and interpreting texts

Year 3

• Explore how different texts appeal to readers using descriptive language.

Year 4

• Explain how writers use figurative and expressive language to create images and atmosphere.

Engaging with and responding to texts

Year 3

- Identify features that writers use to provoke readers' reactions.

Creating and shaping texts

Year 3

- Select and use a range of descriptive language.
- Use layout, format, graphics and illustrations for different purposes.

Sentence structure and punctuation

Year 3

- Compose using adjectives, verbs and nouns for impact.

Presentation

Year 5

- Adapt handwriting for specific purposes.

Starting point: the Friday before the Monday

The unit creates opportunities for making 'unexplained' displays. The purpose of these is to create a sense of mystery and excitement. If children always know what they will do before they do it, there is no need to wonder or speculate. Having to work it out is a useful and brain-friendly way to engage children's attention. If they come to know that these teacher-staged puzzles or mysteries are followed by enjoyable, active learning experiences, their anticipation of this will feed into the process of motivating children.

With this in mind, on Friday, some themed vocabulary around a painting, illustration or photograph is displayed. This could be on any subject or theme which children will find interesting, evocative or puzzling. Each word could be followed by a question mark (see Figure 9.1).

We know this unit of work is not being started in the typical NLS way by reading examples of the text type. Children still need opportunities to experience and browse through shape poems, so they can enjoy and 'explore' this genre. So on Friday afternoon, a box of 'special poems', all available single and multiple copies of shape poems that can be begged, borrowed or reproduced, is added to the resources for a quiet book sharing session. (Any children's work from previous years makes an excellent additional resource.)

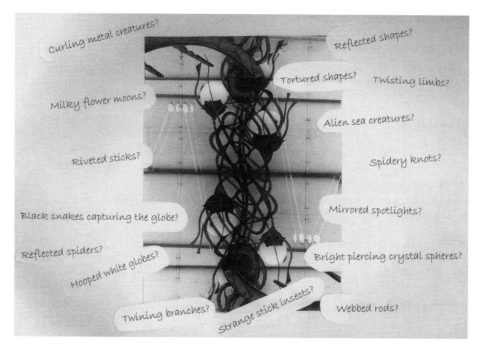

Figure 9.1

The literacy decisions

In this unit the literacy decision is to go through a series of steps which looks something like this:

1. Check that children understand all of the words and phrases.
2. Use the thesaurus to find synonyms they like.
3. Arrange the list in a different order, to exaggerate patterns of sound.
4. Develop artwork for some of the words or phrases.
5. Chosen words and phrases could be linked to music and poems could be performed with musical accompaniment.
6. Arrange the words or phrases into a design which is suitable for the meaning of the poem; develop the design layout to enhance the effectiveness of the language.
7. Use other pictures and objects (with or without words and phrases provided) to build and improve on some original combinations of descriptions and ideas. Use the shapes within the stimulus as starting points for designing a layout.
8. Investigate a range of shape poems to find different layouts and designs.
9. The children make their own shapely poems about anything they choose.

The teaching and learning decisions

These are to get the children into some meaningful talk activities very early on so they are all quickly engaged.

The whole-class shared text session

Give out A4 photographs of the night sky on bonfire night, filled with different sorts of fireworks. It is more effective to do this immediately after bonfire night if we are to use and build on children's own strong sensory experiences. Ask children in pairs to think of words and phrases which describe what the fireworks are doing in the photos. (Their lists could be extended in various ways by changing the groupings, for example by joining pairs to 4s or envoying.) Collect the words and phrases children have come up with, making a flipchart list. Add enough of your own to create an interesting selection. This will be added to as the unit goes on and the thesaurus is used to generate synonyms.

atomise spin
scream screeching
fizzing kaleidoscope wheel
spiralling sparkles arching flashes
scattering light curling crystals
boom crashing spears
choke sprinkling
bangs shooting silver
flying vortex crackling stars

Once some sort of list is written on the flipchart, there are various activities we can do with it to build skills for writing. This introductory session creates and explores the vocabulary with the following activity. Children explore the meanings of the words and phrases, using musical instruments. Each pair or small group is given a share of the phrases, about four or five per group, and each child has an instrument. The groups work for a few minutes around the classroom, working to represent or accompany the words in the phrases. The value of this activity lies in children's attempts to reach an understanding of the language then transform this into some musical phrasing. (What would crashing spears sound like? What sorts of musical sounds would suggest that? How is that different from crackling stars?) Pairs could then perform and compare their musical pieces. This could be done with or without telling the other pair the phrases they were working on!

Spotlight: using the thesaurus to play with words

Children are being shown by the teacher how to use a thesaurus to build on the ideas from the first list of words and phrases. The idea is to add to the bank of ideas already generated. Because the writing is figurative, alternative words gathered in this way are likely to work quite well. So, if the thesaurus is used to find synonyms for **crash** (as a verb), words like collide, collapse, dive, fall, plunge and topple will be discovered. Any of these would sound effective attached to a noun like stars or crystals.

The teacher explicitly models how to try these out to see the tunes and effects of the phrasing:

- 'I like the sound of screeching spears better than crashing spears because the sound patterns of the initial "s" and long "ea" phoneme sound good together.'
- 'Does plunging stars or colliding stars sound better? Or should we keep both?'
- 'What about "the collapsing crystals fall to earth"?'

Once this has been modelled for them, children go off to find their own synonyms and create new phrasings of their own. Ideas are shared between pairs, added to and changed. Children make various illustrations at this stage to capture their interpretations of the language they are using.

Spotlight: making sound patterns – using groups to evaluate work

Children are now working in pairs to make different phrasings or groupings of the language they have collected. Arranging the phrases into an order they like enables them to play with patterns of repetition and sound. They base this on modelling done by the teacher.

Children now join into fours to present their work and get feedback from the other pair. The pair presents a grouping of words, saying why they put them together like that. Each child in the other pair feeds back, saying what they agree with about the grouping and making suggestions. The four children decide on two from each pair to regroup or rephrase and they feed back whether they prefer the new version or their originals in the larger class group.

Once they have done this, they accompany the phrases with musical compositions as before; now though, more time is given, so that a more polished performance is achieved.

Spotlight: making the actual poems – first drafts of firework poems

The teacher has modelled various elements of this at the beginning of the session. Pairs and groups of children are now incorporating their chosen phrasings into a design, so it becomes a 'shape poem'. They do this by making quite large and sketchy illustrations of each part of the poem, and arranging the words onto the illustration; this is shown on Figure 9.2.

Spotlight: guided reading – investigating how writers use layout to appeal to readers

The objectives here are about how different texts appeal to readers and how writers create that appeal.

This session begins by the words from a published shape poem being put into a simple list (this needs to be prepared beforehand). By comparing the rewritten words arranged in a list with the same words arranged into a design, the impact of that design can be

Figure 9.2

brought into sharp relief. Children begin to comment on the effects of the design as distinct from the words. (This can also be done by rewriting a calligram in a plain font.)

The teacher then poses the following questions: 'How has the writer of this poem made it more exciting by laying it out in this way?' 'Do we all like the same ones best?' Shape poems are investigated. Children are invited to describe how different shape poems are laid out and why they think the writer chose to do it in that way. This can be organised so that children are given examples of two (or three) types of shape poem so that different ways of doing it are easy to spot; some could be calligrams, some could represent the actual shape of the subject of the poem, some could suggest aspects of the subject, e.g. the way it moves. This leads into a discussion about how the layout of different types of shape poem in the collection work to enhance the meaning.

There are decisions which need to be made about how to work with different guided groups in relation to this investigation, especially if the guided group is doing the same task as the rest of the class.

- Should work be done with a low ability group, looking at two calligrams and shape poems and supporting their discussion so that they come up with an A1 display of the examples of the two categories of shape poem? This activity could be used to raise their self-esteem by being presented to the rest of the class.

- Would it be useful to complete a similar task with a more confident middle ability reading group? Perhaps choosing to extend their explanation skills by asking each member of the group to complete their own notes about the categories, so that each one can go to another small group in the plenary to explain what they found out?
- Could an abler group of children be challenged by giving them a less deliberately chosen collection of poems and inviting them to find their own groupings for them? The teacher's role here is to help them find several ways to do it, challenging their thinking.

Spotlight: independent and guided writing – using the reading investigation to enhance and develop children's first drafts

Children's first drafts for layout are built upon. The shared session has looked at problems that have arisen, analysing what the difficulties were. The class is now producing more polished versions for a class collection. Various techniques have been explained and demonstrated by children and the teacher.

Some children are using a combination of calligrams and shape poems, carefully making letters which symbolise the firework ideas, then putting these within other shapes. The teacher sits with a guided group who need to work hard at producing *careful* final drafts. She has decided that it is at this stage in the writing process that guidance and support need to be put in. Children think about the needs of the audience and the importance of layout design and styles of lettering.

Spotlight: other ideas which focus on the language, layout and design of shape poems

- Children are using a shape poem with the actual words blocked out. This leaves only a suggestion of the shapes and language, which children could rework, almost like a puzzle (Figure 9.3). They are deciding what the subject of the original poem was, and selecting words to put in each blank. Later they will compare their own versions with those of other children and with the original. Some children develop this by 'extending' the original using linked ideas and connections.
- All of the words have been taken out of the shaped layout of a shape poem (Figure 9.4). Children are putting them into new shape designs, then comparing them with each other and the original (Figure 9.5).

The intention in both of these activities is to value diverse and different ways of completing the activities. Creativity requires divergence and values originality. For children to become risk takers, diversity and difference in approach need nurturing.

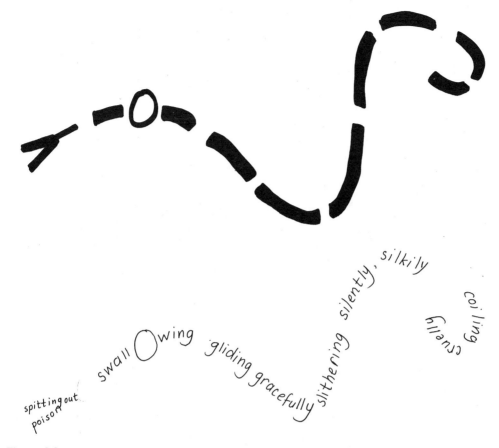

spitting out poison swallowing gliding gracefully slithering silently, silkily cruelly coiling

Figure 9.3

sniffing
snuffling
wagging
bounding
barking
trotting
scratching
scampering
growling
howling
hound

Figure 9.4

Figure 9.5

Spotlight: finding words which use the prefixes un-, de-, dis-, pre-, re-

The teacher has presented a flipchart list of real and made-up words with the above prefixes. Pairs of children are using dictionaries to find out which is which. After a class discussion, 'real' words have a tick put beside them and invented words have a cross.

Next, working in pairs using their spelling logs, children write down and learn to spell the list of 'real' words. They help each other to:

- check the spelling accuracy of the 'real' words they copy into the log
- notice which words they can spell easily
- think of a way to remember the words they find most difficult.

Spotlight: inventing new words to reinforce word level knowledge

Children are inventing their own new word using the prefixes and some of the new vocabulary they have acquired using thesauruses. The pairs have to invent some 'meanings' for their words and write these in their spelling logs.

Spotlight: writing a range of shape poems on other topics

Children are writing poems independently, mostly in pairs, in a range of ways about a range of topics. They are applying what they have learned about shape poems, making poems to add to the class anthology. There is a lot more freedom here about what children write. Children are exploring the genre in a less structured, more open-ended way. Exploration takes time, so a number of sessions are allocated to this writing.

A few children still lack ideas. They are provided with a choice between two prompts:

- **Starting with language**. A list of nouns and adjectives about an animal with instructions about using the thesaurus to change and add to the list. Ideas about selecting the best parts and transforming these into the shape of the animal they represent.
- **Starting with a picture**. A photocopied aerial photograph of a cityscape is used as a stimulus. Children gather some phrases together to describe and represent what they see in the photo. They alter and extend the language using each others' ideas and a thesaurus, then add this to the photocopy. If all the words and phrases are word processed, printed and cut out, blu-tack can be used to draft and redesign a satisfying layout.

Within the unit: alternative starting points

Two other ways of starting this unit could have been as follows:

- Show an evocative picture or object, one where there is uncertainty about what it might be or mean – a sculpture, a photograph, an historical artefact or a reproduction of a painting. Ask children what they think the mystery picture or object is. This tunes children in to the possibilities, gets them speculating and hypothesising – possibly in a very divergent and imaginative way. The idea here would not be to *solve* the puzzle, but to enjoy asking questions and suggesting answers that relate to the puzzle.
- Display a print or photo with a list of words and phrases. Don't say anything about it, and if asked refuse to let on. Children will be left wanting to find out.

Beyond the unit: keep adding to the anthology during the year

- Do this with lists of topic words from any subject to reinforce the subject vocabulary in an imaginative way.
- Try it with topic-related visual images which children create, alter, then add some writing.

10 Dear Giant – Dear Jack

Creating a sequence of letters

Year 3

There is nothing quite like letter writing to give children real and specific audiences and purposes for their writing. This will be an entertaining and dynamic unit of work, which will really give children lots of opportunities to explore, experiment and play to imaginary and real audiences. It will be entertaining and dynamic because we want to explore the connections between each letter and the response to it by acting some of it out, allowing children to empathise with characters, and respond in role by letter. There is an intended progression and link between this unit and the Foundation Stage unit about narrative (Chapter 3). By using drama with the story of *Jack and the Beanstalk* in the Year 3 context, we are suggesting that using these sorts of techniques is just as relevant and appropriate in Year 3 as it is in early years and Key Stage 1.

A central aspect of this unit, then, is the use made of some drama techniques. This starts from two assumptions:

- That some children need help getting and developing ideas for writing. They need some structured inputs to activate and enhance their imaginative, creative powers – giving them a more powerful voice with which to write.
- Kinaesthetic learners may require highly concrete experiences in order to establish effective contexts through which to develop their learning. 'Abstract' contexts cannot give them what they need to make their writing lively and purposeful. When we consider that many underachieving boys may fall into the category of 'kinaesthetic learners', the importance of making the contexts 'real' in this way is highlighted.

As adults we write for a whole range of audiences and purposes. We write to specific people for specific reasons and we are clear about who and what these are. So letters are a very purposeful means of communicating in a non-fiction form. We want children to experience the immediacy of this relevance as they engage with writing this sequence of letters.

We decided that approaches in this unit have to be a bit different anyway. We can't really take a 'text type' approach, because the unit is not based on a single text type. In fact letters do not have a particular text type. (Some may borrow from the structures of the different text types identified in the first NLS framework – such as letters to recount, explain and complain; others do not, having a more generic purpose such as to enquire, congratulate or comment.) This is problematic in terms of the standard NLS approach of teaching through models of a particular text type because here we have a large number of different text types to teach about.

We are choosing here to link this unit of work with previously covered objectives about character. We are also illustrating the approach using a well known traditional story. We felt the need to do this because there is going to be a significant quantity of new material here in terms of the number of different types of letters which will be written. We want children to encounter the text types using a content area that is supportive (known characters in a familiar setting and plot) and motivatingly structured to meet the challenge of the text types.

The final section of this unit looks at the possibilities of developing some work into texting and emailing. This provides rich opportunities for children to explore current language and spelling use. They love it too! Texting in particular is a medium which young people have made their own. Children like it when teachers enter and respect worlds in which they the children are the knowledgeable ones.

What was in the teacher's head when planning this work?

Contexts and coherence

- This work will link into earlier fiction work based on understanding characters' motivation and behaviour.
- This represents good use of time. Children have already met the characters and storyline, so we can work in already established contexts.
- Immersing children in a known context will make them feel secure and knowledgeable, so that the 'playing' can be done in a safe context.
- Texting and emailing will explore increasingly informal styles of language use and presentation.

Motivation

- Children will really enjoy the 'playing' qualities of this interchange of letters.
- Children will get a real sense of connection and communication between themselves and the person they are writing letters to.
- Plenty of drama in this unit will give children a distinct sense of who they are writing to and a clear 'voice' and intention in doing so (in other words, a living sense of audience and purpose).
- Development of this work into texting and emailing is going to be fun!

Content and process

- Some drama techniques will be modelled to develop ideas for the content of each letter in the writing sequence.
- A writing frame will be used in shared writing to teach children about how to transfer their ideas into writing.

- Drama and modelled writing will be used to teach children how to get ideas for and structure their responses to the initial letter.
- Independent and guided writing will be used to help reinforce these skills, in terms of how children organise and express their ideas.
- A focus on reading of children's own writing in guided sessions will support improvement of the writing in terms of its intended audience and what they are trying to make the recipient feel or do.
- Focusing carefully on developing children's rereading and editing skills in guided sessions will support them in applying these independently.
- Developing children's imaginative capacities, using some role play to generate ideas and responses from known story characters.
- The development of this into writing a sequence of letters (also emails and texts) while in role.

Primary National Strategy Objectives

Clustering the learning objectives

While most of the objectives have come from Year 3, some have been brought in from other year groups. Sometimes this is to bring in an objective from another year group which will enrich and extend the topic. At other times, objectives from earlier years are brought in to meet specific learning needs in areas where the teacher knows there are gaps.

Speaking

Year 3

- Choose and prepare poems or stories for performance, identifying appropriate tone, volume and use of voices and other sounds.

Year 4

- Respond appropriately to the contributions of others in the light of differing view-points.

Listening and responding

Year 3

- Follow up others' points and show whether they agree or disagree in whole class discussion.

Group discussion and interaction

Year 3

- Use talk to organise roles and action.

Drama

Year 2

- Adopt appropriate roles in small or large groups and consider alternative courses of action.

Year 3

- Use some drama strategies to explore stories or issues.

Word structure and spelling

- We need to make sure children have a secure phonic skills and knowledge of the long vowel sounds learnt in Key Stage 1. We particularly need to check whether they can *hear* and *identify sounds*, before trying to represent these with letters.

Year 2

- Read and spell less common alternative graphemes, including trigraphs.

Understanding and interpreting texts

Year 3

- Identify how different texts are organised, including reference texts, magazines and leaflets, on paper and screen.

Engaging with and responding to texts

Year 3

- Empathise with characters and debate moral dilemmas portrayed in texts.

Creating and shaping texts

Year 2

- Make adventurous word and language choices appropriate to the style and purpose of the text.

Year 3

- Make decisions about form and purpose, identify success criteria and use them to evaluate their writing.
- Write non-narrative texts using structures of different text types.
- Use layout, format, graphics and illustrations for different purposes.

Text structure and organisation

Year 2

- Use appropriate language to make sections hang together.

Year 3

- Group related material into paragraphs.

Sentence structure and punctuation

This will be the focus of the success criteria which are being used by children as they work in pairs, editing their writing.

Years 1–2

- Use capital letters and full stops when punctuating simple (and more complex) sentences.

Year 3

- Compose sentences using adjectives, verbs and nouns (and pronouns) for precision, clarity and impact.

Presentation

Year 3

- Develop accuracy and speed when using keyboard skills to type, edit and redraft.

Starting point: something exciting on Friday afternoon

This is about finding ways to be imaginative and creative with the teaching, but maintaining a careful structure so that children's understanding, ideas and skills are built upon and layered carefully. Initially it is important to ensure that they have plenty of ideas for their writing.

So, on Friday afternoon:

- Describe a bit of overheard gossip (or read a teacher-written letter from a character in a well known or traditional story). This is intended to be provocative.

- Retell the conversation in role without telling children either who it was about or who is saying it. As the teacher you would be speaking as Jack's mum.

It could go something like this:

> Well, I was just standing there and the old woman was saying that the castle was falling down! . . . Bits are just dropping out of the sky would you believe? So he's crashing around trying to mend it. . . . Serves him right . . . that's what I say!!! But then there's his wife . . . she's really poorly . . . can't get out of bed and no doctor to be had . . . well . . . who in their right mind would go up there?

Invite the children to think about these things over the weekend:

- Who it's about.
- Who is saying it.
- To whom it is being said.
- What has gone wrong.

Monday morning: choices, choices

Where are we going to start? There are many possibilities.

Literacy choices

- Should I start with Janet and Allan Ahlberg's book about letters – *The Jolly Postman* – in the usual NLS way, reading first for enjoyment, then later in the week reading as writers and using the texts as models?
- Would the children be engaged by a session which follows up the overheard conversation introduced on Friday afternoon?
- Should I revisit the dramatic scenario which I described on Friday afternoon, exploring its possibilities using improvisation as a whole class activity?

Teaching and learning choices

- If I choose to start with *The Jolly Postman*, how will I organise this on Monday morning? We could read the whole narrative part of the text together, and then 'discover' who were the writers and recipients of the letters and cards.
- If we use the overheard conversation approach, what will Monday morning look like? Perhaps the teacher should re-enact what Jack's mum said. Then partner work could be used to decide the who, what and why.
- Go to the point where Jack's mum retells this gossip to Jack. Use drama to explore this situation and develop it into a reason to write a letter.

Any of these options could be developed in different groups of sessions within the block. The Ahlberg starting point seems especially useful. The reason for not selecting it as a starting point on this occasion is to provide something different. If we use the Ahlberg text in the usual way, this would mean using the letters as models. This would be challenging and the letters could be difficult to transfer into a coherent context as they vary so much in purpose and structure.

In this unit the literacy decisions are:

- To use the drama starting point as a way in to generating ideas for writing a text. This will need to be set up carefully to provide the necessary scaffolding. The amount of scaffolding needed will depend on the existing language skills, familiarity with improvisation and knowledge about letter writing that children already have.
- To use the structure of the improvisation to form the structure of the letter (as an alternative to using the structure of a text as a model to structure the writing).

The teaching and learning decision is to go for the third option. Action seems a good way in to letter writing. The improvisation will provide lots of opportunities for purposeful talk and problem solving discussions.

The first whole class shared text session

This session is quite different from a standard literacy lesson. Here our shared session is about creating a scenario to set the scene for some shared writing. The shared session will start by setting up the improvisation. The teacher needs to set up the improvisation thoughtfully, including plenty of questions to help children towards the detail.

Improvise some scene(s) to explore what Mum and Jack think about this and how they might respond to the news. For example:

1. **When Jack's mum hears the news**. What sort of a person is she now? Who does she hear the news from? What is she doing at the time? Is she rich or poor? How does she react? What does she say?
2. **When she tells Jack**. Where does this happen? What time of day? How long after the story is this taking place? How old is Jack now? What is he doing in his life? What does he think of the giant now? Is he scared? Guilty? Worried?
3. **When they decide what to do about the giant and his wife**. Using the information from (1) and (2), make up a discussion between the two characters. This must move towards deciding on some possible course(s) of action which they will later communicate to the giant couple. They need to be clear about what they want the giants to *feel* – reassured and grateful? Or sorry for threatening Jack when he came to the castle?

After this groups of two or three will go off and try out the improvisation in the three parts. The teacher will work with a particular group – perhaps the one the teacher will use to model the transferring of the ideas into letter writing.

Spotlight: making notes using a grid to structure the letter

Children are making notes about the outcomes of their improvisations. The note taking grid exemplified in Figure 10.1 enables children to summarise the ideas that they derived from the improvisation. The most useful element of the grid is that it follows the same sequence and structure as both the improvisation and the writing frame for the letter. The three sections become the three paragraphs in the final version of the letter.

Spotlight: using the writing frame to structure the letter – teacher modelling

The teacher is now modelling the use of the frame in a shared writing session. Figure 10.2 shows the writing being produced. The process of the modelling is fundamental here. The teacher needs to demonstrate for children quite explicitly how to take the ideas from the note taking grid and transfer them into each paragraph.

The writing frame is used very explicitly with the teacher talking out loud her or his thoughts and decisions as she or he makes them. The teacher shows children how to write more than one sentence under each prompt on the writing frame: otherwise children see quite limited written outcomes. It is important to do this anyway, because of the richness of the ideas the children have created: doing these justice requires more writing.

Spotlight: what about the tone of the letter? Compose sentences using adjectives, verbs and nouns (and pronouns) for precision, clarity and impact (Year 3)

The drama has given a clear structure to the writing. But what about style and tone? What sort of attitude, and therefore tone, will the writer display towards the giants?

This too comes through the drama. In the first example, Jack's mum has been acted out by children as a kindly, forgiving soul, who wants to let bygones be bygones. She could have been strident and accusatory, or she could have been something else. This link between how the characters were in the drama and how they 'behave' towards each other in the letter needs some teasing out and explicitness in the modelling.

The teacher does this by asking the group she worked with to act out one or two critical parts of the drama to determine what the characters are like. Pairs think about what they've seen and talk about what the characters are like and their attitudes to the giants. These are summarised by the teacher and she shows how to put these characteristics into the letter.

All of this determines some of the purpose. If Jack and his mum are basically kind and friendly, their attitudes to the giants – and therefore their letters – will be helpful and supportive (as in Figures 10.1 and 10.2). If they are antagonistic and aggrieved, their attitudes would be hostile and the letters critical. This is demonstrated in Figure 10.3. The tone of the letter is inextricably linked to the writer's sense of audience and the purpose of the letter.

It is knowledge of the audience and purpose that allows the writer to know which are the best words to choose for the writing. How can we know whether one verb will work better than another if we don't know exactly what impact we are trying to make upon the reader?

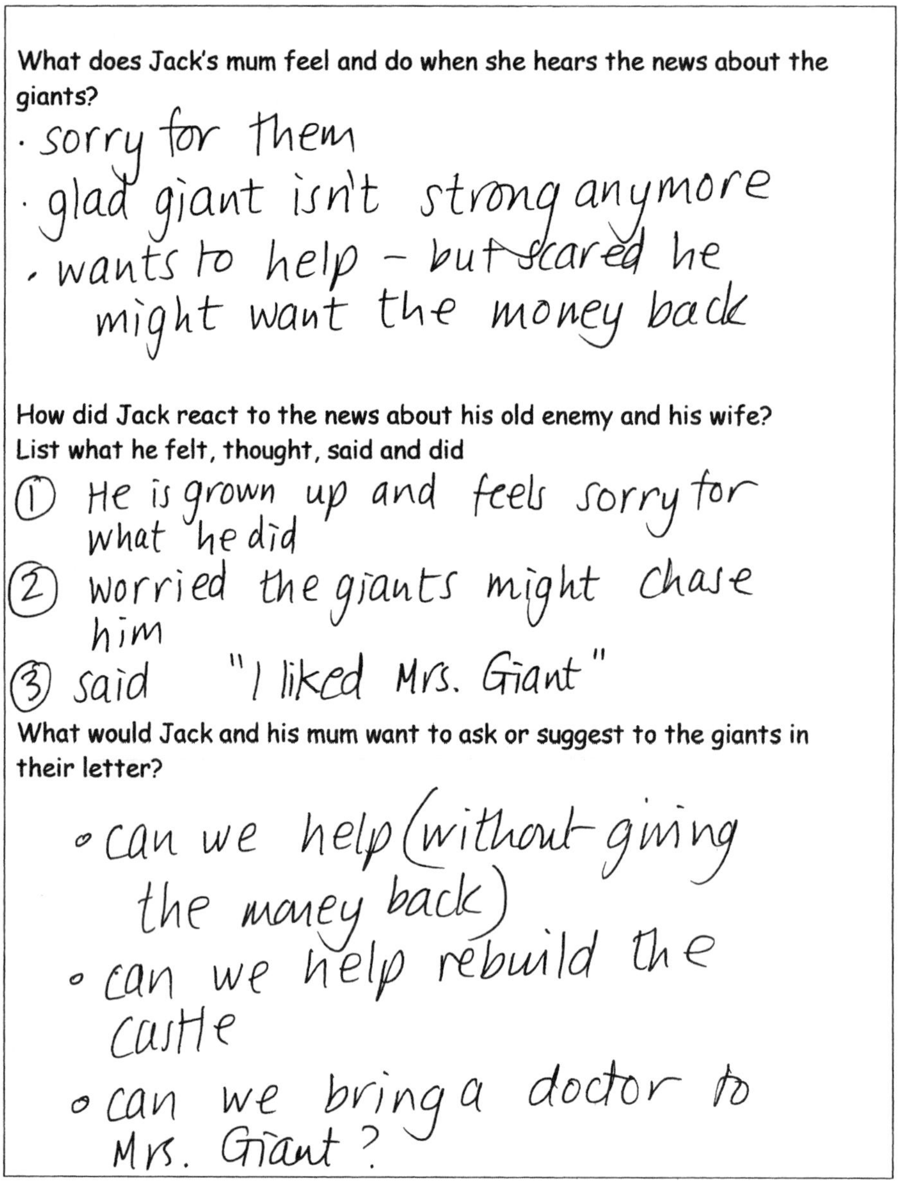

What does Jack's mum feel and do when she hears the news about the giants?

· sorry for them
· glad giant isn't strong anymore
· wants to help – but scared he might want the money back

How did Jack react to the news about his old enemy and his wife? List what he felt, thought, said and did

① He is grown up and feels sorry for what he did
② worried the giants might chase him
③ said   "I liked Mrs. Giant"

What would Jack and his mum want to ask or suggest to the giants in their letter?

○ can we help (without giving the money back)
○ can we help rebuild the castle
○ can we bring a doctor to Mrs. Giant?

Figure 10.1

With this in mind, the teacher draws attention to the objective about 'composing sentences using adjectives, verbs and nouns for precision , clarity and impact' for this session. The teacher demonstrates, using thinkalouds, how she or he is mindful of this when putting the sentences together and how it links to the attitude of Jack and his mum in their letter to the giants. The teacher later shows children how to read the text they have written, using this objective as a success criterion. The teacher asks children in pairs to identify which nouns, verbs and adjectives show Jack and his mum's attitude to the giants. Children will be using this skill later when they evaluate their own writing against the success criterion.

Dear Mr. and Mrs. Giant,

I have been hearing about your sadly changed circumstances.

When I heard the news I immediately remembered how my son Jack had taken some things from you. I wanted to help because now we are rich, and can afford to help!

Later that day I told my son Jack, he felt the same as I did. He feels sorry for what he did! He suggested that we should write to you and ask if we could do anything.

We discussed your situation at length. We decided that we wanted to ask the following three things:

- can your castle be mended?
- what is the matter with Mrs. Giant?
- can we come and visit you?

Please write back and let us know what you think

We feel very

Love from

Mrs. Daisy and Jack

Figure 10.2

Spotlight: children using the letter writing frame independently in pairs

Children immediately apply the ideas used in the modelled writing session to their own writing. They write in the frames, developing the same sort of writing as the teacher showed them. This time though, they use their own ideas from their own dramas and their own notes.

Since the use of frames is intended to support and not restrict children's developing skill in composing text, we need to be careful about how we use them. At some point

When I heard the news I thought it served you right! You nearly killed my son Jack between you. You Mrs. Giant tricked him, and told him to take various things from your house. Then your husband tried to catch and eat him! No wonder you're old and lonely now!

Figure 10.3

many abler children will need to move away from a reliance on writing frames. Deciding when children need and do not need to use a frame can be a tricky business about which teachers need to think carefully. Certainly you will know that children are beginning to find the writing frame restrictive once they start to alter and adapt it. When this happens children may only need to *see* the frame so that they can use it as a prompt for the organisation and/or language style of the letter.

Spotlight: some children write very well without writing frames

Some more able children are writing without the frame. They are avid readers who have internalised a lot of structures and styles for writing through their wide reading. They need freedom, away from the structure of the writing frame, to demonstrate their imaginative capacities and innovative skills. For them a writing frame would be a straitjacket to be avoided.

Two pairs from this group are working on laptops in the classroom. When they finish, they use the same success criterion to check how they have conveyed the characters' feelings towards the giants by choosing vocabulary which creates the right impact.

Spotlight: sorting out nouns and pronouns

This links in to the objective about composing sentences using adjectives, verbs, nouns (and pronouns) for precision, clarity and impact.

In this writing activity children have created confusion by their use of too many pronouns. By observing what children are doing in their writing, it has become clear to the teacher that a few children need to work on creating clarity in their writing by checking how they've used nouns and pronouns. (This particular group needs a distinct target about this later.) What seems to have happened is that in their eagerness to capture their ideas within each section of the letter, which include actions and reactions of more than one character, they have muddled the reader about who is doing what!

One enjoyable way to explore this is by using a teacher-produced muddled text. See Figure 10.4 for an example of this. Children will know it is confused, but may be unsure

Later that day I told my son Jack about him. He said he could go and visit him. If he tried to eat him again, he would use his mobile phone and call in his bodyguards. This would protect him from him.

Figure 10.4

how to sort it out. One simple way is through tracking who does what, using a code. The bits of text which relate to one character can be underlined with a straight line, and the other character underlined with a wobbly line.

There is a fun element which could be introduced and modelled in front of the class. This involves children first acting the sequence out. To do this, the class decides who does what , then the teacher instructs the children to make the sequence of actions. It is after this that children are asked to mark the text with straight or wobbly lines. This additional activity could then be used by children in practising this editing skill, with their own texts, using a target like 'I can make sure the reader understands who is doing what in my letter'.

Spotlight: creating clarity, precision and impact – modelling and trying out some redrafting using A/B pairs

Children have now written their own letter from Jack and his mum to the giants. The teacher wants to improve their revising and editing skills by showing them how to help each other using response partners. This is an ideal opportunity for some differentiation. The success criteria and targets can be adjusted to meet the needs which are being revealed in the first drafts.

As we saw in the last spotlight, some children need to look at clarity in terms of enabling the reader to understand who is doing what. So these children could be asked to do this in pairs using the target we mentioned earlier: 'We can make sure the reader understands who is doing what in our letters'.

Another group's work lacks clarity in terms of missing words and sentence punctuation. These children are asked to help formulate a success criterion or target which goes something like this – 'We can re-read our writing to check it makes sense to the reader and has all the full stops and capital letters'. The teacher models how to clarify meaning and adjust sentence punctuation in the following ways:

- Using 'thinkalouds' to make explicit just what is bothering her about a bit of the writing, which is then underlined. The underlined parts could be adjusted a bit at a time or all at the end. This needs to be done as clearly as possible so that it is easy to reread. (Children rather enjoy doing this with their own teacherly red pen.)
- Children in pairs now adopt A or B roles, and follow the same procedure. A reads the letter aloud while B underlines. They adjust the text together. Then B could reread adding the parts suggested by A. (Using the red pen, children make comments at the end 'self corrected by . . .').

A third group does not need to work on either of the above, and is, instead, asked to underline the words and phrases which show Jack and his mum's attitude to the giants. Having done this, they comment evaluatively on these phrases in their texts, changing anything they feel is lacking in clarity and impact. This group is using the following target which they made up themselves: 'We can choose good words for sentences which make the reader understand what Jack and his mum feel about the giants'.

Spotlight: how will the giants respond?

At a later point children act out the scene where the giant and his wife receive the letter. They work out how the giants respond. Part of this involves preparation to investigate the characters of the giants. Children are not going to know what the giants' response to one of the letters is if they don't know what the giants are like.

This is being done by using 'teacher in role' to develop ideas about the giants. Children could be asked to prepare for this by pairing up to write questions to discover what the giants are like. Teaching and learning issues here revolve around improving enquiry skills. Children work on developing open questions which reveal as much information as possible about each character. Use of teacher in role here enables the teacher to establish a strong character for each giant by the way he or she answers questions. Figure 10.5 illustrates some children's questions.

Once the questioning is completed for each, children in pairs could be asked to select from a list of adjectives to describe the main characteristics of each giant. These adjectives can be quite challenging in terms of the concepts they are developing about the characters, as can be seen in Figure 10.6.

The class is ready now to reread the teacher-modelled letter written to the giants. This time we need two children in role at the front as the two giants, ready to respond to suggestions from the groups after each section of the letter has been read. Some simple 'think bubble' reactions from the giants can be elicited from the watching class, who empathise with and 'think' for each giant. Children are invited to come to the front and speak aloud the character's thoughts. This builds up a bank of possible ideas and alternatives to develop about what response the giants may make to the letter from Jack and his mum. Figure 10.7 gives an indication of what children may think and say 'for the giants'.

But all this relates to the modelled letter. Pairs now need to find out how *their* giants are going to respond to *their* letter from mum and Jack.

Spotlight: pairs discover their own giants' responses to the letter

Around the class pairs are deciding:

- what their giants are like.
- what they say and do when they read the letter from Jack and his mum.

They are engaged in lively discussions: they are improvising the scene where one of the couple reads the letter.

This is shared in the plenary with the teacher helping children to notice what each one may imply for a return letter to Jack and his mum.

Do you like Jack?

Why did Jack steal your hen?

How old are you and Mrs. Giant now?

Are you angry with Jack and his mum because they are rich?

How do you get food to eat?

Would you still chase Jack if he came back?

Figure 10.5

kind

forgiving

grudging

loving

spiteful

angry

bitter

generous

weary

mean

friendly

protective

hopeless

Figure 10.6

Mr Giant (angry and protective)

He didn't <u>take</u> things, he stole them!

So you're rich now and we're poor – that's not fair!

Mrs Giant (generous and weary)

That's lovely ....they want to help us.....

Don't be too angry my dear!

Figure 10.7

Spotlight: writing a response

Now responses are written. There are important decisions to be made at this point about how much the children need structure (more modelling and/or writing frames) and how much they need freedom to express the ideas they have gathered through the drama.

The decision here is to not constrain children with further writing frames. The teacher though does read aloud a lively letter she has written based on the drama with the think bubbles. Children write freely in pairs using their own ideas from the drama. This offers opportunities for assessment later using the same success criteria we identified earlier. It also provides opportunities for self and peer evaluations. Some children choose to compose and shape their texts at the word processor.

Spotlight: word level work focusing on an identified group

This section concerns revision of word level work from Key Stage 1. There are a number of children in the class who are not spelling long vowel sounds well. There are two issues: several children are not discriminating between certain long vowel sounds, particularly **ar** and **or**; additionally, they confuse the various ways of spelling many long vowel sounds. For the two identified sounds (**ar** and **or**), they need to focus on discriminating between the two phonemes. This is done initially with the whole class, because abler children can be expected to help others by using their more developed skill both in hearing and spelling the sounds. This activity is used then as a quick revision for these children, and their skills as a scaffold for the weaker spellers.

Hearing the sounds

It is important to find out whether children can discriminate between **ar** and **or** sounds first. Children are paired (as far as possible stronger and weaker spellers together) to provide support and to make sure that the less able don't just cease to engage with the activity. It is explained that there will be two long vowel phonemes to work with, then a list is read aloud containing various words with the **ar** phoneme: the **ar** sound is emphasised and lengthened. Children are next given the list of words to read together and practise saying in their pairs, using the same emphasis. Their ability to discriminate this phoneme against others is checked, as an intermediate step before introducing the **or** sound. To do this children are asked to stand every time they hear the **ar** phoneme in a word spoken aloud. This is fun and gets them listening carefully. (Other sounds could 'require' a different movement – for example, long **a** could mean both hands in the air.)

The aim of this part of the session is to ensure children are relatively confident with this phoneme before moving on to the next one. If the children seem relatively secure with this sound, it is time to move on. More or less the same could be done with the **or** phoneme, drawing attention to the way our mouths move when we say this sound.

The next step is to get children to distinguish between these two sounds when they are both said aloud in a list of words. Again, an active approach seems best. One way to do this could be to use movements which mimic the mouth shapes used for each sound: so when an **ar** sound is made, a large circular movement is made with the hands, while an **or** sound needs a small circle with hands. This could be repeated with mouth shapes.

Looking at spelling patterns

Next day the class moves on to whole class work on spelling the sounds. Using the written word lists first (which we could have a quick look at again) has given children a preview of the range of possible spellings. Now they need to think about the spelling patterns. Which spellings occur only at ends of words and which ones are followed by other phonemes?

Using **or**

Children are asked in their pairs to find as many different ways as they can to spell some **or** words.

1. claw, saw
2. floor, door

3. caught, taught
4. bought, fought, brought

Note that of the four spelling patterns (1) and (2) can occur only at the ends of words, whereas (3) and (4) are almost always followed by the 't' phoneme. The children's attention is drawn to this. Whether or not they know it comes out in the paired discussions. Some stronger spellers know these spelling conventions, even if they haven't been asked to articulate them before. By asking all children to do this activity, a much greater idea of the implicit understandings of spelling rules and conventions of the stronger spellers is acquired. (Feedback from the pairs, together with a quick look at the whiteboards, will give this information.)

It is assumed at this stage that the children who have only just learned to discriminate between the **or** and **ar** phonemes probably need to do more work to know the range and applications of the spelling patterns for these sounds. (This is checked out later.) For now, using some cursive handwriting activities to link in to the four spelling patterns for **or** is a useful reinforcement. A game or two doesn't go amiss either, before assessments are made of this group to see which of the spelling patterns they are more confident with, and whether they know which ones end the words and which don't. Simple pairs of cards can be made with **or** and **ar** words on them. These can be used for snap, memory games or collecting three of one set or another in a rummy type game.

Spotlight: enjoying a book about letters – *The Jolly Postman*

The class is sharing the text *The Jolly Postman* by Janet and Allan Ahlberg to create:

- experiences of novel and creative approaches based on well loved story characters
- a bigger picture of the range of styles and purposes for which letters can be written.

A letter has been taken out of its 'envelope' and children have copies in which the sender and recipient have been blanked out. The class reads the letter together and pairs of children decide:

- the sender and planned recipient of the letter
- the purpose of the letter – what was it trying to make the reader think, feel or do?

Creating a sequence of emails or text messages

The teacher could write a short sequence of email type communications between characters in this or another traditional story. Children may need some models for what emails look like, and how different they are from letters. After this, some of the above unit might have been adjusted to use emails to communicate. Children will relish the shorter, sharper bursts of writing which are required. We wonder what children and teachers would discover about purpose and audiences in this type of communication. And what would they be finding out about the style that went with these? Emails are generally much briefer than letters. Whereas conventions for letter writing have developed over time, emailing doesn't seem yet to have created such conventions. Obviously though, emails deliver more functional and less expressive messages. Perhaps as a result of this, emails are closer to spoken styles of language than written ones.

This would be even more the case using text messaging. Texting looks even more like speech written down. It is briefer and can fulfil more limited purposes than either letters or emails. Role play linked to text messaging in this unit could involve investigating situations in which Jack might text his mum, either giant, his bodyguards – or someone else they chose to bring in to the story. So, for example, we could pretend that Jack visits the castle, but gets lost and trapped in the ruins of the huge castle kitchen. His bodyguards try to give him directions about how to get out. Children could enact the drama, composing the sequence of messages between Jack and his bodyguards.

Beyond the unit: writing letters to real people

The idea of writing a whole sequence of letters is a powerful one because children learn so much about audience and purpose in this process. Corresponding with real as well as imaginary people is important, so it is worthwhile to try and find contexts in which this can be done. One idea tried out was with older people in day care. They had plenty of time to write and provided a fascinating source of information and different viewpoints.

Reference

Ahlberg, J. and Ahlberg, A. (1986) *The Jolly Postman, or, Other People's Letters*, London: Heinemann.

11 Cyclones!

Information books on same or similar themes: literacy across the curriculum

Year 4

The National Literacy Strategy identified six text types, each of which has particular characteristics at text, sentence and word level: recount, instructions, non-chronological report, persuasive, explanations and arguments.

The recommendation for children to read and write a range of text types, in addition to narrative and poetry, was welcome. However, the focus on specific text types can become an artificial exercise, unrelated to the ways in which texts are produced and used in the world outside school. The front page of a newspaper, for example, may well be composed of some actual 'reporting' (with no persuasive bias), a supposed report which is in fact expressing the viewpoint of the editor, one or more photographs with captions, and an advert. This mix of 'text types' within one text, including both the written and the visual, is typical of the texts children encounter both in paper and electronic form on CD-ROM and the internet. Even specific text types rarely occur purely as written text. Instructional texts, for example, are almost always a mix of writing and illustration – witness any cookery book.

The mix of text types within one text raises interesting questions about writing frames. An exclusively written frame can certainly help children consider the basic structure and appropriate sentences of a specified text type. However, in this chapter we look beyond such frames and the specific, exclusively written, text types they represent with their rigid structure and sentences, towards frames representing texts children recognise and read both within and outside school. In our experience their engagement with such frames is always very positive, especially as they produce work resembling published texts.

What was in the teacher's head when planning this work?

Contexts and coherence

- The work will be linked directly to the geography continuous unit 'What's in the News?'
- The literacy will also be linked to another subject in terms of using the writing frame for a piece of purposeful writing for someone at home.

Motivation

- The children will be fascinated by the awe and wonder of cyclones.
- Children will be immersed in the 'content' of information books – the natural interest of children in the drama of the natural world. This will be used as a way into my focus on strategies for reading these texts.
- Children enjoy writing for someone at home – a powerful purpose and audience for the written outcome.

Content and process

- The layout and features of pages in information books.
- A 'real' information text will be examined rather than an artificial one written to demonstrate a text type.
- There will be a focus on the writing process through the independent tasks and the guided writing groups.
- This unit will be used for vocabulary extension.
- Verbs will approached 'kinaesthetically' by children demonstrating them through action and movement.
- Spelling will be applied in the shared writing, and by the children in their independent writing.

Primary National Strategy Objectives

Clustering the learning objectives

The Primary National Strategy learning objectives are best viewed as end of year outcomes. So, for example, by the end of Year 4 the aim is for children to be able to 'use knowledge of different organisational features of texts to find information effectively'. Planned units will therefore revisit objectives throughout the year, approaching them in different ways, rather than a teacher ticking them off at the end of a unit as having been 'taught'. The 'Group discussion and interaction' objective focuses the children explicitly on developing their ability to take on different roles within groups.

Objectives for this unit have been selected from Year 3 (for children working below age-related expectations), and Years 4 and 5 (to challenge the more able children). By planning in this way we:

- ensure progression both in terms of a child's progress and the progression of knowledge and skills through a school
- differentiate between children of different abilities
- can focus on assessment for learning, being clear where a child is coming from and where the child next needs to go.

Speaking

Year 4

• Offer reasons and evidence for their views, considering alternative opinions.

Group discussion and interaction

Year 4

• Take different roles in groups and use the language appropriate to them, including the roles of leader, reporter, scribe and mentor.

Word structure and spelling

Year 4

• Use knowledge of morphology to spell new and unfamiliar words.

Understanding and interpreting texts

Year 3

• Identify how different texts are organised, including reference texts.

Year 4

• Use knowledge of different organisational features of texts to find information effectively.

Creating and shaping texts

Year 3

• Write non-narrative texts using structures of different text types.
• Use layout, format, graphics and illustrations for different purposes.

Year 4

• Summarise and shape material and ideas from different sources to write convincing and informative non-narrative texts.
• Choose and combine words, images and other features for particular effects.

Year 5

• Reflect independently and critically on their own writing and edit and improve it.

Text structure and organisation

Year 5

- Experiment with the order of sections to achieve different effects.

Sentence structure and punctuation

Year 4

- Clarify meaning and point of view by using varied sentence structure (phrases, clauses and adverbials).

Starting points

A geography lesson

This is all about children looking forward to the work, rather than being surprised by it on a Monday morning. Of the two potential starting points:

- 'Here's a picture of the devastation caused by a cyclone. On Monday we'll be starting some really exciting work on cyclones.'
- 'On Monday we'll be starting some really exciting work on non-chronological reports.'

perhaps the mention of cyclones will make the most impact!

Of course, in our literacy lessons we want the children to focus on text types, their features and how we read and write them, but if we want to create excitement we must not lose sight of a simple idea. All of us (children and adults) read texts because of their content, not in order to develop our higher order reading skills. If, in our desperation to improve literacy, we gloss over the actual content of reading we risk turning literacy into a dry focus on structures and skills. As the lessons accumulate over the primary school years, there is a danger we will lose many children. So, cyclones are exciting, powerful, awesome, and we are all fascinated by them. Focusing initially on them rather than the literacy is more likely to get this unit off to a good start.

In this unit the focus on cyclones takes place outside the literacy hour in a geography lesson. The 'What's in the News?' continuous unit encourages us to link geography to news items of sudden interest, e.g. an eruption of a volcano or a cyclone sweeping through a country. Children should be encouraged to look out for examples in newspapers or on the television news or the internet and reports of 'natural disasters' can be collected for use in units such as this.

The unit can be used flexibly when relevant news events occur.

> Children can practise their non-fiction writing through this unit and consider different styles and forms of written text.
>
> (QCA Primary Geography Scheme of Work)

For the length of the unit, the reading and writing of non-fiction will switch constantly between geography and literacy.

Monday morning: choices, choices

How the literacy itself might start – what will actually happen on Monday morning – involves professional choices.

Literacy choices

- Should the objectives for the unit be introduced at the start?
- Should there be a lively, interactive word level session on a new focus?
- Should there be a quick, couple of minutes' reminder of some earlier work?
- Should the starting point be a reading aloud of the text? Will this be a 'big book' version? Or will the text be projected onto a screen through an interactive whiteboard? Or will copies be handed out?
- Should there be a reminder about the geography lesson(s), the newspaper or internet reports, the videoed news broadcast?

Teaching and learning choices

- Will the children sit on the carpet or at their tables?
- Will the children be 'alone' or with a talk partner?
- Will the whole class teaching be a 'no hands up' lesson?

All of the above will, in fact, happen at different points through the unit, so the decisions for Monday morning will be personal. Teaching is all about making informed, professional decisions – it is what makes teaching so exciting.

In this unit there are two literacy decisions:

- To begin by reminding children of the geography work. The video of the dramatic news broadcast is shown (two minutes) and, with the children in talk partner pairs, they are asked what they can remember about cyclones (three minutes' paired talk).

    As it is a 'no hands up' lesson, some of the pairs are then asked to state what they know about cyclones (five minutes).
- To move into a shared reading of the cyclones text. The text is projected through a data projector.

The teaching and learning decision is to sit the children at their tables, in pairs with a talk partner. The reason for starting in this way is to ensure all children are engaged with the lesson. In talk partner pairs everyone speaks; everyone feels involved.

The whole class shared text session

The lesson begins with a question: 'When you look at these two pages (see Figure 11.1) where do you first look? Where do your eyes go? Talk to your partner.' The resulting discussion (first in pairs, then the whole class) demonstrates how most readers go first to either the heading or the photograph, perhaps switching between the two. There is an exploration of why this happens. And this in turn leads to the **purpose** of these two

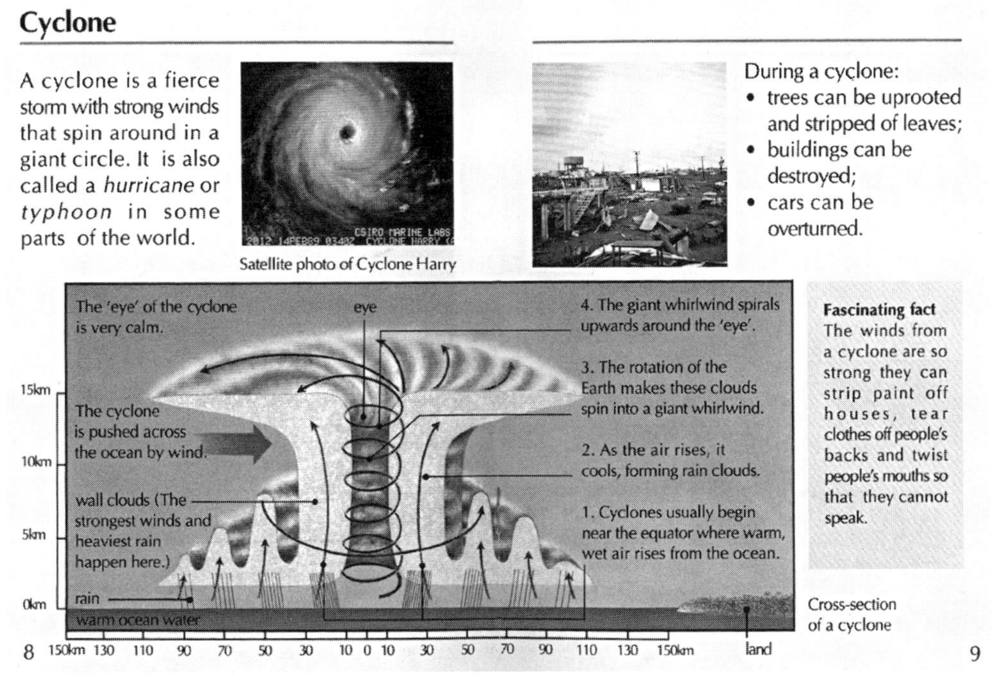

Cyclone

A cyclone is a fierce storm with strong winds that spin around in a giant circle. It is also called a *hurricane* or *typhoon* in some parts of the world.

Satellite photo of Cyclone Harry

During a cyclone:
- trees can be uprooted and stripped of leaves;
- buildings can be destroyed;
- cars can be overturned.

The 'eye' of the cyclone is very calm.

eye

4. The giant whirlwind spirals upwards around the 'eye'.

3. The rotation of the Earth makes these clouds spin into a giant whirlwind.

The cyclone is pushed across the ocean by wind.

2. As the air rises, it cools, forming rain clouds.

wall clouds (The strongest winds and heaviest rain happen here.)

1. Cyclones usually begin near the equator where warm, wet air rises from the ocean.

Fascinating fact
The winds from a cyclone are so strong they can strip paint off houses, tear clothes off people's backs and twist people's mouths so that they cannot speak.

15km
10km
5km
0km

rain
warm ocean water

Cross-section of a cyclone

8 150km 130 110 90 70 50 30 10 0 10 30 50 70 90 110 130 150km land 9

Figure 11.1

elements of the text: the heading to be glanced at so readers know what they are reading and the dramatic photograph to grab the attention.

The text is read aloud with the children watching and listening. There is an emphasis on modelling the appropriate voice for different parts – the heading 'Cyclones', the opening sentences, the bullet points, the 'Fascinating fact' paragraph. In addition there is explicit modelling of how a reader reads the visual elements of the text: the diagram and key, and the dramatic photographs.

There is further discussion about cyclones themselves and how the information in the text confirms and extends what the children already knew.

The shared element of the lesson continues by considering the purpose of each section of the text. A frame on the whiteboard, in landscape, is used to represent the 'Cyclone' double page spread (see Figure 11.2).

First, there is discussion of the text feature in the top left hand corner – the heading or title – and its purpose. Through paired talk the children decide on the purpose of the heading and contribute to a sentence, e.g. the heading tells the reader the subject of the page. Copies of this set of blocks are now given out to children working in pairs, who have to name the features: three sentences, diagram, key, photograph, caption, bullet points, paragraph (fascinating fact), and the purpose of each block. Pairs become fours to compare what they have done. An envoy is sent from each four to find out what another group has written. The envoys then report back and some fours amend what they have written. There is then a whole class sharing of Figure 11.3.

In this first lesson the independent work follows directly from the shared text work, children working in pairs with someone of similar level of reading ability. Copies of information texts are distributed. For the lower attaining readers the text will be from the same book as 'Cyclones', so the design of each page is very similar to that of 'Cyclones'.

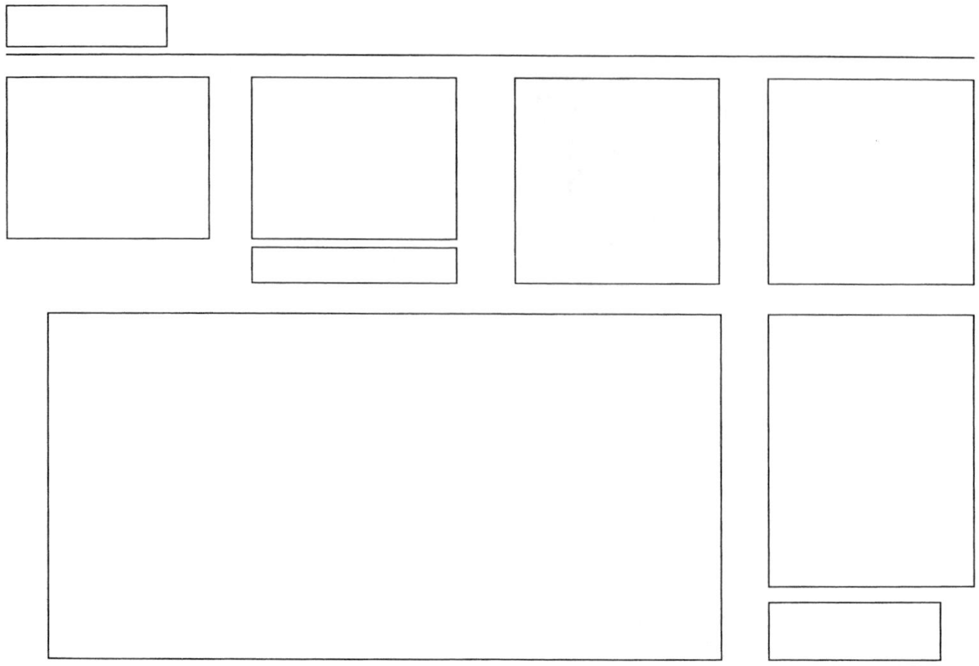

Figure 11.2

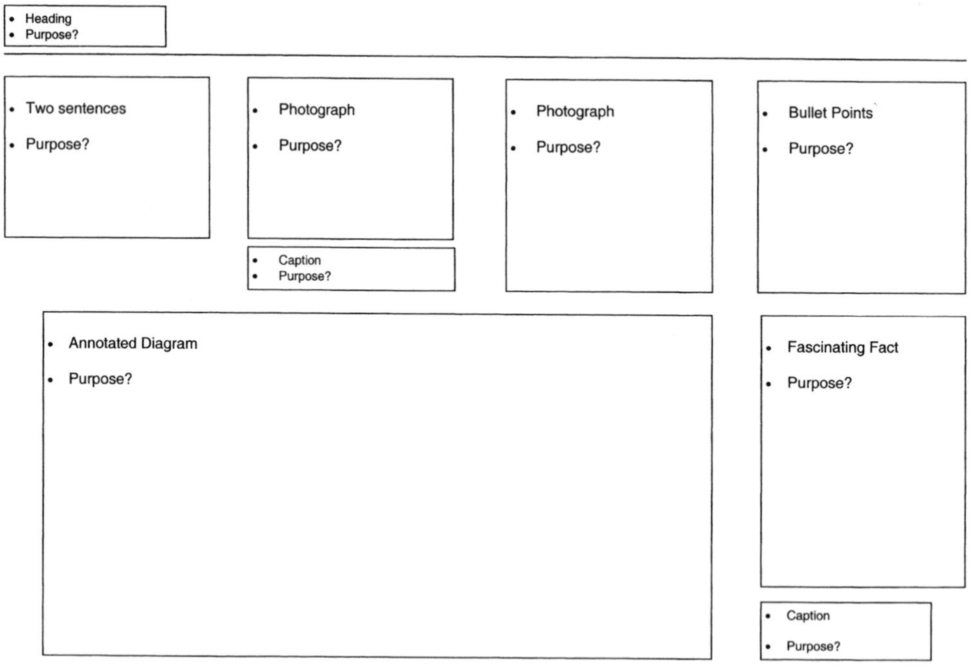

Figure 11.3

For higher attaining readers the text is from a different book. The task is to produce a frame of blocks of text based on the features. The features are named and their purpose summarised in a sentence.

Spotlight: short, sharp revision

We could visit the starts of most of the lessons in this unit. The whiteboard will allow us to revise some earlier work, the children knowing they will be expected to recall this, perhaps from months ago. Such constant, quick revision is so important if we want children to remember and learn. It only takes a few minutes at the beginning of every lesson.

Spotlight: working with verbs

This work, focusing on verbs, verb endings and regular and irregular verbs, is a series of linked lessons involving teaching, children working and learning and then applying their learning, assessment and further planning for teaching.

Teaching

A challenge has been set: everyone likes a challenge and the setting of challenges should be a regular strategy in the classroom. How many verbs can be collected on a large sheet of sugar paper pinned to the wall? Children know they cannot add one to the list unless they are sure the spelling is correct.

The verbs are examined in terms of their meanings – linking spelling to vocabulary. Before a verb is discussed it is demonstrated, so for the verb 'to emerge' all the children crouch down on the floor 'emerging' (slowly) as they stand up. There is exploration of how the action the children have just performed could be captured in words. The children discuss their definitions in pairs before individually attempting a written definition on their whiteboards and holding them up for an instant assessment of who has (and who has not) grasped the meaning of the words.

In another session the tenses of the verbs are being discussed through the construction of a table with verbs from the 'Cyclones' text (see Table 11.1).

Table 11.1

Past	Present
spun	spin
pushed	push
stripped	strip
destroyed	destroy
tore	tear
rose	rise

Spotlight: roles in groups

Children working and learning

The above teaching leads to an independent task in which children in threes collaboratively complete the table. Halfway through this session the work is stopped, envoys are chosen for each three ('Give yourself a letter, A, B or C – Bs are the envoys') and these envoys are sent to another group. The envoys will compare how their group is doing compared to the group being visited, and then report back. This is very challenging, as they have to represent their own group's work and note similarities and differences in the work of the group they are visiting.

The threes now prepare for the plenary. Each child is designated a role within the three. In this case each three requires a leader, a reporter (who will report on behalf of the group in the plenary) and a scribe. The group has to decide whether their presentation will be spoken (what we found and what we learnt), written (this is the table we came up with) or involve active demonstration (when Jane reads the passage, the two of us will demonstrate each of the verbs). They prepare for the plenary.

Developing children's ability to work in different ways in groups is stressed throughout the Group Discussion and Interaction objectives. This will require explicit teaching, perhaps leading to sheets displayed in the classroom e.g. 'When I am the Group Leader I will . . .'. Designating roles may be decided by the teacher initially but as children become more experienced at working in these ways the groups themselves can agree individual roles.

In this lesson the plenary is about the work on verbs. Teacher assessment will involve observing particular children working within the three. However objectives chosen from Speaking, Listening, Group discussion and interaction, and Drama should regularly be the focus of the plenary instead of the content of the lesson. Children know this in advance. In this way speaking and listening can be explicitly considered by the children; this not only develops their awareness and ability but also gives oral work status in the classroom.

Learning spellings

For this unit, verbs have been sorted into five sets of verbs and verb endings, corresponding to the five spelling groups in the class. Within the groups we see the children working in pairs learning how to spell particular verbs and verb endings – both as homework and as independent tasks. At the end of the week the pairs will test each other on the words. The results are treated seriously and collected. Words spelled incorrectly must be learnt for Monday.

Children applying their working

As the spelling and vocabulary work progresses, there is shared writing in which the words are explicitly used and attention drawn to them. Perhaps a selection have been copied onto a 'powerful verbs' list so that they are displayed in front of the children. In their own writing (below) the children know they are also expected to consider verb choice carefully and to add the verbs they choose to the table.

Spotlight: purposeful writing

Here the children are going to use the literacy learning to produce a piece of highly purposeful writing. The work on the frame of the 'Cyclones' double page spread means they now have something which can be used for other purposes and in other curriculum areas. This can be at text level in terms of the multi-modal structure of the page and also at sentence level in that children can use the sentences as the basis for the sentence structures they will now construct. The 'Cyclones' frames are taken to science lessons about gravity (see Figures 11.4 and 11.5).

Apart from engaging children imaginatively in both the literacy and the science, this work has two clear purposes:

- **External** – as with any information book, the purpose is to inform the reader. The work can be sent to another class or taken home to inform parents about the science topic.
- **Internal** – using the frame helps children clarify understandings. They cannot use the frame unless they are clear about the content.

'Outside in' (bringing the curriculum into literacy lessons)

In a literacy lesson we see the children individually producing their science pieces as independent tasks. Group guided writing sessions focus on the purpose of the writing, i.e. to inform a reader about the science unit. Advice will be at text, sentence and word level. So, the teaching itself is purposeful, taking place as it does in a purposeful context.

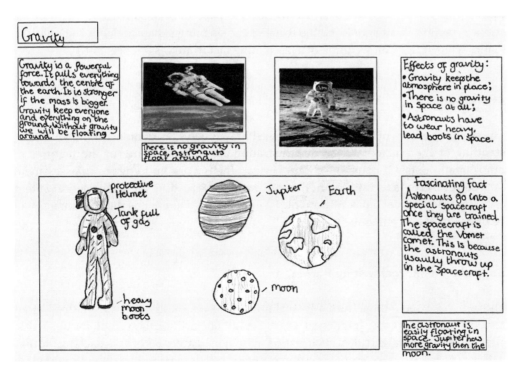

Figure 11.4 Robyn Beaty

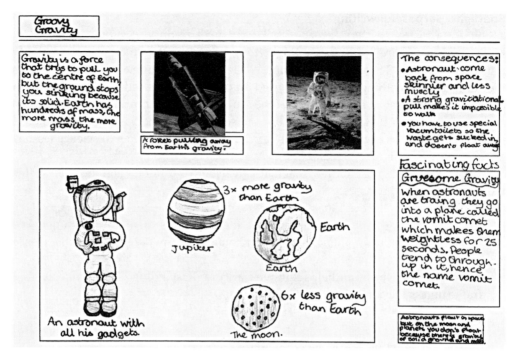

Figure 11.5 Amie Griffiths

Thanks to Nicola Hawkins, teacher at Beaconside Junior School, Penrith for these examples.

'Inside out' (taking literacy into other areas of the curriculum)

In this science lesson the children are working in pairs to brainstorm and then sort the science content. What should be the focus of the opening sentences? What should the diagram illustrate? Can we think of a fascinating fact from this science unit?

Assessment

The resulting pieces of work can be assessed in two ways: as demonstrating an understanding of the science and as demonstrating an understanding of the features of information texts. Of course if children swap their work and engage in assessment themselves there is a further bonus. Because they will be reading the same science content each time they look at a piece by another child, the more likely it is that the science will be understood and remembered.

Beyond the unit: real writing frames

This unit has used a page from a typical information book to teach the children about features of this text type. It is a 'real' example, not one artificially written for this work; all schools have libraries full of such texts. Two major advantages of approaching the unit in this way are first that the main resource is free (it is already in school) and second that the children know they are working with a real example (rather than a literacy worksheet).

The same books can also be used to examine explanations – there are many explanations of processes and how things work within them. Examples of other text types are just as easily obtained (at no cost) because they are all around us in the world outside school. Some examples are listed below.

Instructions

- How to play board games.
- Recipes.
- Car manuals.
- DIY instructions.

Persuasive

- Estate agents' advertisements for houses, both printed and on web sites.
- Junk mail (arrives free through our letterboxes every week).
- Advertisements in newspapers, magazines and on the internet.

Recounts

- Many of the reports in newspapers are actually recounts, e.g. the report of last night's soccer match.

Reports

- One of the school reports to parents or governors?
- A report to members by a local association, club or team?

It is useful to build up boxes of examples of different text types, most of which are a mix of headings, written text and pictures, and apply the process described above. Each text has a purpose and is made up of a number of purposeful elements.

High Expectations of Children

This chapter has been about children in Key Stage 2. Lynn Gill, from Lister School in Germany (Service Children's Education) talked about how she wanted to take ideas and explore how far she could 'push the boundaries' with younger children. Figure 11.6 shows two examples from her Year 1 class. They demonstrate that good ideas for teaching literacy are not constrained by the children we teach. Multi modal texts are a feature of the lives of all children and can be adapted and used to motivate children to write whatever their age.

Ancient Egyptians

The Ancient Egyptians lived about 5,000 years ago.

This is Tutankhamuns sarcophagus .

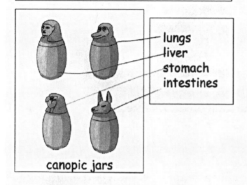

lungs
liver
stomach
intestines

canopic jars

Ancient Egyptians didn't have any toilets.

The boy king cut his leg and died.

They even made cat mummies.

Did you know?

That they put your insides in pots.

Romans

The Romans conquered lots of countries. Romans lived a long long time ago.

Roman Transport.

Helmet
Sword
Shield

They had lots of Gods.

They made mosaics

They had public baths.

Romans used powdered mouse brains for toothpaste.

Figure 11.6

12 Where did our writing come from?

Exploring the writing process

One of the key ideas underpinning the teaching of writing is the reading–writing connection: through reading and examining a range of text types we 'write like a reader'. As a result, the literacy units developed by the Primary National Strategy are based on text types, following a powerful teaching sequence through which shared reading leads to shared writing and into independent writing by the children. However, while some of the units in this book follow this pattern, it is not the only way in which to work, and one of the aims of this book is to provide examples of variations. So, in Chapter 14 poetry begins with a set of illustrations and in Chapter 13 a language based unit explores the differences between speech and writing. Here we focus on a key literacy process, the writing process, working in ways which enable children to explore it and understand how writing can move through a series of stages from initial thinking to a final, polished piece.

Teaching is about both content and process. The former is always explicit in the classroom, with both teachers and children clear about the content of lessons, but processes can be implicit and therefore invisible to learners. Making processes explicit is a key teaching and learning idea. The reading process is drawn to the attention of children in guided reading through 'strategy checks', and in guided writing we join children working at different points in the writing process. This unit, though, has the writing process as its basis and leads to a powerful process display: Where Did Our Writing Come From?

Revising one's writing really is difficult. Realising it is not exactly as good as it should be is a very adult concept. Perhaps there are many children who find the whole idea of doing their best and then having to consider making it better a somewhat strange idea. Left to their own devices would they engage in lengthy revision? Teaching 'revision' is subtle. The key strategy is shared writing in which there is a teacher thinking aloud while composing and revising in front of the children. This 'thinking like a writer' is both internal (the teacher's ideas about the piece of writing) and external (the characteristics of the text type being modelled).

At any stage in the writing process our aim is to teach and get children to think about their writing rather than just doing it. An explicit focus on the writing process means that we can discuss children's writing with them and involve them in important decisions. The key teaching strategy for such work is guided writing, when we join a group of children with similar writing attainment and focus on important aspects of writing. We are trying to produce independent writers who can take hold of the process for themselves. Being an independent writer means being aware of how successful or otherwise a piece of writing might be. Independent writers decide how far to take a piece of writing. In the classroom this might mean a child discussing with us their draft of a story and deciding that enough is enough and the draft will not be taken any further. Our teaching points will be recorded on the draft, so that it has 'status'. The child learns from the task and these points are taken to future story writing, but to 'copy it up' would be a pointless exercise. Such an approach is subtle and sensitive given the range of children in most classes. The child who produces a neat copy of everything without much critical thought is as much of a challenge as the child who dislikes writing and never wants to engage with the process. While the aim is independent, critical writers, how different children are approached is always a challenge. However, if the writing process is not clear to them, such discussions and decisions are unlikely to be meaningful.

The writing process

The full process

Not all pieces of writing go through the full process of pre-writing, writing, revising, editing and achieving purpose. To illustrate the full process we can consider an adult example: writing a letter of application for a new job.

Pre-writing	Writing	Revising	Editing	Achieving purpose
e.g. drawing, discussing, planning	composing	adding, deleting, rearranging	correcting	e.g. informing, persuading, instructing

Pre-writing

We guess there will certainly be a lot of pre-writing! It will involve thinking – in the car, while watching the television – perhaps some notes (words and phrases) or a diagram (a mind-map perhaps showing the key ideas you wish to emphasise in the letter). Thoughts and ideas may well be organised under particular headings. Eventually you will sit in front of a screen or a blank sheet of paper and the pre-writing will be very focused. How to begin? What sort of order for the points you want to make?

Writing

Now you start writing the letter (the hardest part is often that first sentence), but if you are working in long hand, probably not on the actual sheet or form that will be posted. That would be too risky. Word processing allows us to play with our writing as we write it. This means that much revising happens as we write rather than at the end of the writing.

Revising

Now you look critically at your letter. Does it achieve the purpose you need to achieve, i.e. will it get you an interview? You may ask someone else to read it for you and offer some thoughts. You will no doubt find yourself deleting some bits, amending others and adding something new. You might now revise the structure of the letter, reordering some of the sections. You will no doubt focus on the quality of the sentences and rewrite some of them.

Editing

Now you have to ensure the letter is correct. Spelling (especially), punctuation and grammar errors are likely to count heavily against you in the eyes of a potential employer. You might use a spell check and grammar check. You may well ask someone else to check it for you.

Achieving purpose

Finally the letter is posted and you wait to hear if it has indeed achieved the intended purpose of getting you a stage further in the application process.

This example illustrates the full writing process but not all writing goes through every stage from beginning to end. A shopping list will have some pre-writing (thinking plus looking in cupboards and the fridge perhaps), writing and then will achieve its purpose of reminding us in the supermarket. Revising and editing are not necessary (though we may add to the list while sitting on the bus!).

Guided writing

Guided writing means joining a group of children who are all at the same stage in the writing process. We might join them at the pre-writing stage, or while they are writing and revising. They might be editing or feel they have finished. The fact that they are aware of the writing process makes such group sessions meaningful. The key for teachers is to be clear about the sorts of questions we might ask or comments we might make which will be helpful at different points in the process.

The process is more complex than it looks

The writing process looks very simple in the linear way in which it is described above. However, in reality it is much more complex, with elements merging as the writer moves back and forth through it. To a certain extent this will depend on what we might call 'writing personality'. Do you plan in detail before beginning writing or just plan the start or even just get going without a plan because you have a good idea? Is your plan a list down the page or words and phrases scattered about? Do you draw your plan as a mind-map? When you write are you someone who crashes down a first attempt in one rush and then goes back for a lot of revision? Or do you work methodically, revising as you go, so that by the end there is very little revising to be done? Do you correct spelling as you write (on the basis of the words the computer underlines in red) or do you focus purely on composition when you write and leave editing until the end? We all have our preferred ways of writing, and so will children in classrooms. As they move through primary school we need to offer them different approaches so that they can develop what suits them best. By offering variation we let children consider their preferences and also develop the ways they might not prefer. In her research Trisha Maynard (2002, p. 101) found a general dislike of planning sheets among the children in her survey: 'On your planning sheet you put down one set of ideas . . . but when you come to write your stories you've got a whole new set of ideas' (Year 4 pupil).

We believe many children waste time planning because the way they are told to plan does not suit the ways they want to work. This is not to say that planning sheets should not be used, just that their use should be discussed openly and critically with children so that different approaches can be developed, tried and reviewed. Perhaps they are best viewed not as planning frames but as 'thinking frames' – ways in which writers can gather their thoughts, capture sudden new, good ideas, play with an order or even just jot down a particular word so as not to forget it. Such frames are meant to be used flexibly before and during writing.

The writing process is not the same as drafting

As we have demonstrated, the writing process is complex. One element, revising, is often called drafting. However drafting does not mean 'write in rough – correct – copy up in neat'. In our experience there are still classrooms in which children are forced through a simplistic, incorrect view of the writing process during which pieces of writing simply have to be written twice, laboriously. We believe this strategy has been responsible for putting many children off writing, especially those for whom writing is particularly difficult. Mick Waters and Tony Martin (1999) describe a lesson focusing on the writing process and this unit is based on the ideas for that lesson.

What was in the teacher's head when planning this work?

Contexts and coherence

- I want to make links with the ways adults write to achieve a range of purposes.
- The resulting process display will be used in future units when the children are working on a piece of writing.

Motivation

- A key purpose is that children view the writing process positively through engaging with it in a way which is not laborious.
- The children will choose the subject of the writing, which is going to be a place. As experts, they will know the place they have chosen and their teacher will not, so they will be motivated to describe it.

- Because the process will be tightly structured, and the pieces of writing very short, all children will be able to produce writing of which they can be proud.

Content and process

- In this unit the content will be a process: the writing process.
- The children will work with writing partners, so the process of paired writing will also be explored.
- The children will be writing cinquains, five line poems with the pattern:

> Two syllables
> Four syllables
> Six syllables
> Eight syllables
> Two syllables.

Primary National Strategy Objectives

Clustering the learning objectives

The Primary National Strategy learning objectives are best viewed as end of year outcomes. So, for example, by the end of Year 4 the aim is for children to be able to 'develop and refine ideas in writing using planning and problem solving strategies'. Planned units will therefore revisit objectives throughout the year, approaching them in different ways, rather than a teacher ticking them off at the end of a unit as having been 'taught'.

Objectives for this unit have been selected from Years 4, 5 and 6 (to challenge the more able children). The most important in terms of the focus of the unit on the writing process are those from 'creating and shaping texts'. In addition there is a revisiting of a Year 1 objective because the cinquains have a structure based on syllables. Other objectives focus on the strategy used for teaching spelling. By planning in this way we can:

- ensure progression both in terms of a child's progress and the progression of knowledge and skills through a school
- differentiate between children of different abilities
- focus on assessment for learning, being clear where a child is coming from and where the child next needs to go.

Word structure and spelling

Year 4

- Use knowledge of phonics, morphology and etymology to spell new and unfamiliar words.

Year 5

- Group and classify words according to their spelling patterns and their meanings.

Year 6

- Use a range of appropriate strategies to edit, proofread and correct spelling in their own work, on paper and on screen.

Word recognition: decoding and encoding

Year 1

- Identify the constituent parts of two-syllable and three-syllable words to support the application of phonic knowledge and skills.

Creating and shaping texts

Year 4

- Develop and refine ideas in writing using planning and problem-solving strategies.

Year 5

- Reflect independently and critically on their own writing and edit and improve it.

Presentation

Year 4

- Use word processing packages to present written work.

Starting point

The Friday before the Monday

On Friday afternoon the children are asked about places they know well. A brief discussion considers their own houses or flats, their bedrooms, the street they live in, different local shops. They are told that on Monday some work will be started in which they will try to describe somewhere they know very well. When this writing is read the 'atmosphere' of the place will be evoked. There is discussion of how we experience places through our senses: what we see, hear, smell, touch. Sometimes even the cold or the wet can be tasted! The time of day, the seasons and the weather are very important; places change depending on them.

However, there is a challenge involved. There will be a strict limit on the length of these pieces of writing, and they will be very short. Over the weekend the children are asked to look around their own places and to try to think of words or phrases or similes to describe them. On Monday the writing will be a paired writing task (always a popular strategy) so they will need to work with a partner and decide on one place they both know. A teacher may well not know any of the places and so can be a real audience for the writing.

Spotlight: going through the process

This spotlight tracks the progress of the writing through a number of lessons. Each stage of the writing process below is teacher modelled with the whole class in shared sessions followed by the paired writers producing their own independent writing. The pairs are grouped into sixes, each group made up of three writing pairs, and for the guided sessions different groups of children are visited, to help them through the process, drawing attention to and applying the word level objectives.

In addition there are short, sharp sessions on the word level objectives, both of which are about the ways in which words can be changed. When children grapple with the challenge of having the correct number of syllables in each line, there will be direct links to these objectives: the ways words can be changed in particular ways and how words can be extended and compounded.

Each stage of the writing process is worked on a different sheet of paper so that the whole process is collected and can be reviewed. Examples are also used for a powerful process display:

WHERE DID OUR WRITING COME FROM?

| Pre-Writing | Writing | Revising | Editing | Achieving Purpose |

Pre-writing

A real choice has to be made. Should the lesson start with some cinquains in order to show the children what they are aiming at or will the process best be explored as a mystery journey? Either could be chosen, but the choice here is not to introduce cinquains. The process will be worked through together. So the shared work on Monday morning begins with pairs discussing options for the writing and making their choice. They are then introduced to the first part of the process by 'Pre-writing' being written on the whiteboard. There is teacher modelling of the process of thinking through the place, and some words and phrases based around the senses are written. Pairs are then given their own 'Pre-writing' sheets of paper and begin their own as an independent task (see Figure 12.1).

In addition to the shared text level work, this first session is also used as a quick revision of syllables. In terms of the learning objectives, this takes us back to Key Stage 1, where knowledge of syllables is a key element of phonological awareness. Words are called out and, for each word, the children write down a number (for the number of syllables) on their whiteboards and hold the answers up. Very quickly it is clear who is confident about syllables (most of the class) and who might require further revision.

Writing

Now the pre-writing words and ideas are used to create some sentences capturing the atmosphere of the place. The teaching in guided group sessions is all about the power of language to create atmosphere.

Revising

Because revising is so complex, in this unit the children are taken through a structured process and told how the writing will be revised. When, at the conclusion of the process, they are able to appreciate the exact ways in which their revision worked, they take this awareness to other writing tasks. So, the first aim (on the 'Revision' sheet) is to work the atmospheric sentences into just five lines of free verse. Finally, there is a syllable count for the final cinquains, with a direct application of the work on syllables.

The guided writing sessions are now about revision, especially the ways in which poets have to make every word count. The paring down of the writing is an excellent task in itself as it forces children to consider each and every word. Guided writing is about posing questions and being 'positively critical' rather than just encouraging. Is 'the' really necessary in that line? Why 'and' rather than just a comma between those two words? Is 'good' really a strong enough word? In terms of the syllable count, it is not just a matter of crossing out a word which does not 'fit' and finding a different word which is shorter or longer, but of seeing whether any of the words chosen can be modified.

Throughout this stage in the process, children are encouraged to read their writing aloud. As they are working in pairs they can read to each other and consider whether the emerging poems 'sound good'.

Editing

The final cinquains are now edited. Pairs take initial responsibility and then move into fours to help with this exercise. If the pairs are 'mixed ability' there is a good chance that errors will be picked up in a four. However, the final piece must be error free, especially if it is going to be displayed. Errors in the earlier parts of the process can be displayed – they illustrate how writers focus on content first and foremost. But final, published pieces are perfect. Therefore there is a final check before accepting them.

Achieving purpose

These delicate poems are now shared within the class. Their purpose is the purpose of all poetry – for readers to engage with both the ideas and the language – and there is teacher modelling of the reading of them and response to them. Children need to be shown how to read and respond to poetry in order that they can then do so themselves as independent readers.

Figures 12.1 and 12.2 show some Years 3 and 4 children working through the process. (Thanks to Karen Shankland of Broughton Primary School, Cumbria for the examples of children going through the process.)

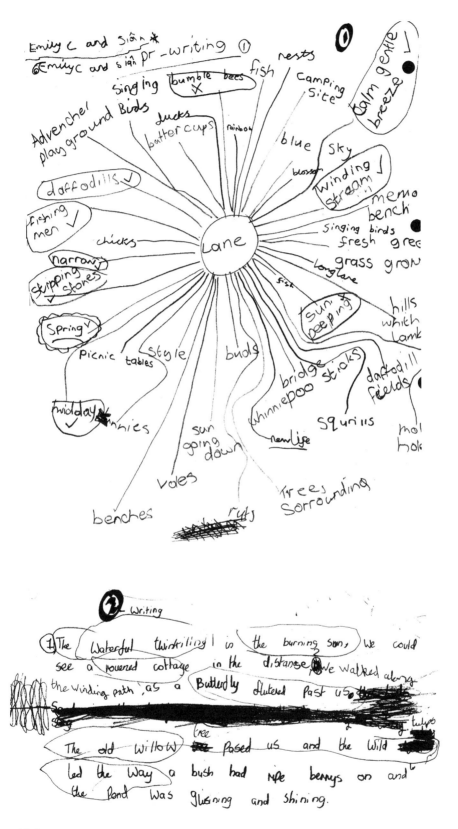

Figure 12.1

 revising

At midday
~~we~~ walked down the long!! narrow lane
a gentle breeze knocking the yellow carpet of daffodills.
~~we~~ ~~I jumped~~ across the winding stepping stones
~~I we~~ spotted the fisher men fishing

2| midday   ④
4| ~~Skipping~~ down lane
6| Carpet of daffodills
8| Jumping across the stepping stones

2| fishing

Midday
Skipping down lane
Carpet of daffodils
Jumping across the stepping stones
Spring time.

By Emily c & Sian

Figure 12.1 continued

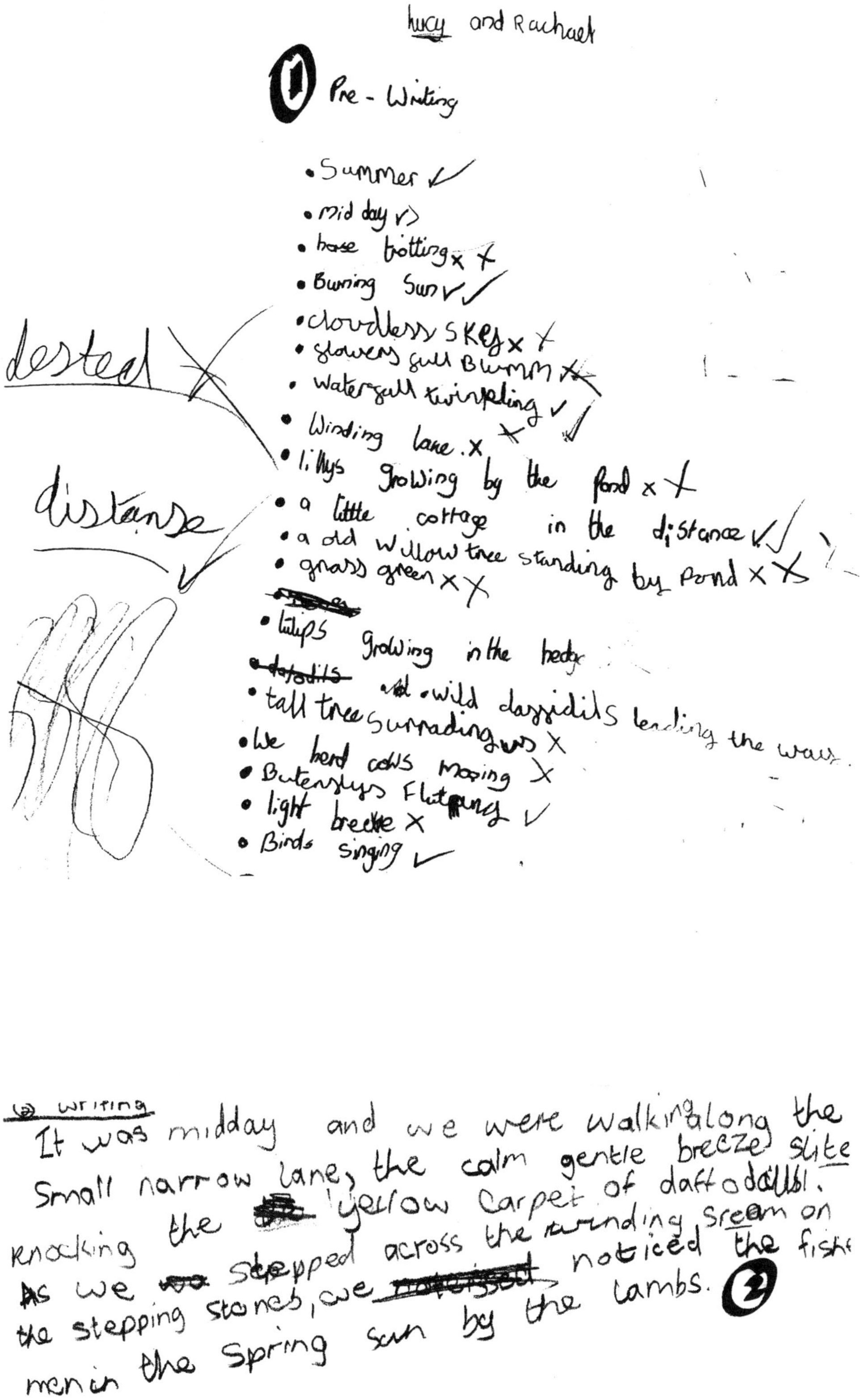

lucy and Rachael

1 Pre - Writing

- Summer ✓
- mid day ✓
- hose trotting ✗ ✗
- Burning Sun ✓✓
- cloudless skey ✗ ✗
- flowers full Blumm ✗✗

~~dested~~ ✗

- waterfall twinpling ✓
- Winding lane . ✗ ✗ ✗

~~distanse~~ ✓

- lillys growing by the pond ✗ ✗
- a little cottage in the distance ✓✓
- a old willow tree standing by Pond ✗ ✗
- grass green ✗ ✗
- ~~~~ tulips growing in the hedge
- ~~dodils~~ wild daffidils leading the way.
- tall tree surrading ws ✗
- We herd cows mooing ✗
- Buterflys flutpung ✓
- light breeze ✗
- Birds singing ✓

2 Writing

It was midday and we were walking along the small narrow lane, the calm gentle breeze slite knocking the ~~~~ yellow carpet of daffodalls. As we ~~wa~~ stepped across the winding sream on the stepping stones, we ~~noticed~~ noticed the fish men in the Spring sun by the lambs. **2**

Figure 12.2

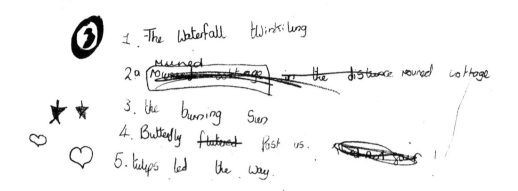

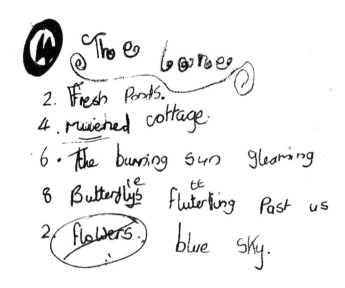

Fresh pond.
Ruined cottage.
The burning sun gleaming.
Butterflies fluttering past us.
Blue sky.

By Lucy Murray and Rachael Mason

Figure 12.2 continued

Spotlight: exploring the process

As well as sharing the final poems, it is important to remember that the key purpose of this work is to make a process, so often hidden within the lesson content, explicit to the children. A spotlight later in the week sees the pairs passing the process around – sharing the sheets, from pre-writing through to the final cinquains. The children are always fascinated to see how the poems began with lists of words and worked through the different stages.

Spotlight: word level work – a collaborative spelling test

The word level focus on extending and compounding words is applied as the children are writing their cinquains. Throughout the unit this spelling focus is explicitly taught and there will be a series of sessions involving the generating of words. Spelling investigations, rightly seen by the National Literacy Strategy as a key teaching and learning approach, are organised as children (sometimes alone, sometimes in pairs, sometimes in groups) explore the data and discuss the impact that prefixes and suffixes have on word meaning and use. Children are also learning words which are felt to be particularly useful, knowing they will be tested by a friend and that the result is important. There is an expectation that spelling will be learnt. Paired testing hands responsibility to children, and also enables spelling to be differentiated.

However, the strategies children are employing when they spell – what they know about spelling – are more important than the particular words they are learning at any one point in the year. A useful way of investigating their spelling strategies is to work with a group and listen in to the decisions the children are making as they try and spell. It's a test, but one with a difference. The group has just one large sheet of paper and chooses a scribe, who holds the pen. The teacher calls out a word and the group has to come up with a spelling of it. There is much discussion and often the word is written a number of different ways before there is agreement on what is thought to be the correct spelling. This is an excellent assessment opportunity: to observe, watch and listen to children's spelling behaviours. The ways different children spell and their thinking about spelling are revealed in the comments and suggestions they make.

Finally, the answers are given but the score is not recorded. The children know this is not really a test, but they are expected to learn the words by the end of the week. As above, there will be paired testing. There is a need for strategies in which we can move spelling away from just individuals learning (or not learning) alone, worrying (or not worrying) alone, towards discussion about spelling and how words work. Children should see words as a source of interest (even fascination) – attainment will follow.

Spotlight: learning from the display

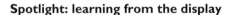

The display 'Where Did Our Writing Come From?' contains examples of this writing going through the whole process. It can be powerful to put up such displays in a public part of the school, so that all teachers in the school, as well as children, learn about the writing process. There are a couple of sessions with the class in front of the display, teaching from it and encouraging children to verbalise how they went about different parts of the process.

Spotlight: repeating the process – haiku, tanka, and on to mini-sagas

This unit now proceeds with children trying a different poetic form, again taking their writing through the whole process. The key here is for the writing to be short so that the process is not exhausting and each stage does not take too long. For the links between the elements to be explicit, children need to move quickly between them. Other types of poetry are well suited to such work, with both haiku and tanka being based on syllabic patterns. Haiku is three lines:

> Five syllables
> Seven syllables
> Five syllables

The tanka extends the haiku with two extra lines each of seven syllables.

This extension work can also be taken into the writing of narrative. A mini-saga is a story in exactly 50 words (49 or 51 are not acceptable) and this is a real challenge for any child!

Beyond the unit: children's writing going through the process

Visits to the classroom following this work will see the writing process being constantly referred to whenever children are undertaking a writing task.

- What sort of pre-writing (a 'thinking frame') might be useful for this piece of writing? A list? A mind-map? A sketch?
- Read your writing aloud to yourself or a partner at regular intervals as you are composing. What does it sound like? How might you revise it?
- Now that you are happy with the composition, is your writing correct? Could a partner help you edit it?

Explicit work on the writing process, such as that described in this chapter, enables children to view future writing tasks in the light of this process. The different stages are now seen to be equal in status and the teacher is able to refer to them, especially in guided writing sessions.

References

Maynard, T. (2002) *Boys and Literacy: Exploring the Issues*, London: RoutledgeFalmer.
Waters, M. and Martin, T. (1999) *Coordinating English at Key Stage 2*, London: Falmer.

13 Writing is not speech written down

Spoken language and written language: a language based unit

Most of the Key Stage 1 and 2 units in this book are text based in the sense that the starting point is a text type. Children's writing is developed from their text and sentence level work on these texts; they 'read like writers' in order that they can 'write like readers'. In this chapter we examine one of the most important aspects of learning to write: the differences between speech and writing. This is so important that we believe it should form the basis of a unit in which language itself is the focus. During this unit, children engage with some of the most fascinating elements of the English language and explicitly consider the implications for their own writing. They analyse their own informal and formal speech, comparing it to writing. They consider accent and dialect and the need to write in Standard English. They also focus on a key issue in terms of their development as writers: the differences between spoken and written language.

The fact that 'writing is not speech written down' is learnt:

- implicitly by many children (younger children who are read to and older children who are experienced readers) who take the lessons from their reading into their writing
- from shared reading – a powerful teaching strategy in which teachers model the rhythms and 'tunes' of written language.

Now, in this unit, children explicitly consider the characteristics of speech and writing.

Exploring speech and writing

The next time you turn on the radio consider how quickly you work out whether the voice you hear is speaking or reading aloud. We guess you will work this out very quickly, but how will you know? Consider the following extracts. What sort of speech or writing are they?

> It's not obvious, is it?
> Well, I . . . er . . . I think . . . I think it's to do with the birthday.
> Yeah. The birthday.
> Oh, right, well in that case.
> But he didn't mean it.

Well, John, I'm here in the very street in which it took place and I have to tell you it's got a really, um, sad feel to it. And with me is . . .

Some of Britain's most beautiful moths, larger and more spectacularly coloured than many butterflies, are tumbling in numbers, sparking fears that the nation's moth population is in serious decline.

Captain Everard Gault wounded the boy in the right shoulder on the night of June the twenty first, nineteen twenty one. Aiming above the trespassers' heads in the darkness, he fired a single shot from an upstairs window and then watched the three figures scuttling off, the wounded one assisted by his companions.

We guess you have worked out very quickly that the first two are examples of speech. The first is 'informal conversation', in this case between a teacher (who poses the initial question and then adds the fourth utterance) and two 9-year-old children. In fact the act of transcribing such a conversation makes it appear much neater than it was in reality – the voices were cutting in on each other as they do whenever a group engages in discussion. This is informal speech, with its lack of complete sentences (contrary to popular belief, we do not often speak in complete sentences), its use of words such as 'well' and 'right' to indicate the start of speaking, and its lack of clarity to an outsider because there is no need to be clear except to the members of the group.

The second one we could call formal speech (not a written down speech, which is a form of writing), spoken either off the cuff or on the basis of a few notes. This is the sort of speech you use when you are explaining something to your class. In this case it is a radio reporter. Notice again the 'well' at the start, the pause, the gap filler ('um') to buy some time for the thinking to turn into speech and the 'And' to begin the second sentence. While formal speech is closer to writing than informal speech, we can tell it is not writing. The reporter would not have written it as he spoke it.

The remaining examples are writing. As an experienced reader, you will be able to work out the different text types they represent: the third is the beginning of a newspaper report, and the fourth is the opening of a novel, *The Story of Lucy Gault* by William Trevor (2003). It is, however, much more difficult to analyse each of them in terms of their characteristics. Exactly how are they working at text level (structure and organisation), sentence level (sentence construction) and word level (vocabulary)? As we teach the different text types to children, we draw attention to such characteristics so that children can write such texts for themselves. For the purpose of this unit, though, we want to be able to examine speech and writing in more general terms. What can we say about them? Have a look at Table 13.1.

Writing has to be more explicit than speech: a sense of 'audience'

If we consider the differences between speech and writing, one key idea emerges: writers have to be more explicit and detailed than speakers. Because the speaker has the listener present, she can constantly adjust her speech. She knows if she is being understood and the context for the conversation is shared, at the time. Writers on the other hand have to imagine their target reader (e.g. the bank manager) or readers (e.g. 12-year-old boys) and construct and express their writing in such a way that they feel will be understood and

Table 13.1

Speakers	Writers
Generally do not speak in sentences.	Generally write in sentences.
Usually have the listener(s) present (though may be a long way away at the end of a phone).	Usually write for a reader who is not physically present.
Can use volume and intonation to make meaning clear.	To indicate how the writing should be read can use punctuation (e.g. exclamation marks) or can underline or use capital letters. But reliant to a great extent just on the words.
Can use non-verbal communication (eye contact, gesture) to make meaning clear (though not on the phone).	Cannot use non-verbal communication.
Can check that their meaning is clear (and that listeners are paying attention!) with expressions such as 'OK?'	Cannot check that the reader understands (though can use expressions such as 'it should now be clear' in the hope that the reader understands!).
Can be asked questions by listeners.	Usually have no such contact with readers.
Use gap fillers, to give themselves time as they turn thinking into speech 'off the cuff' ('um', 'er', 'you know').	Have more time to consider the choice of words.
Indicate the start of speaking with expressions such as 'well'.	Indicate the start in different ways depending on the text ('*Earthquakes*', 'Once upon a time', 'Dear sir').
May use non-standard dialect.	Generally write in Standard English.
Have accents (which may affect the listener's attitude to them and what they say).	Do not write with an accent.

appreciated. This 'sense of audience' is of vital importance for teachers trying to develop children as writers. Is a child consciously thinking about the needs of a real or potential reader when they write, or are they simply writing something which makes sense in their own minds?

Consider just two text types:

- **Narrative**: the writer will no doubt have some sort of picture of the setting and characters in his/her mind. Now they have to turn these pictures into words for the benefit of the reader.
- **Instructions**: the writer usually knows the subject matter well. They now need to stand back from their own knowledge, imagine someone who does not have the knowledge, and write with them in mind. Are they writing for totally new learners ('Recipes for Beginners') or readers who already know something about the subject ('Advanced Bread Making')?

The same sorts of considerations can be explored for other text types.

(Of course, if the reader is always the teacher, children soon learn how to focus on those elements they think will please the teacher. This is not to say that children should never write for their teacher, just that providing a range of real or imagined audiences for writing is vitally important.)

Skills and fascinations

We believe that language study is fascinating in its own right, whether it be word level or sentence level. Our aim is to share this fascination with the children we teach. If we view spelling, vocabulary, sentence construction and punctuation simply as skills which have to be learnt, then children are unlikely to engage with them deeply. If it is true that in life we get better at something in which we are interested, then attainment is more likely to rise if children see word and sentence level work as interesting for their own sake.

Punctuation

This unit also allows us to focus on punctuation from a particular viewpoint – its purpose being to aid the reader. Many children regard punctuation as something they have to do as writers for its own sake. They think writers punctuate because that is what learning to write is about. However, in fact, writers use punctuation in order to try and ensure that the reader reads the meaning they are intending.

A more general point about punctuation follows from viewing it from the reader's rather than the writer's viewpoint. This ought to become a general way of approaching it throughout the primary years. When asking a child to punctuate an unpunctuated passage, there is a real difference between:

* punctuate this correctly

  and

* punctuate this in order to make it easier for a reader to read.

Punctuation is part of the developing sense of audience in children as writers – the ways in which they realise that they are writing for a reader and have to help the reader read the writing.

Standard English, dialect and accent

This unit is about creating a climate of respect for and interest in the different ways people talk. We would hope that just such an ethos has been developed throughout the school and, indeed, it is a whole school issue. One example will be used to illustrate what we mean:

'She were a right canny lass.'

Children often include non-standard, dialect words and sentence structures in their writing. Here we have both non-standard vocabulary: 'right' and 'canny' (how do you view 'lass'?), and non-standard grammar 'She were'. How do we react to such writing? The danger is that we simply correct it, giving the message to the child that it is wrong. The child then goes home and hears grandma using exactly the same vocabulary and subject/verb in her speech. So, the teacher is saying that grandma cannot speak properly?

Immediately a gulf can open up between the child and the school, which at the very least can make the child defensive about language. Anyone's language is highly charged with powerful notions of who they are, where they belong and how they view themselves. Language is closely tied to personal identity. The key condition for children to engage with the work described below is a confidence in the way they speak, and a belief that the teacher respects their language. Their language has to have 'status' in the classroom.

Examples of non-standard grammar in children's writing – children writing like they speak – can be approached on the basis that 'writing is not speech written down'. By correcting the writing we are not criticising the speech.

In general we believe 'appropriateness' is a better way of approaching language than 'correctness'. Children quickly appreciate (as do adults) that certain situations demand more formal language, while at other times informality is fine.

What was in the teacher's head when planning this work?

Contexts and coherence

- This unit is highly contextualised in the everyday language of the children.

Motivation

- A major aim is for children to be fascinated by this study of language.
- Children will be reflecting on something they do every day: speaking and listening.
- The unit will give status to children's accents and dialect.

Content and process

- The content will be the children's own language.
- Through their understanding that 'writing is not speech written down', children will be able to recognise the need to use Standard English when they write.

Primary National Strategy Objectives

Clustering the learning objectives

The Primary National Strategy learning objectives are best viewed as end of year outcomes. So, for example, by the end of Year 5 the aim is for children to be able to 'identify some aspects of talk that vary between formal and informal occasions'. By the end of Year 6 the expectation is that children can 'select words and language drawing on their knowledge of . . . formal and informal writing'. This distinction between formal and informal uses of both speech and writing lies at the heart of this unit. Planned units will therefore revisit objectives throughout the year, approaching them in different ways, rather than a teacher ticking them off at the end of a unit as having been 'taught'.

Objectives for this unit have been selected from Year 4 (for children working below age-related expectations) and Years 5 and 6 (to challenge the more able children). By planning in this way we can:

* ensure progression both in terms of a child's progress and the progression of knowledge and skills through a school
* differentiate between children of different abilities
* focus on assessment for learning, being clear where a child is coming from and where the child next needs to go.

Speaking

Year 5

* Use and explore . . . different ways words are used, including formal and informal contexts.

Listening and responding

Year 5

* Identify some aspects of talk that vary between formal and informal occasions.

Year 4

* Identify how talk varies with . . . familiarity . . . purpose.

Year 6

* Listen for language variation in formal and informal contexts.

Creating and shaping texts

Year 6

* Select words and language, drawing on their knowledge of literary features and formal and informal writing.

Sentence structure and punctuation

Year 5

* Adapt sentence construction to different text types, purposes and readers.

Starting points

The week before

During the week before this unit begins, a homework task is set. Children have to think about and try to collect any words and expressions they think are connected with the ways people speak in their area. They could ask parents or grandparents. Other adults in school are often a real mine of knowledge. Some examples might be provided so they know what is meant:

> Look at they children
> They done it very nice
> I didn't do nothing
> Aye lad
>
> She's a right canny lass
> We was going home
> I'm after eating my tea, amn't I?
> You'm alright

Monday morning

The first lesson begins with a sharing of what the children have brought. As some examples are offered they spark off others which suddenly spring to mind. There is debate about how to represent some of them in writing on the flipchart.

The terms 'accent' and 'dialect' are introduced and discussed:

- **Accent:** the sounds our voices make.
- **Dialect:** the vocabulary and grammar.

The two are closely bound up in the sense that people with particular accents will live in or be from areas where particular dialect expressions are used.

Different accents can be discussed – some children will have picked them up from people they know or from television. Do they have an accent? Is it the same as their parents'? Their grandparents'? Why might there be differences? The dialect expressions are spoken with the strongest accents the children can muster.

This just gives a flavour of what might be included in the first session. Its overarching aim is to generate excitement and interest in language use. Its main criterion for success is how far it achieves this. The flipchart is left up for the duration of the unit, with children adding new expressions as they come across them.

Spotlight: Standard English

In a future session the concept of Standard English and non-standard dialect is explored. Some history helps with this, so the children have explained to them the origins of Standard English.

If we go back to the year 1500, there were five main speech areas: Northern, West Midlands, East Midlands, Southern and Kentish. And they really did speak differently! An anonymous quotation from that time states: 'I translated it for northern people who can read no other English.'

Where, then, did Standard English originate from? It was all to do with power and influence! The 'East Midlands Triangle' was based on:

Oxford   Cambridge

London

This area was the centre of power (the court and government), trade and learning. It shared the same kind of English, and this became the basis for Standard English. If the court had resided in Cumbria, say in Whitehaven, and the major universities had been established in Workington and Maryport, then Standard English would sound very different today (those who know the west coast of Cumbria will know what we mean!). Standard English is simply a dialect which attained high status.

Within this teaching, mention is made of the different influences on English throughout history. How wonderful for children as far apart as Newcastle in the east and the coast of Cumbria in the west, to realise that their local dialects have much in common from the Vikings. In addition, people able to speak Geordie can converse with Norwegian sailors on the ferries.

Two pieces of writing are used with the class to reflect on the idea of language change at this point. The first was written by Caxton in the fifteenth century:

> In so moche that in my dayes happened that certayne marchauntes were in a shippe in tamyse, for to have sayled over the see into zelande, and for lacke of wynde, thei taryed ate forlond, and wente to lande for to refreshe them. And one of theym named Sheffelde, a mercer, cam in-to an hows and axed for mete; and specially he axyd after eggys. And the goode wife answered, that she coude speke no frenshe. And the merchaunt was angry, for he also coude speke no frenshe, and wolde have hadde egges, and she understode hym not.

The second is the Chinese character for 'Woman' (see Figure 13.1). The link between language change and social change (not to mention power) is brilliantly illustrated here and accessible to children.

Figure 13.1

Primary children are not taught the detail of language change, just the 'big idea' that it has changed (dramatically) over the centuries and will continue to do so. The language they themselves use is dynamic and living and ever changing.

Now lots of examples are worked on both in whole class sessions and as independent tasks. For instance:

- The dialect examples collected by the children are 'translated' into Standard English.
- A news broadcast is written as a shared writing exercise and then translated into dialect.
- Raps are translated into Standard English.

When children have grasped the idea (and the vast majority seem to do so very quickly) it is fascinating how they are able to grapple successfully with the sort of task indicated above. Perhaps this is due to their hearing so much Standard English on television. Some years ago a class of Year 6 children in Carlisle, north Cumbria were asked to compose news broadcasts which they taped. Some had to be in Standard English (as they would expect to hear on television) and some in their local dialect. With a minimum of teaching they were able to do this, and the parts where they were not correct were focuses for teaching. The above work is a good opportunity for assessing exactly what different children know about Standard and non-standard English.

Correct or appropriate?

Such work can also lead to consideration of whether there is such a thing as 'correct speech'. We would argue that a stress on correct speech is likely to make the above work extremely difficult. It undermines the ethos we argued for above, an ethos within which children feel the way they speak has status and is welcome in school. As we argued above, a far more useful idea is to discuss 'appropriateness' in terms of when we might be expected to use Standard English and when it might be appropriate to use dialect. This includes discussion of different situations, the people we are speaking to and the degree of formality. Children appreciate that if someone was to read the news in broad dialect, only a small percentage of the population would be able to understand it. 'Standard' means just that – standardised so everyone can understand. It can be spoken in any accent.

Spotlight: speech and writing – an in-service session with teachers

We begin with an in-service session run on many occasions for teachers. This session is described here because the examples of speech and writing generated by teachers demonstrate that we all use language in these ways, not just children. It reinforces the fact that speech and writing really do have their own characteristics.

First, the teachers consider the differences between speech and writing contained in Table 13.1. This always leads to a great deal of discussion, not least about accent and dialect. The session then moves on with the teachers responding to a Peanuts cartoon. The cartoon itself is not important – any subject known to the teachers could be used – but it is used to collect examples of three different types of response:

- **Informal speech:** a group discussion. Some teachers are taped discussing the cartoon 'informally' in groups.
- **Formal speech:** a talk. Some individual teachers are taped giving a talk about the cartoon 'off the cuff'.
- **Formal writing:** some teachers write about the issues raised by the cartoon.

Written transcripts are made of extracts from the informal and formal speech. This means that the characteristics of these different types of language use can be examined and discussed. The characteristics are recorded on a proforma, as shown in the box.

INFORMAL SPEECH	FORMAL SPEECH	FORMAL WRITING

The Peanuts cartoon is about a young girl sitting a test in a classroom. We do not know what the test is about. Her thoughts are shown in think bubbles: *'These tests are going to drive me crazy . . .'*. She is concerned about whether she should express her own views or those she thinks the teacher expects: *'Do you want us to write what we think, or what we think you want us to write?'* Finally after much deliberation she writes: 'George Washington was a good man.'

The teachers were simply asked to respond to the cartoon. In fact all of them focused on the implications of it for teaching.

Informal speech

Here is an extract from one of the group discussions.

Heather I feel that it, it . . . has to be something that has to be trained into a child – it's something that takes over a number of lessons.

Jude It's it's part of the ethos isn't it?

Heather Yes em

Voices Yes

Jude Cause I can remember actually doing this with reception – getting again – just doing simple predictions – and they – none of them wanted to be right – or none of them wanted to be wrong – so they wouldn't offer an idea that was their own.

Voices Yes

Jack What would you do then if a child didn't express an opinion – had no bias on it one way or another?

Heather Maybe if you did it in group work

Voices Paired – paired – yes

Michelle They'd feel less intimidated

Formal speech

Here is an extract from one teacher giving a talk about the cartoon. She has discussed what she might say with some colleagues and is now on her own, talking into a tape recorder.

> Er right erm what we decided was to try and help children to express and develop their own opinions – we were concentrating on perhaps – erm – a Year 2 class and we were thinking that – erm – you could start with maybe like – erm – carpet time sessions to introduce a topic – it could be something as simple as – erm – school uniforms – favourite colours – whatever – and to get the children to work in small groups and to talk about how they felt about a certain thing . . .

Formal writing

Here is an extract from a piece of writing by a teacher in response to the cartoon.

> This cartoon looks at how children interpret questions and how they often strive to find what is in the teacher's head, rather than expressing their own opinions. We felt that children needed to be trained how to express their own opinions throughout their time in school, so that they grew in confidence in speaking out and forming independent views. This might begin in Reception with simple views on what they liked and disliked, and be developed throughout the school.

Using Table 13.1, the teachers list, and discuss the features of the different types of language use.

In the classroom

The same sort of session can be run in the classroom. Table 13.1 is shared with the children so that they are actively involved in considering the differences between speech and writing in the table. As with adults this is always a lively session and provokes lots of thinking – it might be the first time they have considered these characteristics and linked them to their own speech and writing.

A focus for the talking and writing is then chosen: not the Peanuts cartoon this time, but it could be almost anything: a photograph, a character in a story they all know, a sport. The only criterion is that all the children know something about it. The class is divided as follows:

- Some of the children in groups of four having a taped discussion.
- Individual children speaking 'off the cuff' on tape about the focus.
- Pairs of children writing about the focus.

The aim is to compare these different forms of language use in a series of whole class sessions. Having been involved in producing the examples, either in a group or as a 'formal talker' or writer, all children then help the teacher in the production of written transcripts of the speech. Trying to punctuate speech so that the transcript can be read as it sounded is a lovely exercise, and enables the purpose of punctuation to be raised and clarified.

The proforma used by the teachers (p. 227) is now used with the children in conjunction with the list of differences between spoken and written language to consider their own examples of the three different types of language use.

This exercise is extremely powerful at drawing children's attention to the issues described in this chapter, especially:

- the need for them to be more explicit in writing than they need to be in speech
- the need to write in Standard English, while dialect is quite appropriate in many social situations.

Both of these vitally important aspects of writing can be referred to from now on in both shared and guided sessions.

Spotlight: spoken and written vocabulary

In a word level session, a word is chosen, say, *upset*. The children are in mixed ability pairs and each pair has to think of synonyms. These are collected on the flipchart together with teacher examples to extend the vocabulary of all children. Now five are chosen to show shades of meaning – a move from the 'most upset word' to the least. Each word is written on a sheet of paper and held up by children standing in a line in front of the class. There is discussion and agreement is reached about whether the order is correct.

The focus now shifts to words we use in everyday speech and those we would only expect to come across when we read or use when we write. The former will be known to most children while the latter list will contain new vocabulary for many.

For independent work a challenge is set. This challenge is in two parts. First, mixed ability groups of children are each given a word, for example one group has *angry*, another *sad*, another *happy*. Each group has a scribe who lists words the children contribute. Are they all generally used in speech? Are some 'literary' words? To extend the lists, groups consult a thesaurus – can they add words to what they already have? Do they know the shades of meaning of these words? Dictionaries are consulted for definitions. Second, groups then present their five words to show the shades of meaning from most to least.

This work begins during the unit and develops throughout it – word level work directly linked to the language focus.

Beyond the unit: talking about writing – a poster

One of the key ideas in this book is that of children being able to stand back from something they do (read . . . write . . . speak . . . listen) and reflect on how they do it. In terms of writing, this means children thinking about what they do as well as doing it. Such 'metalinguistic awareness' enables them to consider their own writing as well as the writing produced by other children. From this unit a poster is developed with the class:

WHEN WE TALK ABOUT WRITING WE COULD TALK ABOUT:

➤ The purpose of the writing
➤ The structure of the writing
➤ The sentences
➤ The grammar: speech or writing?
➤ The vocabulary: speech or writing?
➤ The spelling
➤ The handwriting

This poster is used by children as a reference point for discussions with a 'response partner' as well as when considering their own writing. At the end of the unit we can imagine a child reflecting positively on what she has learnt: 'Ee miss that were reet good!'

Reference

Trevor, W. (2003) *The Story of Lucy Gault*, London: Penguin.

14 Whatever happened to Lucy Gray?

Classic poetry

Year 5

On not beginning with the text . . .

One of the problems all teachers face when set ways of working are developed (such as a literacy hour divided into timed sections) is that of the work becoming 'ritualised' in the classroom. If each literacy hour follows exactly the same format, and I'm a child in my eight hundred and forty third, the danger is that I might stop really engaging with the process and just go with the flow (or demonstrate that I've had enough by shuffling on my backside to the edge of the carpet – 'Not another big book!'). The challenge we all face as teachers is wrapped up in the word 'variation'- how can varied experiences and ways of working be provided so that children are kept on their metaphorical toes? Everyone likes novelty and tends to take notice when something is different.

Variation also relates to learning styles and the preferred ways in which different learners access learning and might demonstrate what they have learnt. Visual, kinaesthetic, auditory, interpersonal and intrapersonal learning can be the basis for planning for variation in our teaching of a text and can also be offered to children in terms of different ways they might produce work based on the text.

In this chapter we offer an approach to poetry which does not begin with a shared reading of a poem. The initial text is actually a series of pictures with no writing. The pictures tell the story of Wordsworth's ballad 'Lucy Gray' (1800) and are designed to provoke speculation and creative thinking. This visual beginning then leads to a teaching sequence of short activities involving individual thinking (intrapersonal), much speaking and listening in different pairings and groupings (interpersonal) as well as sorting with cards (kinaesthetic). 'Lucy Gray' is not read until a great deal of work has been completed. But this work enables the children to access a classic poem.

The children are not read the poem in advance but they are told in advance that the next literacy unit will be about poetry and they are going to be investigating something mysterious. But now, on Friday, they will have to wait until Monday to find out what this mysterious happening is all about.

By now you may be wondering about the ballad of Lucy Gray, wanting to read it for yourself (see Martin 2004). This chapter is structured so that you can experience the work leading up to the reading of the whole ballad, thereby appreciating the way it works for children.

What was in the teacher's head when planning this work?

Contexts and coherence

- Lucy Gray is a powerful narrative with echoes of modern day cases of children who 'disappear', so connections can be made with the children's awareness of current or recent news stories.
- Having investigated and worked on Lucy Gray, the children will be well prepared to tackle other ballads.

Motivation

- Children are fascinated by mysteries and will engage with trying to solve the mystery of Lucy Gray.
- Beginning with a visual representation of the narrative will appeal to all children, but especially the visual learners.

Content and process

- Through writing a modern version the children will engage with the way Wordsworth wrote the ballad, especially in terms of the setting and his use of vocabulary and sentence structures.
- In school we explicitly emphasise our fascination with language and words. The children are therefore used to investigating word meanings and how language changes over time. They will enjoy discussing the old fashioned language in ballads.
- This unit can be used to embed ideas about rhythm and rhyme.

Primary National Strategy Objectives

Clustering the learning objectives

The Primary National Strategy learning objectives are best viewed as end of year outcomes. So, for example, by the end of Year 5 the aim is for children to be able to 'reflect on how working in role helps to explore complex issues'. Planned units will therefore revisit objectives throughout the year, approaching them in different ways, rather than a teacher ticking them off at the end of a unit as having been 'taught'.

Objectives for this unit have been selected from Year 4 (for children working below age-related expectations) and Years 5 and 6 (to challenge the more able children). By planning in this way we can:

- ensure progression both in terms of a child's progress and the progression of knowledge and skills through a school
- differentiate between children of different abilities
- focus on assessment for learning, being clear where a child is coming from and where the child next needs to go.

Speaking

Year 4

• Tell stories effectively and convey detailed information coherently for listeners.

Drama

Year 5

• Reflect on how working in role helps to explore complex issues.

Engaging with and responding to texts

Year 4

• Interrogate texts to deepen and clarify understanding and response.

Understanding and interpreting texts

Year 5

• Infer writers' perspectives from what is written and from what is implied.

Year 6

• Understand underlying themes, causes and points of view.

Creating and shaping texts

Year 5

• Experiment with different narrative forms and styles to write their own stories.

Year 6

• Select words and language drawing on their knowledge of literary features.

Starting point

Flexing the hour

The starting point for this unit is the need to flex considerably the structure of the literacy hour. So, on Monday for the whole hour we are whole class teaching, moving through a set of activities in which the children work in different ways engaging with and responding to a powerful story. There is no set half-hour whole class teaching or twenty minutes' independent work. In addition, working through these activities with different classes always produces variation in how long they last. Exactly how much will be achieved on Monday is difficult to forecast. But in our experience the children are always engaged and that surely is the most important criterion.

We begin with a set of pictures which tell the story of Lucy Gray (Figure 14.1). These are the work of Nancy Martin while she was education officer at the Wordsworth Trust, based at Dove Cottage, where Wordsworth lived when he first moved to the Lake District. The pictures are designed to encourage speculation.

What story do they tell?

Before reading on, look at the pictures on pages 235–6 and decide what you think is the story of Lucy Gray.

The sheet of pictures is distributed, one between two children. The suggested teaching sequence is as follows.

1. Individual, silent thinking for a minute or so. 'What story do you think is being told by these pictures?'

As we state in Chapter 2, during whole class teaching there should be regular opportunities for children to think something through on their own. This really does mean giving them time to think, rather than expecting instant hands up all the time. Some questions do require instant answers, e.g. 'we have been working on words beginning with **bi**, hands up if you can write me one of those words.' In such a spelling lesson the pace may well be fast. But for many questions children need to know that they are expected to think first – and this reflection requires time. Pace does not always equate with fast – we do hope poetry is not being taught quickly.

2. Now the children work with their partners. 'Decide who is going first. Tell your partner what you think happens in the story. If you are the listener, listen for differences to your own version. You will then explain these differences (if there are any) back to your partner.'

Developing listening skills means giving the listener something specific on which to focus. If each child simply tells the story, then the listener is likely not to be listening, but waiting to begin her own version. We can all recall times when, in the pub perhaps, someone is telling a story about their recent holiday and we can't wait for them to finish so that we can jump in with our own favourite story! So we don't really listen. In this activity the listener really does have to listen for something specific and is only meant to respond on the basis of it. We know full well there will be lots of retelling in some pairings – but it is always enthusiastically done.

3. Whole class sharing. Some children volunteer to explain their versions of the story

This establishes we are not saying 'anything goes' – the pictures provide the basis. However, they have been produced to encourage lots of speculation. We have heard children whose versions are very close to Wordsworth's, with Lucy Gray being the girl and the man her father who sends her on an errand and she gets lost. Others suggest she has been sent to this man by her parents for some reason and gets lost on the way home. The final two pictures raise lots of ideas, though mostly they are seen as showing Lucy's

Figure 14.1

ghost, as she has drowned in the stream. One child did announce the story was about Jesus and Moses – which was difficult to respond to!

4. The children in their pairs are asked to designate themselves A or B. The As move on to form a new pairing. Now the focus moves from talking about the story to storytelling, as the pairs have to generate a telling of the story which will capture the interest of the class. They have time to sort this out and practise, before moving into fours to tell their story to another pair. A couple of pairs then volunteer to tell their version of Lucy Gray to the whole class.

The shift from talking about a story to telling the story is very powerful. The 'Speaking' learning objectives for this unit draw attention to its importance. It can also be used before children are going to write a story. One element of 'talk for writing' is the use of talk as a rehearsal for writing. Talking about what might be written and then beginning to tell it, can help the writer sort out both ideas and language. At the very least it means the child writer is less likely to view the blank page as a problem: how to start is often the hardest part.

Creating new pairings within one whole class session is an important teaching strategy. Over a relatively short number of lessons, each child can work with just about every other child in the class. We are sure you will be able to list the advantages, ranging from the contribution to speaking and listening, through social skills, classroom ethos and behaviour. In one Year 3 class, where the teacher worked in this way, there was an autistic boy and a girl with Down syndrome, each with an adult helper. The other children knew that they would regularly be paired up with one or other of these children. Observing the ways in which they dealt with this situation was a privilege, illustrating how 'schooling' is about so much more than targets, attainment and league tables.

5. By now the children really have done a lot of thinking and sharing about this story, so the time has come to introduce some written text. Not all of the ballad (not yet!), but a verse for each of the eight pictures (see Figure 14.2). The task for the pairs is to match the verse with the appropriate picture (Figure 14.3). They then check this out with another pair.

A hands on, kinaesthetic activity. Some pairs may require some help but in our experience not much. The key here is mixed ability pairs with at least one child in each pair able to read the verses aloud. Because of the previous activities, Wordsworth's language has become far more accessible than if it had just been read aloud to them. 'Accessibility' is one of the major challenges of poetry, which by definition is 'concentrated language' and therefore often difficult for any of us to take in at a first reading.

6. Having agreed the order of verses (the last two cause the most discussion) they are read aloud – a 'shared reading' in which the voice of the text is modelled and there is discussion about the meaning of the text and the words in which it is composed.

Now the full ballad can be read aloud, with the verses already discussed shown in italics. This could be done through an overhead projection or an interactive whiteboard, but because of a key reading activity to come, we suggest it is actually given out, one per pair (Figure 14.4).

The poem is discussed and this may be the time to remove the pictures. The text is now the ballad written by Wordsworth. We have found children still eager to base their

'To-night will be a stormy night,

You to the Town must go,

And take a lantern, Child, to light

Your mother through the snow.'

Over rough and smooth she trips along,

And never looks behind;

And sings a solitary song

That whistles in the wind.

And now they homeward turned, and cried

'In heaven we all shall meet!'

When in the snow the Mother spied

The print of Lucy's feet.

No Mate, no comrade Lucy knew;

She dwelt on a wide Moor,

The sweetest Thing that ever grew

Beside a human door!

Yet some maintain that to this day

She is a living Child,

That you may see sweet Lucy Gray

Upon the lonesome Wild.

The storm came on before its time,

She wandered up and down,

And many a hill did Lucy climb

But never reached the Town.

The wretched Parents all that night

Went shouting far and wide;

But there was neither sound nor sight

To serve them for a guide.

They followed from the snowy bank

The footmarks, one by one,

Into the middle of the plank,

And further there were none.

Figure 14.2

thoughts on the pictures as if the evidence is contained within them. But the pictures are just one person's interpretation of the poem.

The aim is always discussion. Any teacher will have questions prepared but the aim is to use these questions as a springboard for discussion. This means listening to the answers and using them to probe further, clear misconceptions, encourage personal response. There is always the danger of us seeing the aim being to get through our questions – and children quickly pick up on the fact that this is the name of the game. So, no real thinking, just try and read what is in the teacher's mind and come up with something to please her.

Figure 14.3

The other issue is the difficulty of involving all children if the discussion is all based on 'teacher in charge discussing with the whole class'. Strategies already discussed, such as some silent thinking time followed by short paired talk, increase involvement and inclusion (in terms of whole class teaching the key inclusion issue is how to include all of the children in the lesson). At times the 'no hands up' edict can be used – when the paired talk time is up, different pairings are asked to contribute, with no hands up by anyone else.

In Lucy Gray, discussion will be about the mystery of what happened to her, examples of unfamiliar vocabulary (faggot band, blither, etc.) and the text level objective concerning figurative language.

7. The children now listen to one verse read aloud, with their focus being the teacher's voice – intonation, pace, changes in volume. The verse is read at least twice before each child reads it aloud to their partner, modelling their reading on the teacher's. What effect is created by this reading? Can anyone read it differently to create a different effect?

A key element of shared reading (see Chapter 2) is children hearing the text from their own mouths. How this is done develops from the early years of the whole class being encouraged to join in with the teacher's reading.

8. The children can now engage in some more creative thinking through group hot seating. In 4s they come up with questions they would like to ask Lucy: her life in 'the Wild'; her 'solitude'; the night she died; her continued existence as a spirit.

One of them volunteers to be Lucy and, when all are ready, the Lucys move to another group to be questioned.

Lucy Gray

Oft had I heard of Lucy Gray,
And when I crossed the Wild,
I chanced to see at break of day
The solitary Child.

No Mate, no comrade Lucy knew;
She dwelt on a wide Moor,
The sweetest Thing that ever grew
Beside a human door!

You yet may spy the Fawn at play,
The Hare upon the Green;
But the sweet face of Lucy Gray
Will never more be seen.

'To-night will be a stormy night,
You to the Town must go,
And take a lantern, Child, to light
Your mother through the snow.'

'That, Father! will I gladly do;
'Tis scarcely afternoon—
The Minster-clock has just struck two,
And yonder is the Moon.'

At this the Father raised his hook
And snapped a faggot-band;
He plied his work, and Lucy took
The lantern in her hand.

Not blither is the mountain roe,
With many a wanton stroke
Her feet disperse the powdery snow
That rises up like smoke.

The storm came on before its time,
She wandered up and down,
And many a hill did Lucy climb
But never reached the Town.

The wretched Parents all that night
Went shouting far and wide;
But there was neither sound nor sight
To serve them for a guide.

At day-break on a hill they stood
That overlooked the Moor;
And thence they saw the Bridge of Wood
A furlong from their door.

And now they homeward turned, and cried
'In heaven we all shall meet!'
When in the snow the Mother spied
The print of Lucy's feet.

Then downward from the steep hill's edge
They tracked the footmarks small;
And through the broken hawthorn-hedge,
And by the long stone-wall;

And then an open field they crossed,
The marks were still the same;
They tracked them on, nor ever lost,
And to the Bridge they came.

They followed from the snowy bank
The footmarks, one by one,
Into the middle of the plank,
And further there were none.

Yet some maintain that to this day
She is a living Child,
That you may see sweet Lucy Gray
Upon the lonesome Wild.

Over rough and smooth she trips along,
And never looks behind;
And sings a solitary song
That whistles in the wind.

Figure 14.4

Hot seating is one of the most powerful teaching techniques for engaging children with learning (see Chapter 2). In a hot seating exercise around such an open text as Lucy Gray, the children are almost forced to think inferentially both in terms of 'reading between the lines' and 'reading beyond the lines'.

This sequence of teaching has been described in full, as each element flows in to the next. Trying to achieve it all in one lesson really does mean building up momentum and excitement, and because the activities are so varied we have had no problems keeping the children involved and engaged. However, there is no reason why the sequence could not be spread over a number of lessons.

Spotlight: further discussion of the story

Later in the week children are continuing their discussion of Lucy Gray. As time passes, the poem and its mystery clarify in their minds (poems often need time for this process) as well as producing further questions. The focus is on the thinking. Through homework tasks, children are given an opportunity to think through such issues as:

- Should her father have sent Lucy out on her own to meet her mother?
- Are there any further thoughts about what happened to her?
- Wordsworth gave the poem a subtitle: 'Solitude'. Why do you think he did so?
- Could this have happened nowadays?

There is further paired, small group and whole class discussion.

Vocabulary

As an independent task, in pairs, children pick out the words they do not understand. In fact, there are never that many, and most occur in the first half of the poem. Some words are old fashioned, while others are still in general use nowadays but not known to some children. Beginning with all the unknown words is generally better than going straight to the old fashioned (archaic) language – for many children, words taken for granted by adults are not part of their vocabulary, so whether they are old or new is not obvious. These words are looked up in dictionaries and form the basis for much discussion.

From reading to writing

This task addresses the sentence level objective: to understand how writing can be adapted for different audiences and purposes, e.g. by changing vocabulary or sentence structures. The class is challenged to write its own ballad, based on Wordsworth's. First structure is established:

- A series of four line stanzas
- A rhyme scheme of ABAB
- First and third lines have eight syllables
- Second and fourth lines have six syllables

Children tap out the syllables all together and then in groups, establishing the patterns. The last word in each line is highlighted and the rhymes checked. What do they make of the half rhyme with which the poem finishes? (There is no right answer! What do you think? Does it work?) Children search for full rhymes with 'behind' – would any of them have been a better choice for Wordsworth? Can the last line be rewritten? It is wonderful for children to begin to realise the way poems have been crafted.

In this unit, we have decided to write a modern version of Lucy Gray, so there will have been discussion of the way the poem resonates with today's tragedies of missing children. There is no suggestion of abduction, just that Lucy has disappeared. Where will our modern Lucy live? In terms of structure, a rhyme scheme ABAB is really difficult, so a decision has been made to use the simpler ABCB, with only the second and fourth lines needing to rhyme.

'Teacher demonstration writing' is used to compose the first verse. The modern day Lucy lives on a housing estate on the outskirts of a city. Old fashioned expressions ('Oft had I heard') are modernised ('I'd often heard'), while others '(and when I crossed') can be left untouched.

What do you think of this as the first verse of a modern Lucy Gray?

Lucy Gray
or, Solitude

I'd often heard of Lucy Gray,
And when I crossed the park
I saw her standing by the swings,
Alone, and in the dark.

Now the children join in with the composition (scribed writing). The next two verses are not easy in terms of bringing them up to date, so the teacher is very much in control with her own suggestions:

She had no friends of her own age,
Though there were people all around,
The prettiest girl who ever lived
In city or in town.

You've seen the pictures on TV
This child – what does it mean?
Now the sweet face of Lucy Gray
Will never more be seen.

From this point (three verses into the ballad) Wordsworth's poem becomes fairly straightforward – the narrative of that evening drives the verses and children can come up with ideas. They are gripped by the drama unfolding in a way they realise is very relevant to them and their lives. The modern version brings home to them how a poem written over two hundred years ago can speak across the centuries and move us today.

Have a go at writing modern verses to match those in the original ballad.

Reading other ballads

Within a two or three week unit, other narrative poems will be introduced, and may include well known ones such as 'The Highwayman' (chosen for the Primary National

Strategy exemplar classic poetry unit) or 'The Lady of Shallot'. In this unit there will be some contrasting narratives: Michael Rosen's 'Eddie and the Gerbils' (from *Quick, Let's Get Out of Here*, 1985) and the traditional Scottish ballad 'The Twa Corbies'. The contrast could not be more pronounced.

'Eddie and the Gerbils' begins:

> Not long ago
> We went on holiday with some people
> Who've got gerbils.
> We haven't got any pets
> And Eddie (he was two years old)
> He thought they were
> WONDERFUL.
> He was always looking in their cage
> Going
> 'Hallo gerbils, hallo gerbils, hallo gerbils.'

The tone is conversational, easy for children to understand. Written in free verse, Michael Rosen's poem is one of a series written about his young son Eddie.

'The Twa Corbies' is hundreds of years old. Perhaps originally there were more details, explaining who the knight was and why he died. However, like many traditional ballads, which were passed on over the years through singing rather than through being written down, the details got lost. The narrative is pared down to its absolute essentials: mysterious, cold, dark and disturbing. Having heard it read aloud on a couple of occasions, groups of children are set the task of unlocking the mystery. What do the words mean? What story do they tell?

The Twa Corbies (ravens)

> As I was walking all alane
> I heard twa corbies making a mane:
> The tane unto the tither did say
> 'Whar sall we gang and dine the day?'
>
> 'In behint yon auld fail dyke
> I wot there lies a new-slain knight;
> And naebody kens that he lies there
> But his hawk, his hound and his lady fair.
>
> His hound is to the hunting gane,
> His hawk to fetch the wild-fowl hame,
> His lady's ta'en anither mate,
> So we may mak' our dinner sweet.
>
> Ye'll sit on his white hause-bane, *(neck bone)*
> And I'll pike out his bonny e'en:
> Wi' ae lock o' his gowden hair
> We'll theek our nest when it grows bare.

Many a one for him maks mane,
But nane sall ken whar he is gane:
O'er his white banes, when they are bare,
The wind sall blaw for evermair.'

Beyond the unit: teaching poetry

A visual approach

The approach to 'Lucy Gray' looks for a way into a poem and uses a visual approach. We may not be able to produce pictures of the quality used here, but it is not difficult to find illustrations of poems. In most poetry anthologies for children the poems are illustrated. Photocopying an illustration and using it as the starting point can be equally effective.

Another visual approach is to read the poem aloud to children with their eyes shut. They have to imagine a photograph or film of the poem. How do they visualise it?

A poem a week: just listening

If the aim is for children to become readers who love reading poetry, they need to be regularly immersed in it. Experiencing poetry only in the poetry units is scarcely going to achieve such an aim. One idea is for children to hear a poem every day, as a poem of the week. This poem (which can be chosen by either the teacher or a child) is read five times, once at the beginning of each day. There is no discussion until Friday. The children just sit, listen and then the school day begins. On Friday we can structure some brief discussion of the poem, which the children have now heard five times. However, the point is not to analyse the poems, simply to read them aloud and immerse the children in them.

Choral reading: active involvement

This is about immersing children in particular poems through involving them as part of a choral reading. The whole class takes part in this exercise with teacher coaching and modelling to ensure a powerful, dramatic reading. Some children have lines or phrases or words to say on their own (often a mix of all three scattered through the poem), others speak in pairs or small groups. At times perhaps half the class will speak together or even the whole class. Some children sit, others stand (on the floor? on tables?) so that the voices come from different parts of the room. Each child has their own copy of the poem which they annotate with their own parts. Everyone is involved. Through such an experience the power of poetry is felt by children, as they experience it from inside a poem.

Once children have grasped the potential of dramatic, choral readings, groups can be encouraged to produce their own with poems they enjoy. If, over the year, children build up their own individual, illustrated anthologies of favourites, these can form the basis for a group to choose one poem for a reading.

Reading poems in advance

This approach is underpinned by another key idea – the danger of surprising children with texts. One can imagine a worst case scenario in which 9-year-old Jennie arrives at school, in the rain, on Monday morning. Her mind is full of the weekend and she can't wait to share it with her friends. She has no idea what is going to happen in literacy. Suddenly she is on the carpet and the teacher is pointing at a poem. Before she has time to gather her thoughts it is being read and (like a great deal of poetry) it is not easy to follow. Then the questions start . . .

We know we have exaggerated in this example, but we do feel it illustrates a real issue in many literacy hours. How can we guard against it happening? The most obvious way is to read the class the poem on a number of occasions before they ever see it in shared reading. Perhaps at the end of Monday, Wednesday and Friday the previous week the poem is read aloud. No discussion. The children just listen. There are twenty seconds of silent thinking after the reading. By Friday we notice some of the children moving their lips quietly during different parts of the poem. They are beginning to remember it. Now they all know that on Monday they are going to see, read and discuss this poem, and that this will begin with them working with a talk partner. What is it about? Can you remember any words or phrases or longer bits?

Analysing poems

Poems can be the basis of wonderful discussions with children, where we focus on how they respond to the 'meaning'. However, in the 'Lucy Gray' unit, the writing of the modern ballad led to a consideration of how the poem was constructed. The analysis of poems in terms of their structure, vocabulary and use of poetic techniques such as simile, metaphor, alliteration, onomatopoeia can be fascinating but there surely needs to be a light touch in the primary classroom. We would not want young children to view poems as texts to be analysed.

- **Begin with the children's responses:** perhaps the best advice when considering analysis is to base it on the children's responses. If the poem made us laugh, feel sad, feel scared, how did the poet achieve this?
- **The key words:** one strategy that works well before any discussion of the poem (once the children have heard it on a number of occasions) is to get them to work in pairs underlining what they think are the key words. There should be a number limit imposed which will vary with the poem but which forces the children really to consider only the important words. Pairs can become fours to compare and/or envoys sent to hear about another group's words. The words must always be justified. These words always seem to lead into a discussion of the theme of the poem.

Analysing poems in these ways should be fun. If it becomes a sterile exercise the magic of poetry will be denied to children. While knowing the meaning of 'simile' might be a useful piece of general knowledge, we believe teaching poetry is aiming at much greater outcomes.

References

Martin, N. (compiler and illustrator) (2004) *The Golden Store: A Selection of Poetry by William Wordsworth*, Grasmere: Wordsworth Trust.

Rosen, M. (1985) *Quick, Let's Get Out of Here*, Harmondsworth: Puffin.

15 'We made the story!'

Making whole stories with underachieving, uninterested boys

Year 6

The ideas in this unit have been developed over several years of working with all sorts of children in all kinds of schools. They have been developed in response to the particular difficulties faced by those children whose achievements in reading and writing are behind those of their peers. For many of these children, the gap widens (relative underachievement increases) as they progress through Key Stage 2. A significant issue in many primary schools is how to support these children, many of them boys, before they give up the struggle and become disengaged from learning and disaffected at school. How then can we make writing lively and significant enough to avoid this happening?

There are some important challenges and questions about working with narrative that we address in this unit: many of these coincide with current national practices and issues about raising attainment in writing. Writing narrative is very complex. Teachers as well as children find narrative writing challenging. Writing stories well *is* a daunting task.

It is not surprising that children struggle at many different points in the process of putting together a narrative. Here are some of the difficulties they face – difficulties which are reflected in the type and quality of the stories they often write:

- Problems with getting and developing ideas for their writing. How do children use their limited life and sometimes reading experiences to get and develop their ideas? (These limited experiences often lead children to write stories based on cartoons and TV programmes they have watched. When this happens, the stories may 'read' like a long dialogue, because children have written down the story in the way it was experienced – as a dialogue between characters.)
- Problems manipulating the chosen content and storyline so that there is an effective narrative voice, controlling the pace and build up of events in the story.
- Making characters interesting and creating interactions between them which link to the purpose and direction of the story.
- Using styles of suitably 'writerly' language.
- Developing the knowledge, experience and skill to vary sentence structures.
- Understanding and knowing, then making vocabulary choices by using a sufficient variety of language orally before applying it in writing.

Critical questions for teachers must be:

- How can we make the shared experience of building and writing stories supportive, so that the complexity and challenge of story writing is taken seriously?
- What could some stepping stones leading through this process look like in practice?
- Can we do it in such a way that we create delight and success for children?
- Can we somehow retrieve and recreate that love of hearing and making stories, which children display naturally in the early years?
- Can we be flexible and innovative – within the structures and supports we provide – and build and develop these and other approaches?
- Can we develop our ways of teaching writing to support children in various ways as they think about and get their ideas for writing?
- Can we provide them with some useful structures to help shape and direct their stories?
- Can we bring the writing process alive so that children really begin to think about how to develop their own writing?

Many of our children who give up the struggle to achieve in writing lack the experiences of story which could support their development as writers. Lack of reading fluency has reduced their access to good stories. Current curriculum pressures in primary classrooms have often reduced the amount of time that teachers read stories aloud. So the very children who have difficulties accessing the type of children's literature which they need to acquire the structures and language patterns of narrative, have less access to story than they used to. This needs to be thought about carefully and addressed, if we take ideas about the connections between reading and writing seriously.

This unit of work will be more useful if it is part of a whole school approach to story making and writing. Children need many frequent, lively experiences of building up whole stories. There has been a tendency both for the reading and writing of stories to be fragmented. Interpretations of the first literacy framework of objectives emphasised coverage of objectives rather than the provision of coherent literacy contexts and experiences. The Primary Strategy Framework provides a structure in which teachers are more likely to plan for writing whole stories.

The unit presented here could be used in a slightly modified version in any year group. Attention does need to be paid though to the level of difficulty at which the shared writing is demonstrated. Some schools moderate their shared writing, which is useful because it gives teachers more confidence that they are teaching at a challenging enough level. It's useful anyway to see how other teachers write stories – it doesn't come particularly easily to many teachers, and moderating gives teachers lots of ideas.

Careful thought needs to be given to the types of thinking and planning frameworks we give children. If different frameworks are used in different year groups – which is generally beneficial, because children are being offered variety – this creates the danger of a lack of coherence. There are no right or wrong frameworks. Teachers though need to know which planning formats have been used in previous years. They need to be able to refer back to them and to know why each was used. Considerations, such as which learning styles are promoted by each format, seem important, as do issues about the types of creativity and thinking skills we are attempting to develop. Exploring the learning and teaching issues associated with these is absolutely essential if we wish to develop children's writing.

Narrative writing can be a very abstract activity, more or less wholly disconnected from children's real experience. When teachers despair of children's 'lack of imagination' while they are teaching story writing, they are possibly reflecting this very disconnection. So one of the areas that will be addressed in this story writing unit is how to create significant multisensory experiences in the classroom, experiences which help to bridge gaps for children. These are gaps between concrete and abstract thinking; gaps between understanding about the parts and whole of a story; and gaps between writing stories for no particular reason, with no particular reader in mind and being sure of who a story is for and the effects you therefore intend to achieve.

There is a strong connection in this unit to the Foundation Stage chapter entitled 'Tell me a story' (Chapter 3) and to some of the ideas in the Key Stage 1 chapter 'Dance your way to a story' (Chapter 7). Somehow it is accepted that enacting and retelling stories is an essential element of story making for children in the Foundation Stage and Key Stage 1. The suggestion in this chapter is that this remains a powerful need and support for children as they master the complexities of composing narrative.

What was in the teacher's head when planning this work?

Contexts and coherence

Context and coherence in this unit depend upon:

- Providing a sequence of story making learning activities which build coherently upon children's earlier experiences of these from the Foundation Stage onwards.
- Highlighting the reading–writing connection: this depends on previous enjoyment of hearing or reading historical adventure stories, which provide ideas, structures and styles for creating new stories.
- Writing with an explicit sense of audience and purpose: coherence is given to children's writing when they have thought about the people they are writing for and what they want to make those people feel or think.
- Using and applying material from any historical topic work. (In this unit the topic of Britain since 1930 is used.) Immersion is created through linking literacy with subject work in history.

Motivation

The main aim of this unit of work is to motivate uninterested pupils – those who just don't seem to be able to muster the skills to put together an effective piece of writing. This will be done by:

- Developing some approaches to generating writing content which involve visual, auditory and kinaesthetic (VAK) approaches.
- Using teaching strategies which access children's imaginative capacities.
- Doing this in a range of ways that activate children's pleasure in playing and the creative process. (Even at the top of Key Stage 2 children are only 11: they are still children! Their abilities to conceptualise imaginative scenes and interactions in an abstract and decontextualised way may be very limited.)
- Creating writing experiences which present high levels of challenge and expectation.

Content and process

- Skills will be built first through providing structured, **concrete experiences** (visual, auditory and kinaesthetic – dramatic). These experiences are designed to contribute in specific ways to written texts.
- Experiences will need to be transformed **explicitly** by the teacher during shared writing. During this process the teacher will link the events of the experiences very closely with the writing up of that part of the narrative. In this way, concrete experiences are translated into an outcome which is highly abstract – narrative writing.
- The work begins by teaching children to build up and develop imaginary situations surrounding a sequence of events in a narrative. This will involve work on the following:

  - improvisation of events in the story
  - work in role to develop ideas about character.

- These 'tools' will be needed by young writers. They form part of the learning process:

  - strategies to develop vocabulary, so that it can be used expressively in 'writerly' ways
  - a variety of thinking frames which help in planning and writing a story for a specified audience and purpose
  - some varied and motivating revision and editing activities, so that strategies to improve writing can be used and applied consciously by children.

Primary National Strategy Objectives

Clustering the learning objectives

What is needed here for a Year 6 teacher are learning objectives which cluster around teaching children about planning and writing a brief short story. (To an extent this may make the story seem simpler than the level required for Year 6. But the building in of challenging and varied sentence structures and evocative language needs to be designed to address this. Shared writing has to be aimed at the appropriate level.)

Speaking

Year 5

- Use the techniques of dialogic talk to explore ideas, topics or issues.

Years 6 and 7

- Use exploratory, hypothetical and speculative talk as a tool for clarifying ideas.

Group discussion and interaction

Year 6

- Understand and use a variety of ways to criticise constructively and respond to criticism.

Drama

Year 6

- Improvise using a range of drama strategies to explore themes such as hopes, fears and desires.

Years 6 and 7

- Develop drama techniques to explore in role a variety of situations and texts or respond to stimuli.

Word structure and spelling

Years 6 and 7

- Draw on analogies to known words, roots, derivations, word families morphology and familiar spelling patterns.

Understanding and interpreting texts

Year 4

- Explain how writers use figurative and expressive language to create images and atmosphere.

Year 5

- Compare different types of narrative and identify how they are structured.
- Explore how writers use language for dramatic effects.
- Infer the meanings of unknown words using syntax, context, word structures and origins.

Engaging with and responding to texts

Year 4

- Read extensively favourite authors or genres and experiment with other types of text.
- The Year 4 objective here is being used to build confidence and facilitate 'volume reading'.

Creating and shaping texts

Objectives are being taken from different year groups here and clustered because of the need to write a *whole* story, using and applying a range of skills.

Year 3

- Make decisions about form and purpose, identify success criteria and use them to evaluate their writing.

Year 4

- Use settings and characterisation to engage readers' interest.
- Show imagination through the language used to create atmosphere or suspense.

Year 6

- Use different narrative techniques to engage and entertain the reader.

Text structure and organisation

Year 6

- Use varied structures to shape and organise text coherently.

Sentence structure and punctuation

Year 5

- Adapt sentence construction to different text types, purposes and readers.

Using text in the unit

This unit assumes that children will have been offered opportunities to read and hear well written short stories. (Multiple copies are useful for this.) Children need to have been able to respond in a feeling way to the glory and excitement of the stories, before a cold analysis of text features takes place.

As well as longer stories though, children in Key Stage 2 need to see very short stories from which they may derive ideas and models. In fact, explicit teaching needs to be centred on this type of very short story, since this is the sort of story children are often encouraged to write (e.g. in Key Stage 2 tests). If we take the reading–writing connection seriously, we know that children will need to explore how authors achieve effects in very short stories (if they are to be encouraged to generalise from these reading experiences!). They need to think about the following questions:

- What has this author been able to 'miss out' in his narrative and still make it a good story?
- How much dialogue/description/action is there?

- What is the timeline like for this story? How much time passes and what is the pace like in different parts?
- Is there much elaboration of character? What do we think the characters are like, and how do we know it?
- Does the format of introduction/build up/dilemma/resolution work well here – or is it foreshortened?

Starting points

The Friday before the Monday

The unit is preceded by a staged event, designed to mystify and intrigue children. The class has a 'visit' from a 'witness' of a strange wartime occurrence. (The teacher works in role as that person in the hot seat.) Children have to find out as much as possible about the mystery incident, by asking open questions. (This is linked to work on questioning: questions are recorded on a flipchart and the three most likely to obtain the most revealing information voted for by children.) The teacher can control the flow of information to the children giving them tantalising glimpses of a mysterious tale which will be created next week.

Monday morning: literacy choices

Mostly the choices are about how we time and sequence the activities we have thought of. We want children to experience activities that will progressively back up the experience of supported composition. This requires us to think carefully about the order in which we present them with ideas about writing.

In this unit it is decided to use the Friday afternoon hot seating activity to give ideas for work on Monday morning. The teacher will present key aspects of the story they are going to write together in a novel and appealing way, which also reinforces the story elements contained in the planning format she is going to use. So questions are answered in such a way that attention can be drawn to the introduction, build up, dilemma, etc.

The whole class shared text session

Initially this will be about gathering and developing ideas for the story. Gathering ideas and developing them into some sort of plan is the first stage of the writing process. The plan in this case comes directly from the hot seat activity: information obtained from the witness will be written up in the introduction or build-up flipchart format.

The aim of this is not to create one particular format for story planning, but to show one starting point for story writing and how to make a useful record of this. It is intended to provide a **framework for thinking** about stories. The intention is to allow children to meet such frameworks with consistency and explicitness, so that the thinking processes which lie behind the creation of novel and imaginative ideas become explicit and accessible to them.

So we might well end up with a flipchart record of today's session which looks something like Figure 15.1.

This is just a skeletal beginning. It is the outline of the main story events. To transform this into something meaningful, there is a need to be clear about the following:

- **Audience:** who is the story for?
- **Purpose:** what are we trying to make them feel or think or imagine?
- **Characters:** who are they and what are they like?
- **Setting:** where does the story take place; what is it like?

Issues of audience and purpose can be simply dealt with through paired discussion with teacher-managed feedback to the whole group. This efficiently resolves these key issues and enables a decision to be made quickly.

For 'audience' the paired discussion is initiated by wondering aloud about the age and interests of children who are likely to enjoy wartime adventure stories. It is useful to

OPENING
In the kitchen after tea ......

BUILD UP TO: (PROBLEM.)
Bomb falls
↳
House ruined
↳
Family trapped
↳
Firemen arrive
↳
Can't find baby

RESOLUTION
Terry helps save the baby

Figure 15.1

ask Key Stage 2 writers to write for an audience *older* than they are, as this requires them to aspire to more than if they write for younger children. (There is an interesting conjecture here about NC levels and the levels of expectation when teachers model how to compose text with children. How difficult is the shared writing? At which NC level is the shared writing demonstrated?) It is important to challenge children to come up with realistic ideas about who is likely to want to read this story.

When discussing 'purpose' children will come up with ideas like making the reader:

 (i)   excited
 (ii) scared
(iii) wanting to be there (or not be there) in the adventure
(iv) wondering what it's like to live in that time
 (v)   imagining how they would feel if it happened to them.

Points (i), (ii) and (v) are selected and put onto the flipchart (see Figure 15.2).

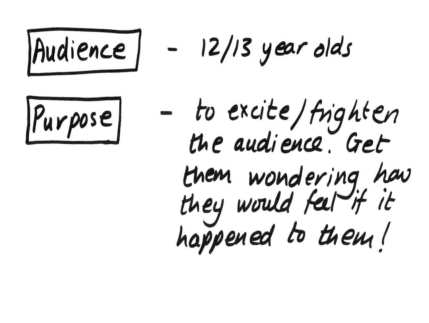

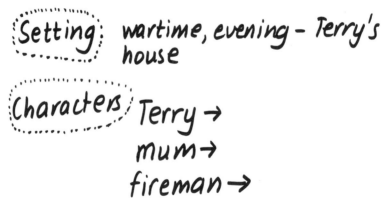

Figure 15.2

That's really enough for the first shared session. An interesting way to develop this into independent work may be to ask pairs to create any sort of visual representation such as a story 'map' or board with illustrations and speech bubbles, to give a concrete shape to their stories. They will need A3 for this. Coloured pens and self-adhesive notes can be used, so that dramatic or layered incidents can be represented.

Transformation of the flipchart notes into a more visual medium can be valuable for more visual learners. The collaborative discussion aspect of this will enhance inter-personal skills *and* allow children to make their own sense of the story. Pairs are then asked to join into fours in the plenary to explain their illustrations. After this, pairs are given a couple of minutes to add to their own A3 sheets. (This may need to be modelled at each stage if children are unfamiliar with the process.)

Issues of characters and setting will come from the following spotlights.

Spotlight: getting to know the characters

So far we know only that we have certain characters in the story: Mum, Terry, baby Molly, Dad, who is away at war, and some firemen. Children need to find out a bit more about each. This can be done so that children infer some characteristics for each person. These are added to the planning notes and referred to as we write. Knowing one or two definite and clear things about the character helps children make the story real and alive. They are more likely to create strong characters if the central characteristics are strong.

One simple and useful technique is through envoying. The class is split into two sections, half being asked to think about Mum, half to think about Terry. Each group is given a picture of the character, with a series of captions about what the character thinks, says and does. They make some notes in a spider diagram format, giving as much information as they can. Pairs from the two groups are then joined together and asked to explain their own character. The listening pair could make notes and ask questions to help the speaking pair to clarify and refine their ideas.

This will need to be summarised and processed onto the thinking frame. This should be very concise, for example:

- Mum – tired, funny, worried.
- Terry – scared but overcomes it, protective of his family.

Spotlight: ideas and language for the main story setting

Children need support to gather ideas and descriptive language for the setting. One powerful way to do this is through visualisation activities. The children are asked to relax and close their eyes as a 'guided visualisation' is voiced by the teacher. They are asked to try to see, smell, hear, feel and taste the things described to them. It is useful if the voice changes as different parts of the scene are described. Sometimes the voice needs to be soft and drifting (describing comfortable or pleasant scenes); at other times it needs to be hesitant, worried or searching (where there is an element of danger, threat and fear). It could go something like this:

You are in the kitchen . . . there's a comforting oniony smell of gravy and potatoes coming from the cooker. You sit back on the rocking chair feeling the soft cushion

under your bottom and the baby's silky blanket hanging against your face . . .
it's fluffy and tickly at the same time! It smells of baby Molly . . . giving you a
warm, proud, important feeling like you get when you hold her and give her
a bottle of warm bubbly milk . . .

You can see mum looking tired, but scrubbing all the pots at the sink . . . the
bristly brush launches water at your face and you hear your mum laugh softly at
you in that gurgling, gentle, kind way she has . . .

The wooden clock is ticking loudly as the big hand approaches 12. Nearly 8
o'clock . . . you sit up in your chair . . . any minute she'll tell you to go up . . . up
those cold stairs . . . away from the warm fireplace. You think of the chilly sheets,
imagine them clinging to your shivering legs and shoulders . . .

In a sense here, the story structure is being reinforced for children, with an 'introduction'
and the beginnings of a 'build-up'. If it is done briefly but evocatively, they will adopt a
similar style when writing the story. If interesting vocabulary is used, children will now
use it themselves in discussion. The character plans we've worked on are also being
contextualised here.

Mostly though, at this moment, the intention is to put pictures and sensations in their
minds. These will connect with the ones that are already there, making both more real.
Afterwards they discuss, extend and find language for the places they experienced in
their imaginations.

As soon as the visualisation is over, children go into A/B pairs and take turns to tell
each other everything they saw, smelled, heard and touched. This always includes things
they have imagined – delightfully those 'unimaginative' children are as imaginative as
everyone else in this activity. Usually children imagine additional things which weren't
said – in this type of context, care needs to be taken with these parts, as there is a strong
chance that some will be anachronistic.

In pairs they are given ten minutes to draw the scene they visualised. They will have
to agree on the main elements. Next the pairs are asked to caption the drawing – placing
an adjective and noun next to three or four of the parts they have included in the drawing.
They might include captions for smells, physical sensations, etc. (This will need to be
modelled at each stage.)

To develop and improve the language elements being used, pairs then join to make
fours and 'read through' each labelled diagram. The task now is to think of different

- nouns for each caption
- adjectives to describe each noun.

The aim is to get a number of language choices for each caption. Children may regroup
a number of times to ensure that enough alternatives have been generated. A sample of
this is given in Figure 15.3.

Now children can explore which adjective and noun combinations sound good
together. Because of the way we have generated alternatives here, children will
have some unusual choices. The teacher will model some of the thinking processes
involved in moving children away from ordinary, clichéd language combinations.
Lots of work has been done around this, discovering as many different ways as possible
to combine the pairs of words, and then ranking them in terms of the most and least
clichéd.

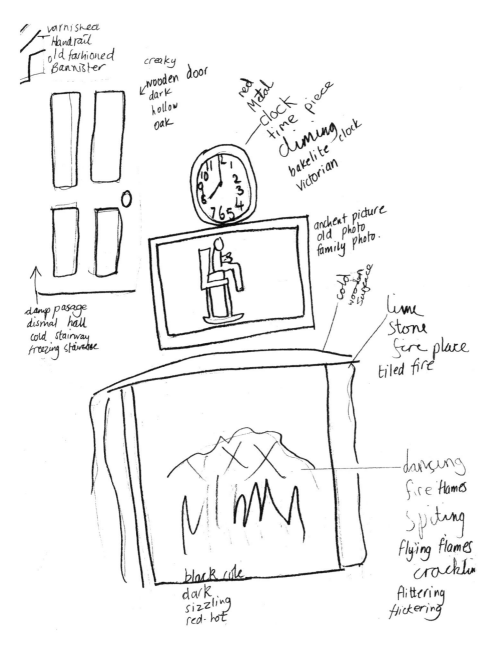

Figure 15.3

—— and —— sound a bit ordinary. I like the sound of —— and —— together –
they sound unusual, but not so different that readers won't understand. What do
you think?

Spotlight: making a word game

This is to explore the use of the following roots and affixes: aero, aqua, audi, bi, cede,
clude, con, cred, duo, log(o) (y), hyd(ro) (ra), in, micro, oct, photo, port, prim, scribe,

scope, sub, tele, tri and ex. Though the word level work here is planned to be discrete – it doesn't link in to the nicely coherent sentence and text level work around story writing – some of the language could be intentionally used during modelled writing or supported composition. The activities are really valuable, encompassing knowledge about both word meanings and spellings. Understanding more about where words come from and how they are connected in meaning gives children access to a greater range of spelling strategies.

This work on word roots and affixes begins with children preparing to make a card game using the word chunks. They need a basic understanding of what the given chunks mean. This can be done in a range of ways, using prior knowledge of the affixes, finding words with those chunks in them, then inferring meanings using a dictionary, etc.

- Pairs of children start with a stack of small cards to write on. Using the listed affixes they invent words, by attaching one or two affixes to a noun. Nouns could be specified by the teacher, thus intentionally restricting the choice, so that the challenge of the game rests with the difficulties presented by the roots and affixes, not the nouns. Children's examples might include micro-octocruise, telehomescribe, subphotomeasurementscope. Figure 15.4 is a copy of instructions used with children for this activity.
- For each invented word, they write a 'definition'; so micro-octocruise could be a tiny cruise boat which visits eight places, or a short journey of a group of octopi. Later (during another session of independent work later in the week?) they can challenge another pair to match invented words to invented definitions, before playing a 'memory' or 'snap' card game.
- Another way to process the material that children have made is to get pairs to show each other the definitions, and challenge counterparts to suggest what the word chunks might have been.

The point of the activity is that it is fun!

- It gets the most uninterested children playing with word meanings in a thoroughly original way.
- It provokes an interest in the word chunks they need to use.
- It makes children question how to spell the roots and affixes when they combine them.

Spotlight: modelling how to use the work so far to write an opening

The teacher demonstrates how to use the visualisation and captioning activity to write a story opening. She uses the unusual vocabulary choices. At intervals she checks out how the text 'sounds': how good do the sentence structures and language choices sound? The teacher also demonstrates the use of colons and semi-colons. Children are now asked to write their own openings based on their drawings and captions.

Use these word roots / affixes

aqua	maxi
hydro	micro
bi	mini
octo	aero
scope	ject
sub	tri
super	quad

Make a card game

1 Combine one or two affixes with a noun.

2 Write a definition on a card.

3 Try matching definitions to invented words.

Figure 15.4

Spotlight: enacting a dramatic moment and writing the narrative

The class has reached the point where the whining of the bomb can be heard coming down towards the house. How can this be expressed succinctly in a couple of sentences, still encapsulating the drama and fear of the moment?

The class uses freeze frames. Children go off in pairs and improvise the activities in the kitchen until the teacher says 'Freeze'. Thought and speech bubbles are used to explore what Mum and Terry could be thinking, feeling and saying. Figure 15.5 gives an example of how this may look in practice.

The writing up of this can be modelled immediately (Figure 15.6). Children then redo theirs, writing the thoughts or speech onto laminated thought or speech bubbles, then incorporating this into text for the independent section. Plenary time could then be efficiently used to review and assess how well children were able to transform the drama into well punctuated sentences.

Figure 15.5

Teacher scribed text written from this:

Terry stopped in the middle of wiping the plate in his hand.
"What's that whining noise?" he wondered, straining to hear more.
Mum reacted quickly. "Get under the table Terry – NOW!"

Figure 15.6

Spotlight: playing with words

The children are now engaged in a teaching and learning activity that will prepare them to write more expressively.

This begins with the introduction of a list of adjectives and adjectival phrases which suggest some of the sensations which may be experienced in the bombed house. (Many children will 'know' some of the words, but won't use them independently in their writing, because they need a bit of scaffolding first. They need to explore and discuss the shades of meanings of the words and phrases, grouping them and understanding degrees of intensity. They need to have used the language verbally before they are able to apply it in their writing!)

Here are some of the words and phrases that could be introduced:

Dusty blackness
Spluttering sounds of water escaping
Blank darkness
Soup mixed with dirty clothes
Dank odours
Dimly lit reflections
Icy dripping water
Glowing partially lit reflections
Water pooling in clammy layers along my side
Freezing gathered moisture
Steady breathing
Icy smoking moisture
Water hissing in the darkness
A muddled stench of tonight's mouthwatering tea and a fear of death

Mewing, tiny cries
Poisonous odours combined with . . .
Burnt onion mixed with gas
Bone chillingly icy fog
A smell of broken lives
Reflected darkness
Steadily quiet breaths
Hardly audible cries
A confusing stink of powdery baby clothes and burst drains
Gasping noises
Almost silent gasps of air
Dark blankness

Children investigate ways to group the words and phrases. Here is one possible grouping – done in regard to different sights and sensations that may have been experienced.

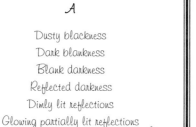

A
Dusty blackness
Dark blankness
Blank darkness
Reflected darkness
Dimly lit reflections
Glowing partially lit reflections

B
Icy dripping water
Water pooling in clammy layers along my side
Freezing gathered moisture
Bone chillingly icy fog
Icy smoking moisture
Water hissing in the darkness
Spluttering sounds of water escaping

Groups now explore and experiment with these using the two activities that follow:

- Children innovate with different groups of words to create new phrases – so for D they might combine and develop ideas to get phrases like gasping, hissing breaths; hissing gasps and soft crying; steady, soft mewing cries.
- Each child in a group selects the phrase they like best, and writes it onto landscape A4 paper with a flipchart pen. The group stands at the front, each person holding an A4 sheet: the sheets are arranged according to the strength and intensity of the phrases by another group or the whole class.

Spotlight: making the words in the text more powerful

Here children are being taught about how to change and improve written drafts. It builds on the previous spotlight, which provided language for this activity and a chance to explore and use that vocabulary.

During shared writing the teacher has modelled ways of making language choices more expressive and figurative. This is illustrated in Figure 15.7. Now children are each

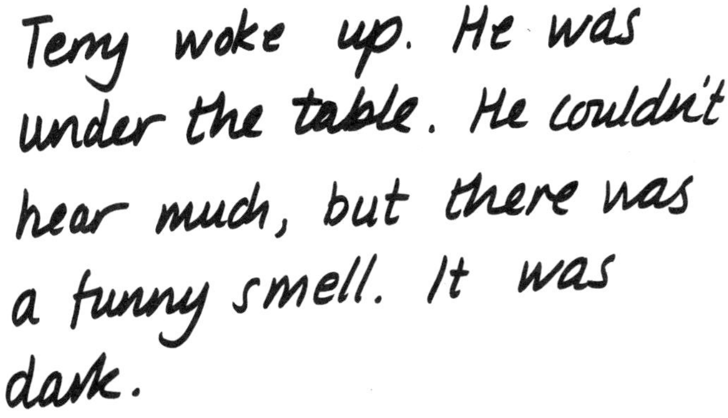

Terry woke up. He was under the table. He couldn't hear much, but there was a funny smell. It was dark.

Figure 15.7

given a teacher-written scene just after the bomb has devastated the house. There are three sentences of unimaginative description. In A/B pairs they improve the language using some of the ideas introduced in the preparatory vocabulary development activity with adjectives and adjectival phrases.

Each A then joins another B to compare and discuss the changes they have made. The As could move on again and obtain more ideas, before returning to their original pairs for a final comparison and decision.

The whole class could now use the technique of dialogic talk to manage a larger group discussion. When this is first being used, some teacher help and management might be a much needed support. This technique will enable children to hear and discuss a larger range of possibilities for the phrases that they are unhappy with in the text. This also allows the teacher to assess how children's skills in using more expressive language are developing.

Further ideas to use as the story is being composed

- Use freeze frames to improve the drama and tension at any point in the story, e.g. improving the suspense as Terry saves the day. Exploring Terry's thoughts allows children to empathise. This is important! Children **can** empathise really well with characters, but they won't necessarily do it automatically. They probably need some carefully timed interventions to help. This also slows down the telling of the story and generates ideas with children.
- If this type of activity is done regularly with the whole class, children can do it independently with ease, as they think about or write their own stories.
- Do some more visualisation and artwork around the scene of devastation. Develop this into captioning as before, and develop it into some poetry as in Chapter 8.
- If there had been darkness, the visual senses would be limited. What could they smell, hear, touch and taste?

- Make musical representations of the noises the family could hear after the bombing.
- Firemen improvisation – outside to in – how did they move? Enact this first in the hall as a movement/drama activity.
- Get a list of verbs from a general list and select ones that will suit the firemen's movement into the house. Will they move the same way all the time? Will the 'clambering' become more tentative as they approach people? Do children know how to enact this? Can we represent the expressive movements with verbs/adverbs? Is figurative use of language useful here?

Spotlight: from 'We made the story!' to using the strategies and skills to write independently

The title of this chapter – 'We made the story!' – is a quote from a boy in a Birmingham school, who went through this process of enacting and working through a story. Up to now in this unit, children have been taught, in a tightly scaffolded and very structured way, how to develop and write a story about a wartime event. Children need to practise applying the strategies and skills they have been taught. They need the freedom to be creative and experimental, incorporating the ideas used in the unit.

Children are now asked to write their own stories about another wartime incident. They do this in pairs, planning in their own ways, adapting as they go. Pairs may wish to try out their ideas by explaining them to another pair. They may need to enact parts of the story to make it concrete for themselves, as they compose the story: they stop and do this.

When pairs have finished their stories, they join into fours to say what works well and suggest ideas and improvements. Some are working with self-adhesive notes and red pens to evaluate and improve the writing.

The finished writing is used as an assessment by both children and teacher, to notice what has been achieved and what still needs to be worked on. If children start off with group writing targets linked directly to the objective about using language to create atmosphere or suspense, they can judge how well they have achieved their target using the type of proforma shown in Figure 15.8.

Beyond the unit

- This type of story making could be used in any history topic to help develop and embed the learning.
- It could have been a geographical setting: e.g. work related to different locations (Struay in Year 2).
- It could be used in science, creating a storyline for solids, liquids and gases using their attributes to generate a plot.
- The word game could use a list of topic-related nouns that children are learning about.

Name

I think this piece of work shows I have achieved

_____

_____

_____

_____

from my writing target

Figure 15.8

16 Enjoying a good argument?

Writing discursively

Discursive texts are probably more unfamiliar to many 10 and 11 year olds than any of the other text types introduced in the first NLS literacy framework. It is important to think carefully about what it may mean to a child, to be expected to write effectively using a complex and unfamiliar genre within a short, two or three week block of work.

What also seems important here is the vastly different home experiences that children bring to school with them. Some children will be very familiar with the vocabulary and language structures contained within discursive writing. Some children will have had plenty of experience of hearing family members talking articulately about their views and beliefs. They may also have heard measured responses, disagreeing, perhaps in a careful and discreetly impersonal way with the ideas expressed. Spoken discussion – talking about, agreeing and disagreeing on ordinary family matters – is not identical to the formally written forms we are considering here, but it may have a number of similar features. This will depend on cultural patterns of talking in families, and brings in lots of issues about how much and what sort of talking happens. We do know that there are all sorts of social forces that seem to be reducing the quantity (and quality) of such talk. Recent social trends – ready meals not eaten at a table, TVs in bedrooms and computers for example – can all reduce the opportunities for extended periods of face-to-face interaction.

While some children do have these valuable experiences of discussion, some don't. To guarantee that oral practice with some of these language structures has been established, plenty of speaking and listening experiences need to be planned in to literacy and subject work. This will increase children's use and application of the language needed in both oral and written discussion.

Learning how to articulate your own ideas backed up with supporting evidence, and how to balance these against some opposing views is a valuable social and communicative skill – an important component of personal, social and health education (PSHE). Learning the oral skills of supporting and adding to another person's ideas and viewpoint, or, alternatively, expressing partial or total disagreement seem to be important elements of the bigger picture of the work within this unit.

What was in the teacher's head when planning this work?

Contexts and coherence

Importing content from other subject areas for both reading and writing creates coherent contexts for children in the following ways:

- Providing familiar material for writing arguments: this creates security for children and reduces the complexity of dealing with both unknown text types and unknown information.
- Reinforcing the subject knowledge.
- Creating scaffolding for the literacy skills.
- Avoiding the arbitrariness of the content within a published scheme, which may have nothing to do with anything the child either knows about or is interested in.

Motivation

- Children love argument and controversy.
- They like to feel powerful among peers – being better at mustering their arguments enables children to make a case powerfully. Emphasising this 'competitive' aspect of discursive writing gives it a value that treating it as yet another text type to be mastered fails to do.
- We need to move away from the tendency to complete a thorough but quite coldly dispassionate analysis and reconstruction of text. Argument is about feeling and expressing views which are often passionately held.
- In teaching children about this text type, we are transforming something personally meaningful and passionate into a prescriptively structured and impersonal format. It seems important that we emphasise the feeling aspect as well as the logical, analytical part.

Content and process

This follows a fairly standard NLS pattern of approaching a unit of work by immersion in the reading of a text type. This is followed by shared guided and independent writing activities.

There are two significant differences, however. The first is in the amount of active preparatory work which provides ideas and dramatic contexts for writing. The second is in the emphasis on speaking and listening as an integral part of the unit, in DARTs activities (see Chapter 8) and in 'talk for writing'. The process follows this shape:

- Ideas for arguments and counter-arguments are generated using a variety of active and interactive approaches, including research, drama, interviews, group discussion and hot seating.
- Specific DARTS activities are used to draw out the key features of the texts read – in terms of structures and language features.
- Lots of structured group discussion to build on understandings of how argument texts are built up (comparing, evaluating and extending texts using DARTs activities).

- Use of writing frames to make notes of two 'for' and two 'against' points – and evidence to back up the points.
- Use of teacher modelling and supported composition to demonstrate how these notes can be written up.
- Teacher modelling followed by paired and group tasks to review and redraft writing in terms of language features.

Some of this work will take place inside and some outside the literacy hour. It is *all* being included and described here as part of a coherent and sequenced process because if we just assume the 'non-literacy' ancillary bits will be done, without saying what those bits consist of, the whole process is stripped to the minimum and perhaps left like that. How we use content from other subject areas has to be dealt with here if we are going to wean ourselves away from the use of publishers' schemes and texts which have absolutely no connection with work children are doing in subject areas.

Primary National Strategy Objectives

Clustering the learning objectives

While most of these objectives have come from Year 6, some have been brought in from Years 4, 5 and 7. Sometimes this is to bring in an objective from another year group which will enrich and extend the topic. At other times, objectives from earlier years are brought in to meet specific learning needs in areas where the teacher knows there are gaps.

Speaking

Year 6

- Use a range of oral techniques to present persuasive arguments.
- Participate in whole class debate, using the conventions and language of debate.

Years 6 and 7

- Use exploratory, hypothetical and speculative talk as a tool for clarifying ideas.

Listening and responding

Year 6

- Analyse and evaluate how speakers present points effectively through use of language and gesture.

Group discussion and interaction

Year 6

- Understand and use a variety of ways to criticise constructively and respond to criticism.

Years 6 and 7

- Adopt a range of roles in discussion, including acting as a spokesperson, and contribute in different ways such as promoting, opposing, exploring and questioning.

Drama

Year 6

- Improvise using a range of drama strategies to explore themes such as hopes, fears and desires.

Word structure and spelling

Years 6 and 7

- Record and learn from personal errors, corrections, investigations, conventions, exceptions and new vocabulary.

Understanding and interpreting texts

Year 6

- Understand underlying themes, causes and points of view.
- Understand how writers use different structures to create coherence and impact.

Creating and shaping texts

Year 6

- In non-narrative text, establish, balance and maintain viewpoints.
- Select words and language, drawing on their knowledge of formal writing.

Text structure and organisation

Year 6

- Use varied structures to shape and organise text coherently.

Sentence structure and punctuation

Year 4

- Clarify meaning and point of view by using varied sentence structure (phrases, clauses and adverbials).

Year 5

- Adapt sentence construction to different text types, purposes and readers.

Presentation

Year 6

- Select from a wide range of ICT programs to present text effectively and communicate information and ideas.

Starting point: assessment for learning

It is important to find out quickly how much children already know about reading and writing discursive texts. Children may have done work on this in previous years or they may not. Now that the Primary National Strategy framework for literacy does not specify the text types to be covered in particular year groups, it is more important that teachers complete some sort of assessment to understand current learning needs.

So a quick revisiting activity is planned to establish some baselines about reading and writing skills. The children will read one argument text and look at an argument writing frame, before completing a writing task as an assessment to give some relevant reading and writing targets. Once this is complete, a very clear idea of what children need has emerged. This will inform both the selection of objectives, and the emphasis given to the objectives selected.

Evidence from written assessments indicates the following learning needs, split into reading and writing.

What the assessment shows

Reading at a whole class level

- Children need to understand the sequence and structure of a discursive text. They need to understand the way in which the text contains paragraphs with arguments for and arguments against the main idea being disputed. They need to know how evidence can be expressed, and what constitutes effective evidence when it is being used well.
- Children need to appreciate the formal and logical (almost legalistic) tone of the language used in this type of text. They need to be able to recognise ways in which this is done (by the use of technical language; also careful sentence construction and sequencing to present evidence for a case).

Writing

- Children need practice in first constructing, then putting in a sensible sequence, each separate paragraph of the argument.
- Children need to work on linking ideas in sentences and paragraphs. This will be done first by experiencing how to use contrasting connective words and phrases

(e.g. *however, on the other hand, whereas, in contrast to this*). These will highlight the distinction between one viewpoint and the opposing viewpoint. Second, the children will be working with other connecting words and phrases which add on information or evidence in this sort of text.

- Children need to establish and maintain a sufficiently impersonal writing style, using response partners to reread and revise.

Spotlight: tuning children in

It is important to get children tuned in to the geographical content by introducing them to the pleasurably combative aspects of the opposing points of view in the text. This is being done outside the literacy hour and rather than start with the text itself, children are working on an improvisation based around some ideas contained in the text. Children are given a scenario of a proposed 'improvement' in their area. They are told that the improvement is a large production plant, and that it will bring prosperity and regeneration to the area, reducing crime and unemployment. The information is given in the form of a simple persuasive flier (Figure 16.1).

Different groups are asked to speculate in role about the proposed plant and think whether it is a good idea. (Groups include parents, children, pensioners, shopkeepers, bus companies, teachers.) Groups are also asked to think about points and questions they may wish to put to the company, given the fact that the flier gave very scant and one-sided information. These are illustrated in Figure 16.2. There are a lot of ideas here about the difference between seeing one and two points of view. Groups then question a company representative separately (played by the teacher in role), thus acquiring expert

Figure 16.1

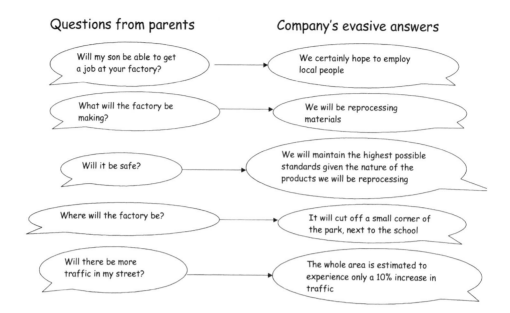

Figure 16.2

knowledge about the possible effects on their interest group. Opposing views begin to emerge at this point, because children begin to see through the 'spin' and realise that the company is not necessarily telling the truth about the production plant.

The 'expertise' of groups could later be pooled in a jigsaw activity, in which a representative of each interest group joins with others to decide on follow-up questions for a public meeting. These follow-up questions differ from the first set of questions, because they are a result of pooled information and expertise: we would expect them to have more 'depth'. (See Figure 16.3 for examples of the questions and answers.)

The opposing views are brought out fully when a representative of the company (teacher in role) attends a public meeting. The disadvantages of the location of the production plant are now becoming clearer to children. The teacher in role is becoming extremely provocative in her dismissal of the public's concerns and fears. Children are becoming more impassioned as a result. This gives us a genuine conflict of interest, in which children are immersed and partial (particularly since it is their own area). Putting children in role like this makes it easier to see the issues in a complex and multidimensional way.

There is no attempt to resolve any of the issues, simply to raise awareness and leave the difficulties to ferment.

Spotlight: following the improvisation, choices, choices . . .

Literacy choices

What should be done first as a follow-up to the improvisation?

- Should children be told the literacy objectives?
- Should it be pointed out that they will not be told the objectives, but asked at the end of each session what they think they have learned?

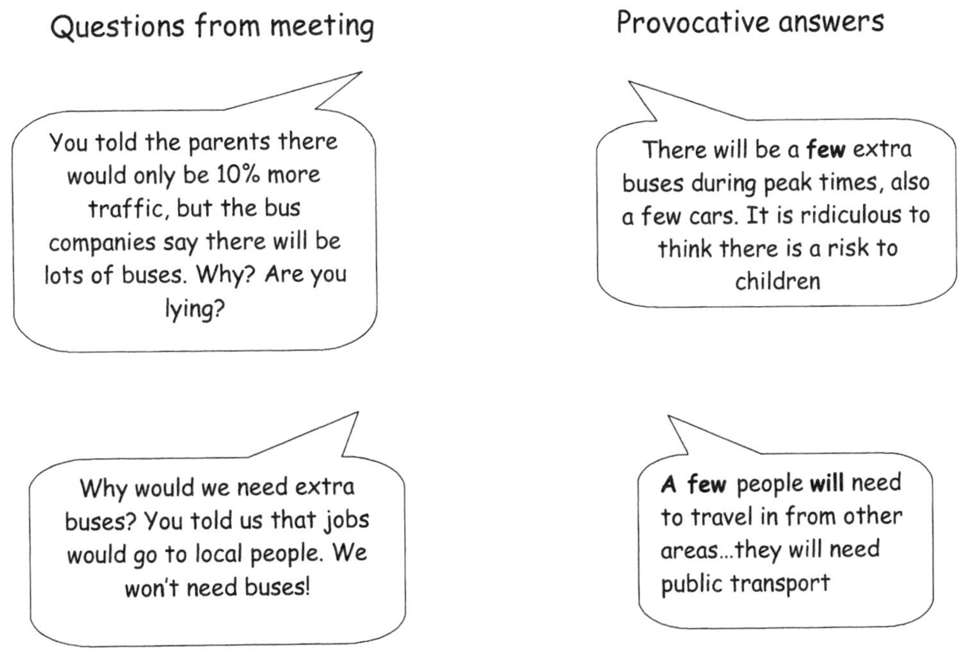

Questions from meeting

> You told the parents there would only be 10% more traffic, but the bus companies say there will be lots of buses. Why? Are you lying?

> Why would we need extra buses? You told us that jobs would go to local people. We won't need buses!

Provocative answers

> There will be a **few** extra buses during peak times, also a few cars. It is ridiculous to think there is a risk to children

> **A few** people **will** need to travel in from other areas...they will need public transport

Figure 16.3

- How should the reading and writing elements of this unit be interspersed within it? Will the experience of reading a number of argument texts over a week or so, followed by a solid block of writing, be more useful than integrating the two so we move into writing more quickly?

Teaching and learning choices

Here the big question is about how to combine the subject-based content with the literacy part of this work. Is it possible to make sure that both are motivating and enjoyable? (It would be easy to develop a sequence of teaching which creates the idea that the fun parts never happen in the literacy hour.) The main way that this will be done is by making the work involve as much speaking and listening as possible, but there are still choices to be made as to how to do this:

- Should the teacher keep the class group more or less together, in mixed ability pairs, completing the same task which they compare in plenary time?
- Should the teacher create more tasks and then form ability groups?
- Should the teacher create more tasks but keep the pairs, or groups, mixed ability and ask them to compare their tasks with groups who have done the same thing, before explaining the outcomes to pairs?

The decisions

In this unit the literacy decisions are:

- *not* to tell children the objectives. We want to create a problem-solving approach to the lesson – can they identify what they are learning?
- to read and work on a number of argument texts before we begin to write. We want children to be thoroughly familiar with the structure and language styles of the genre because it is so unfamiliar to many of them.

The teaching and learning decisions are to create more tasks which will ensure the following:

- A good pace to the lesson, with pairs completing tasks so that their outcomes can be compared and justified with a pair who have completed the same activity.
- Opportunities to regroup with a pair who have completed the other task. This enables each pair to explain what they have done and why they did it. Because they do this after checking out with the first 'same task' pair, they have rehearsed and adjusted their ideas already, giving a more thorough grounding and context for explaining them.

With these four decisions in mind, we embark on the first activity.

Spotlight: shared reading of an argument text

This is done by reading the first argument text and simply noticing what is in each paragraph. This is discussed in pairs, and a 'running log' is established noting what is found. This is shown in Figure 16.4.

Follow-up work for this involves two groups of children in mixed ability pairs. Finishers will be asked to write literal and inferential questions about the text.

Group 1 will complete a DARTs activity which requires them to cut up the shared text and stick it onto a writing frame which takes the same format as the original text (Figure 16.5). Other argument texts will be provided so children can compare the structure with the one used for shared reading.

Group 2 will take the shared text and a more formally written version of the same text. They will find differences between them, and say what they think the differences do in the reader's head. An example of this is given in Figure 16.6.

Spotlight: investigating the language of arguments

A number of argument texts have now been read. Pairs are using all the argument texts read so far to make a collection of words and phrases which open the various paragraphs. These will be compared and extended by regrouping pairs to fours. Then a display edition can be prepared for the classroom wall. This will be referred to by the teacher in modelled writing. (This is also fulfilling the requirements of the word level objectives: this is a vocabulary extension and display activity.)

INTRODUCTION

Telling us what both sides are and that they are different

Two different opinions were expressed at a local meeting about the redevelopment of the Scotland Road/Hepton Avenue site. Whereas many of the local residents have welcomed the news of a new factory, others regard it as a threat to an already dangerous and noisy environment.

3 different paragraphs, making 3 points in favour

Those residents in favour of the scheme welcomed the fact that local unemployment will be reduced by the new development. Information from ESL states that 500 new jobs will be created.

A spokesperson told the meeting that this would bring new life back into the area. 'Everyone will benefit' she said, 'Shopkeepers, schools, families and businesses. There will be more money and a better environment because of this. Rawlingstone will be a better place to bring up your kids'.

It was even suggested that the crime rate would decrease as a result of the new jobs. Research by Newcastle University has shown that crime is often caused by unemployment and poverty.

ONE SIDE
Residents who want the factory

Advantages of the factory

Paragraphs begin with words and phrases which bring in opposing ideas

However the opposite view has been expressed by another group of residents. They say that the factory will make the environment less safe for their children, because it will bring more traffic to the streets. There would have to be more cars, buses and motorcycles so that people could get to their new workplace. This would cause more pollution. Similarly, the factory would be bound to increase pollution. Parents argue that the number of road accidents would increase, because there would be more cars.

They also suggest that instead of bringing increased employment to the area, ESL is planning to bring in people from other parts of the city to work in Rawlingstone. They say that this fact emerged at a public meeting, when it was revealed that bus companies were scheduling new services to bring employees to ESL from all over the city.

Another important issue for these parents is the fact that part of Rawlingstone Park will disappear when the factory is built. They complained, 'Our children will lose the one safe place there is for them to play in'.

OTHER SIDE
Residents who <u>don't</u> want it!

Disadvantages of the factory

Opposing opinions are being held on both sides. Although we have considered the fears of some residents that their children will suffer, it seems likely that this development will bring enormous benefits to the people of Rawlingstone. They are set to regain the lost days of full employment and a thriving community.

Think it <u>is</u> a good idea overall! SUMMARY

Figure 16.4

Spotlight: finding questions for argument texts in other subject lessons

Children are benefiting from setting their own questions for discussions in various subjects. One simple way to do this is to ask children to think of open questions for a hot seat activity! Hot seating gives children opportunities to think of very provocative questions directed at a real person (see Chapter 3). These are then transformed into the more impersonal language of formal arguments.

History

- Was it a comfortable existence to live as a slave in Roman Britain?
- Should Victorian children have helped their parents by working in mines and mills?
- Should children have been evacuated into the countryside during the Second World War?
- Should people in the countryside have been pressurised to take in children evacuated from the cities?

Geography

- Has this area got too much traffic?
- Should we recycle more waste?
- Should dangerous industries be located away from cities?

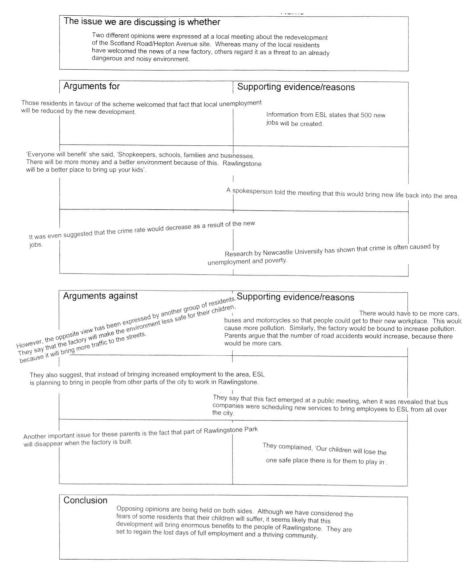

The issue we are discussing is whether

Two different opinions were expressed at a local meeting about the redevelopment of the Scotland Road/Hepton Avenue site. Whereas many of the local residents have welcomed the news of a new factory, others regard it as a threat to an already dangerous and noisy environment.

Arguments for	Supporting evidence/reasons
Those residents in favour of the scheme welcomed that fact that local unemployment will be reduced by the new development.	Information from ESL states that 500 new jobs will be created.
'Everyone will benefit' she said, 'Shopkeepers, schools, families and businesses. There will be more money and a better environment because of this. Rawlingstone will be a better place to bring up your kids'.	A spokesperson told the meeting that this would bring new life back into the area.
It was even suggested that the crime rate would decrease as a result of the new jobs.	Research by Newcastle University has shown that crime is often caused by unemployment and poverty.

Arguments against	Supporting evidence/reasons
However, the opposite view has been expressed by another group of residents. They say that the factory will make the environment less safe for their children, because it will bring more traffic to the streets.	There would have to be more cars, buses and motorcycles so that people could get to their new workplace. This would cause more pollution. Similarly, the factory would be bound to increase pollution. Parents argue that the number of road accidents would increase, because there would be more cars.
They also suggest, that instead of bringing increased employment to the area, ESL is planning to bring in people from other parts of the city to work in Rawlingstone.	They say that this fact emerged at a public meeting, when it was revealed that bus companies were scheduling new services to bring employees to ESL from all over the city.
Another important issue for these parents is the fact that part of Rawlingstone Park will disappear when the factory is built.	They complained, 'Our children will lose the one safe place there is for them to play in'.

Conclusion

Opposing opinions are being held on both sides. Although we have considered the fears of some residents that their children will suffer, it seems likely that this development will bring enormous benefits to the people of Rawlingstone. They are set to regain the lost days of full employment and a thriving community.

Figure 16.5

PSHE

- Should all people's beliefs and customs be respected equally?
- Are designer clothes made in third world countries too expensive?
- Could anyone in the world become an asylum seeker?

Design technology

Conducted orally, this discussion activity is promoting evaluative and critical thinking. It is then used to lead to a more effective evaluation report:

- Is this design for a TV chair healthy?
- This design for a classroom meets every child's needs. Do you agree?

Bits underlined ᴍᴍᴍᴍ are stronger words

more of an argument!

Two distinct and hostile opinions about the redevelopment of the Scotland Road/Hepton Avenue site, were expressed at a meeting for local residents. Whereas many of the local residents have expressed positive views about the proposed production plant, others regard it as a threat to an already dangerous and noisy environment. The meeting ended in anger.

stronger Those residents in favour of the scheme welcomed the fact that local unemployment will be enormously reduced by this initiative. Reliable sources of information from ESL suggest that at least 500 new jobs will be created and that retraining will be given to local people who have been unemployed for longer than two years.

official sounding

A spokesperson told the meeting that this would inject new life back into the community. 'Everyone will benefit' she said, 'Shopkeepers, schools, families and businesses. There will be more money and a better environment because of this. Rawlingstone will be a better place to bring up your kids'.

make the reader believe it is fact! Residents were told that there would be less crime in Rawlingstone when the plant was built. It has been proved that the crime rate decreases as a result of increased employment. Research by Newcastle University has shown that crime is caused by unemployment and poverty.

seems more certain

However, the opposite view has been argued forcefully by a group of residents. They have evidence that the plant will create a dangerous environment for their children, because it will bring more traffic to the streets.

They also have proof, that instead of bringing increased employment to the area, ESL intends to bring in skilled workers from other parts of the city. They have no intention of retraining local people, as it would be far too expensive. No one but a naïve fool could believe that ESL, with their disgraceful employment record was going to go out of their way to help a community! *very definite* *suggests ESL really bad!*

really important Another vital issue for these parents is the unavoidable fact that a substantial part of Rawlingstone Park will be lost to the redevelopment. They complained, 'Our children will lose the one safe place there is for them to play in'.

Although many people are optimistic that this development will improve their future, anyone with any intelligence must realise that the days of a thriving and healthy community in Rawlingstone, are long gone, and unlikely to return just because of this development.

Different ending — makes the reader think it can't be good if ESL win.

Figure 16.6

Spotlight: 'doing' the argument

Are designer clothes made in less developed countries too expensive?

As we move towards writing we have chosen this example from those above because this PSHE question has already been discussed up to a point in the forum of the school council. Here the focus was on school uniform and the social bullying which surrounds peer pressure about what children wear. The issue of wearing school uniforms was first discussed in classrooms, then again in the council meeting: this, together with a follow-up report back to classes, meant that at least some of the types of language that children need to use confidently to frame their points of view were being heard and rehearsed repeatedly.

To move the discussion on, children are introduced to provocative and quite shocking information about the exploitative conditions under which designer gear is manufactured. The intention here is to move them beyond their own personal worlds and interests, without losing their emotional involvement in the issues being discussed. Some improvisation is used to develop empathy with the people working in sweatshop conditions.

Children are now split into two groups representing the two opposing sides in this argument. The two sides are manufacturing companies and parent groups. This will ensure that they gather together all their ideas properly, thinking of evidence and illustrations to add weight to their assertions. Each side can then be used to 'interrogate' and challenge the ideas presented by the other side.

This takes the form of a 'yes but' game. This is played in pairs. Each pair from both sides prepares two points, recording them as statements on speech bubbles. It is aimed to develop children's skill in making and anticipating objections to their ideas. The speech bubbles in Figure 16.7 provide examples of points and responses in the 'yes but' game.

Figure 16.7

Before the 'yes but' game, we might have chosen to input some background ideas for children by setting up a question setting or hot seat activity. This can be done in various ways. Maybe the simplest is to have the teacher in role, giving out information in response to children's questions (generated in pairs). This input can deepen children's understanding of the complexity of the issues and their awareness of why people have such different interests in many situations.

Spotlight: 'doing' the debate

We are now going to hold at least one formal debate in the classroom, as an oral rehearsal for writing. The structure and language of a debate mirrors almost exactly the structure and language features of a discussion text. They both start with an introductory statement summarising the two sides of the argument and proceed with the points and evidence from both sides. Both conclude by making a decision about which side to opt for.

Children work in fours using writing frames as note-making tools to prepare themselves for this. The teacher might want to model an appropriately formal (or 'posh') register for this oral presentation. It is probably best to start with a group of four who will be good role models for the others.

Another way of doing this as a presentation is to ask children to select an ICT program to present this to the class as part of the debate. The ICT presentation would then become the verbal prompts for each part of the debate.

Spotlight: using the argument ideas to build up a text

This is a conventional modelled writing session inside the literacy hour which demonstrates how to use a writing frame to write:

- the opening paragraph
- the two manufacturers' arguments against the idea that designer sports wear is too expensive.

One way to organise this is to use the notes from the group of four children who modelled the class debate in the previous spotlight. The session is composed mainly of teacher-modelled writing rather than supported composition. The teacher modelling will involve speaking the thoughts aloud. Some examples of these are given in Figure 16.8: the teacher is also making reference to a list of prompt phrases to start the paragraphs.

The teacher also uses a combination of modelling writing and supported composition to maintain the involvement of the more lively groups. In pairs children are asked to write in their partner books a next phrase or sentence, using a given prompt. This has the specific focus we identified as a target area initially, such as the phrases we use to add evidence or illustrations, or how to use the **contrasting** or **adding on** connectives. The teacher-modelled writing is now removed from view, and an independent collaborative task set that asks pairs to write the same three paragraphs. Writing frames may or may not be used, depending on teacher or child evaluation of how much support is needed.

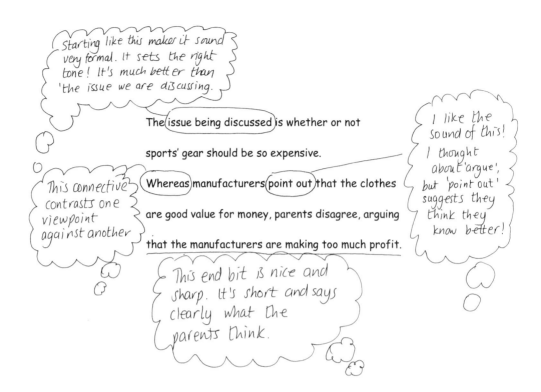

Figure 16.8

Spotlight: rereading and revising strategies

Unexpected issues about the language features of children's written texts have arisen. The teacher has noticed from discussion that children don't seem to realise what is needed here. They are still inconsistent about adopting an impersonal style and using connectives (Figure 16.9 shows two examples of this).

The class is using an overhead projector (OHP) and photocopies of a short (five sentences) piece of writing that the teacher has 'assembled' with a range of children's 'impersonal style inconsistencies' (so that no one child's mistakes are singled out and a fuller range of misconceptions can be addressed). The teacher asks pairs to read through

Two opposing opinions have been expressed about sports products being extreemly expensive! On one hand the manufactres tried to explain that the prices are not expensive at all, but the parents would not have it. On the other hand the parents and children say that they are drop dead really expensive aspeshly when they have four and five kids.

Figure 16.9a

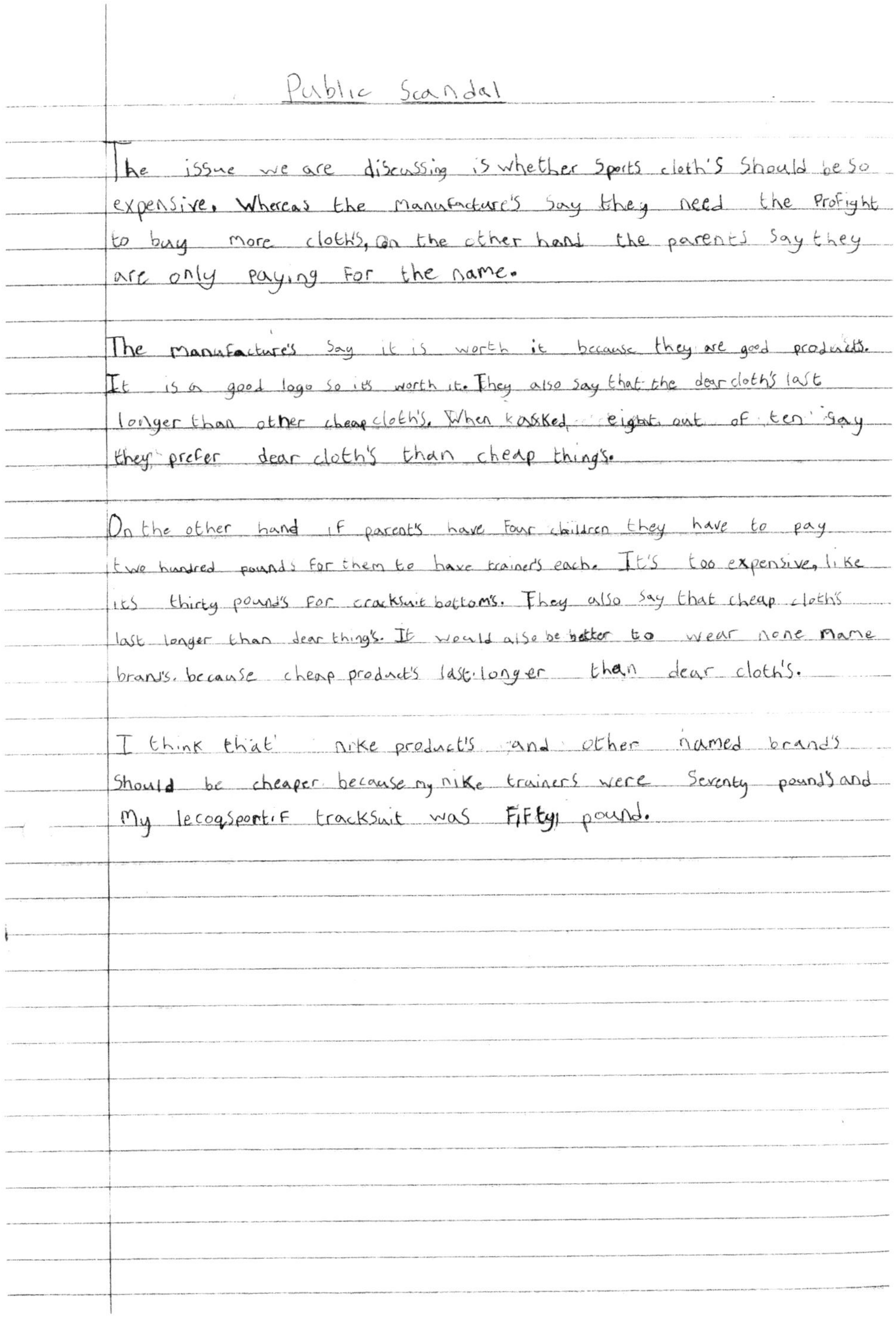

Public Scandal

The issue we are discussing is whether sports cloth's should be so expensive. Whereas the manufacture's say they need the profight to buy more cloth's, on the other hand the parents say they are only paying for the name.

The manufacture's say it is worth it because they are good products. It is a good logo so its worth it. They also say that the dear cloth's last longer than other cheap cloth's. When kasked eight out of ten say they prefer dear cloth's than cheap thing's.

On the other hand if parent's have four children they have to pay two hundred pounds for them to have trainer's each. It's too expensive, like its thirty pound's for cracksuit bottom's. They also say that cheap cloth's last longer than dear thing's. It would also be better to wear none name bran's. because cheap product's last longer than dear cloth's.

I think that nike product's and other named brand's should be cheaper because my nike trainers were seventy pound's and my lecoqsportif tracksuit was fifty pound.

Figure 16.9b

the text themselves, underlining parts that seem to lack the required formality. Pairs then join to fours to compare which bits they've underlined and talk about why they thought the style was wrong, what exactly made it seem personal rather than impersonal. This can then be processed as a whole class using the OHP, with the teacher underlining the parts that need redrafting. Dissent may well arise about some parts children think could be improved, but which don't really fall into the 'too personal' style category. (Perhaps a way of discriminating between the different redrafting needs can be created?)

Spotlight: connectives

Further ideas for work on connectives could include a classifying activity where pairs are given some cards with connecting words and phrases to sort into those which:

- express contrast or opposition (*however, in contrast to this, on the other hand, on the contrary*)
- indicate more is to be added (*furthermore, in addition, moreover, another view commonly expressed*)
- link the presentation of evidence to the point being made (*this is shown when, research scientists would argue, views published by experts prove*).

These could be made into sets of small cards or fans and used with an OHP of a discussion text with connectives blanked out. Individual thinking time combined with paired talk could precede a 'show me' activity for pairs to hold up the missing word or phrase.

Lots of practice may be needed for children to use some of these words and phrases confidently. In some ways, we shouldn't be surprised by this as children are almost having to learn the conventions of a new language as well as how to use the language. It is much better that these 'cloze type' activities are used in a real writing context than with decontextualised exercises.

Spotlight: parallel spelling work

Here we see children being encouraged to problem-solve their own spelling difficulties. Children of similar levels of ability are working in pairs on their own spelling errors and/or uncertainties. They are using writing produced earlier in an independent session. This sequence shows what children are doing:

1. Children are normally encouraged to write initial drafts without worrying about spelling, but pausing to underline whole words they are dubious about. This is done to promote a 'flow of and linkage of ideas' rather than the possible disjointedness which can happen when children pay too much attention to the detail of spelling. Children are prioritising the text and sentence level aspects of their writing over word level, because it is simpler to edit spelling later.
2. Children are seen highlighting those parts of previously underlined words that they don't know how to spell. This focuses their attention down onto which exact part of the word they are unsure about. It will help them later to identify either a spelling strategy or a spelling rule that they need to use to fix the correct spelling in their memories.

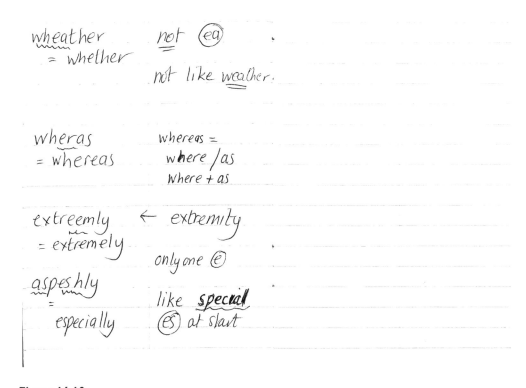

Figure 16.10

3. Children now write a given number of their 'query' spellings into their spelling logs to work on. The use of a log provides a more permanent record than whiteboards or scraps of paper. This is useful for the teacher as a monitoring device: although it is important that children develop independent spelling skills, it is also important to keep an overview of how successfully they are developing strategies to remember spellings. The spelling log provides opportunities to assess children in very useful ways. It is also a tool for children to go back and recheck spellings they have had trouble with in the past.

Figure 16.10 gives an example of a page from a spelling log.

Spotlight: writing discursively on paper or on screen

Children are now assembling their own ideas about a different issue, in note form on a writing frame for discursive writing. This time there is a much less structured approach, as children try out independently the strategies that were modelled in such a staged way in the earlier parts of the unit. Some will then work directly on screen, editing and revising as they go.

In a later session children are asked to compare their writing with their earliest attempt at the very start of the unit. Children themselves comment evaluatively on the progress they have made and on what they have learned.

Beyond the unit

The spotlight on 'Finding questions for argument texts in other subject lessons' suggests ways of extending some of this work orally at other points in the term. Because the structure of formal debates mirrors the structure of this type of discussion text, children could keep visiting and revisiting this spoken genre throughout the year. This will hone the literacy skills at the same time as working on the subject objectives in an economical and enjoyable way.

Index